Reasoning
from the
Scriptures
with

CATHOLICS

Ron Rhodes

HARVEST HOUSE PUBLISHERS
Eugene, Oregon 97402

REASONING FROM THE SCRIPTURES WITH CATHOLICS
Copyright © 2000 by Ron Rhodes
Published by Harvest House Publishers
Eugene, Oregon 97402

Rhodes, Ron.
    Reasoning from the Scriptures with Catholics / Ron Rhodes.
        p. cm.
    Includes bibliographical references and indexes.
    ISBN-13: 978-0-7369-0208-3
    ISBN-10: 0-7369-0208-2
    1. Catholic Church Controversial literature. 2. Evangelistic work. I. Title.
    BX1765.2.R52 2000
    282—dc21   99-43335
                                                                    CIP

Printed in the United States of America

05 06 07 08 09 10 11 12 / BC-PH / 13 12 11 10 9 8 7 6 5

To the friends and supporters of
Reasoning from the Scriptures Ministries

Acknowledgments

I am indebted to a number of individuals whose books and articles have been of great benefit in the researching and writing of this book: Norman Geisler, Ralph MacKenzie, John Ankerberg, John Weldon, James White, James McCarthy, and Ken Samples. I am very appreciative of the work these individuals have done in this field—and I highly recommend their books (see the Bibliography).

Thanks also to Tom Ulrich, a former Catholic, who went through part of the manuscript prior to publication. I appreciate his suggestions.

My wife, Kerri, and two children, David and Kylie, deserve special mention. Thank you for your support and encouragement. As has always been true, my work of ministry would be impossible without you.

If you run into witnessing trouble, feel free to contact
Reasoning from the Scriptures Ministries.
We will help you if we can.

Ron Rhodes
Reasoning from the Scriptures Ministries
P.O. Box 2526
Frisco, TX 75034
Email: ronrhodes@earthlink.net
Web: www.ronrhodes.org
Phone: (214) 618-1912

Contents

Preface

The subject of witnessing to Catholics is one that is close to my own heart since I have friends and family who are members of the Roman Catholic Church. In view of that, I want to say right up front that I don't attack Roman Catholics in this book. Rather, it is my compassionate and heartfelt desire to help Catholics truly understand the wonderful gospel of God's grace.

To be sure, this book contains strong biblical arguments against a variety of Roman Catholic doctrines. But the motivation behind these arguments is one of love. Like you, I want to see my Roman Catholic friends and family members in heaven.

Reasoning from the Scriptures with Catholics was written to provide helpful information that will enable you to witness effectively to Roman Catholics. My prayer is that God would use this book for His glory and for the extension of His kingdom.

Evangelizing Catholics

"Abounding grace is the hope of mankind."[1]
A. W. Tozer (1897–1963)

Vatican City is an ecclesiastical state. It is the seat of the Roman Catholic Church. Within the walls of this city in Italy is a miniature nation that was built during the fourth century and rebuilt during the sixteenth century.

The city has its own banking system and coinage, its own stores, pharmacy, telephone system, radio station, and post office, as well as an army of over 100 Swiss Guards. The most imposing building within the walls of the city is St. Peter's Basilica, which is said to cover the shrine of St. Peter the apostle. The city also includes the Sistine Chapel, the Pauline Chapel, the pope's palace, five museums of antiquities, libraries, the archives of the Roman Catholic Church, and two art galleries. The city publishes its own newspaper, *L'Osservatore Romano*. Various utilities and supplies— water, food, gas, electricity, and the like—are imported from outside the city.

11

The pope exercises sovereign control over Vatican City. He has absolute executive, legislative, and judicial powers within its walls. He also appoints the members of the Vatican's governmental organs. From this city the pope also rules over the Roman Catholic Church, said by Roman Catholics to be the one true church on earth. It was allegedly established by Christ through Peter as the first visible head of the church.* The governance of the church is said to continue generation after generation via Peter's successors, the popes.

Throughout history, under the leadership of various popes, many of the distinctive Roman Catholic doctrines emerged far after the first century. Here are a few notable dates:

— A.D. 593 — belief in purgatory
— A.D. 600 — prayer to Mary and the saints
— A.D. 709 — the practice of kissing the pope's foot
— A.D. 995 — the canonization of dead saints
— A.D. 1079 — celibacy of the priesthood
— A.D. 1090 — praying the rosary
— A.D. 1215 — transubstantiation and confessing sins to a priest
— A.D. 1439 — belief in the seven sacraments.[2]

Protestants, who believe the Bible alone is the final authority and source of divine revelation (*not* tradition, and *not* the ex cathedra pronouncements of the popes), hold that such doctrines are human inventions and go against the teachings of Scripture. This will be demonstrated throughout the rest of the book.

---

* Non-Catholics, however, would establish the beginning of the Roman Catholic Church in A.D. 590 with Gregory I, who consolidated the power of the bishopric in Rome (see Paul Enns, *The Moody Handbook of Theology* [Chicago, IL: Moody Press, 1995], p. 529). I will discuss Peter as the alleged first visible head of the church later in this book.

Salvation and the Roman Catholic Church

Previous to Vatican Council II†, those who held beliefs akin to those of modern Evangelical Protestants—such as salvation through *grace alone* by *faith alone*—were considered "anathema," in the words of the Council of Trent.* And indeed, throughout its history a major emphasis of Roman Catholicism has been that union with the Roman Catholic Church is essential to salvation. Cyprian (circa A.D. 200–258) said: "No one can have God as Father who does not have the Church as Mother."[3] In the twelfth century the Fourth Lateran Council affirmed: "There is only one universal Church of the faithful, outside which none will be saved."[4] This was reaffirmed by Pope Boniface VIII's Bull, *Unam Sanctam*, in 1302.[5] Then in 1854, Pope Pius IX declared: "It is to be held as a matter of faith that no one can be saved outside the Apostolic Roman Church. It is the only ark of salvation and anyone who does not enter it must sink in the flood."[6]

This one "true" church is said to be the dispenser of the seven sacraments, which are necessary for salvation. We can immediately understand, then, why many Roman Catholics have historically said that to be faithful to God one must necessarily be faithful to God's one "true" church—the Roman Catholic Church.[7]

Since Vatican Council II, however, all who are named "Christian" (including non-Catholics) are viewed as part of God's family. Non-Catholics are now considered to be "separated brethren." Vatican II concluded that "the church knows that she is joined in many ways to the baptized who

---

† The Second Vatican Council was an ecumenical council of the Roman Catholic Church held in Rome for four sessions: the first during the pontificate of Pope John XXII (October 11 to December 8, 1962); the other three during the pontificate of Pope Paul VI (September 29 to December 4, 1963; September 14 to November 21, 1964; and September 14 to December 8, 1965).

* The Council of Trent was an ecumenical council of the Roman Catholic Church held in 25 sessions between A.D. 1545 and 1563.

are honored by the name of Christian, but who do not however profess the Catholic faith in its entirety or have not preserved unity which unites them to Christ."[8]

These "separated brethren," however, are not in the most advantageous position—for, as noted previously, Roman Catholicism represents the one true church on earth. After all, Rome's bishops are allegedly the successors of Christ's 12 apostles. And the Catholic pope has allegedly inherited the throne from Peter (see Matthew 16:18). Clearly, then, there can be no other true church than that of Rome. It is only in the Roman Catholic Church that "the *fullness* of the means of salvation can be obtained."[9]

It is highly revealing that even though the Second Vatican Council has displayed a more open attitude toward non-Catholics, it has repeatedly reaffirmed past councils—including the Council of Trent, which pronounced anathemas against those who believe as Protestants do today in regard to the doctrines of justification and salvation. In fact, the recent *Catechism of the Catholic Church* (1994) cites the Council of Trent 100 times.[10] And what should be of concern to modern Protestants is the fact that these anathemas uttered by Trent have never been recanted by the Roman Catholic Church.

Categories of Roman Catholics

Despite the Roman Catholic Church's claims to be the one true church, it is a fact that not all Roman Catholics believe the same. Ken Samples, after an extensive study, concluded that there are six primary categories of Roman Catholics today: the ultratraditionalist Catholics, traditionalist Catholics, liberal Catholics, charismatic/evangelical Catholics, cultural Catholics, and popular folk Catholics.

Ultratraditional Catholics defend old time Catholicism and are critical of the changes brought about by Vatican II. Traditionalist Catholics, while critical of liberalism and modernism within the Church, generally accept the reforms of Vatican II. Liberal Catholics have replaced the Bible and Church authority with the authority of human reason and have questioned the infallibility of the pope, Church councils, and the Bible itself. Charismatic/evangelical Catholics are more evangelical in belief and affirm conservatively orthodox doctrines, and they emphasize the gifts of the Holy Spirit, the importance of being baptized in the Holy Spirit, and the Spirit-filled life. Cultural Catholics are "womb-to-tomb" Catholics—they are born, baptized, married, and buried in the Catholic Church, but are relatively unconcerned about spirituality. Popular folk Catholics predominate in Central and South America. They are very eclectic in their beliefs and combine elements of an animistic or nature-culture religion with a traditional medieval Catholicism.[11]

Why is it important to understand these categories? Roman Catholics cannot be lumped together into one big bucket. There are distinctions in what individual Roman Catholics believe. There are *some* Roman Catholics who *do* believe what is taught in the Bible about grace and justification and are, in fact, saved (despite some of the official teachings of Catholicism). This book is written to reach the many Roman Catholics who believe in the distinctive Roman Catholic doctrines as historically understood. This, as noted earlier, is in my view a vast mission field. These individuals desperately need to hear the gospel of grace.

Blinded to God's Grace

For a moment, imagine a tortuous journey through a desert wasteland where the heat depletes your strength and your throat craves even a single drop of water. The heat is oppressive. Your tongue feels like a dry piece of leather. You are literally coughing dust.

You then pass by a huge neon sign pointing to a wonderful and deep well full of cool and refreshing water. You walk right by the sign and, instead, pick up an old rusty shovel and start to dig your own well in the parched soil. It is a desperate effort.

Such folly. You've just passed by a well of cool, fresh water, free for the taking, but are blind to it and try to find another solution on your own.

In Jeremiah 2:13 we read, "For My people have committed two evils: They have forsaken Me, the fountain of living waters, to hew for themselves cisterns, broken cisterns, that can hold no water." In context, this verse speaks of how Israel had forsaken God, the only true Source of life-giving nourishment and power. But this verse also paints a vivid picture that is applicable to the Roman Catholic Church.

I do not mean to be disrespectful, but is seems that many Roman Catholics walk right by the huge neon sign of Scripture that points to the free grace-gift of salvation by faith in Christ. Instead, they seek to "dig their own wells" by participating in numerous rituals and engaging in various works of penance that have no basis in Scripture. Their efforts—in what amounts to a works system of salvation—are as futile as trying to store water in broken jars.

There is another metaphor that comes to mind when I think of Roman Catholicism. It is a story told by Jerry Bridges about a visit he paid to a doctor's office. While there, he was drawn to a picture of a man being sculpted: "The sculpture was complete down to about mid-thigh, and the finished work showed a robust and muscular man with the kind of physique all men would like to have. The striking thing about the picture, however, was that the artist had put the hammer and chisel in the hands of the man being sculpted."[12]

Bridges marveled at how the picture depicted the way people often try to change themselves in their own strength: "We take what we think are the tools of spiritual transformation into our own hands and try to sculpt ourselves into robust Christlike specimens."[13]

Certainly these words aptly describe the "I-will-try-to-make-God-like-me" trap that Protestants sometimes fall into. But I think the words also describe the typical Roman

Catholic who, through an endless succession of various rituals and "meritorious" works, seeks to earn God's favor and make himself or herself acceptable to God. Somehow, the Roman Catholic has missed the fact that those who trust in Christ are *already* made acceptable to God forever—with nothing that anyone can do to add to it (2 Corinthians 5:21; Hebrews 10:14).

In this book it is my goal to help you reason from the Scriptures with Roman Catholics on a variety of issues— many of which deal in some way with the doctrine of salvation. It is here, in my estimation, that Roman Catholics have most seriously gone astray in their doctrine. I do not question their sincerity. I know my Roman Catholic friends and family members are sincere. But, as even my Catholic friends agree, sincerity does not make a person right. As Solomon put it, "There is a way which seems right to a man, but its end is the way of death" (Proverbs 14:12).

What is of particular concern is that today there are nearly 945 million Roman Catholics in the world. That means that almost 18 percent of the world's total population has bought into a works-oriented system of salvation. It is my desire to reach these people with the glorious gospel of God's grace. God's Word says, "By grace you have been saved through faith; and that not of yourselves, it is the gift of God; not as a result of works, that no one should boast" (Ephesians 2:8,9).

Why It Matters

According to the current ecumenical spirit of the times, it might not be "politically correct" to say that many Roman Catholics are lost and are in need of evangelization.* I am aware of the controversial "Evangelicals and Catholics Together" document, signed by both evangelicals and Catholics. This document declares evangelical–Catholic unity,

---

* To be fair, there are also many people who attend Protestant churches who are lost and are in need of evangelizing. *All people need to hear the gospel of God's grace.*

and its signers promise to refrain from evangelizing one another's flocks, labeling this activity "sheep stealing." In this document we read: "Evangelicals and Catholics are brothers and sisters in Christ."[14] "We thank God for the discovery of one another as brothers and sisters in Christ."[15] "The love of Christ compels us and we are therefore... resolved...to explore patterns of working and witnessing together in order to advance the one mission of Christ."[16]

Certainly I concede that Catholics and evangelicals can work together for the betterment of society, actively countering secularism, moral relativism, societal decay, and the like. But I also believe there must be a line drawn when it comes to biblical doctrine. At God's command, we cannot compromise here: "I...write to you appealing that you contend earnestly for the faith which was once for all delivered to the saints" (Jude 3).

Because eternal souls are at stake, there can be no other policy than to share the gospel of grace with all those whom we believe have likely not heard it or have not understood it correctly. Because the teachings set forth in Rome's catechisms, creeds, encyclicals, and conciliar documents are in a number of ways a far distance from what the Bible teaches on key issues, especially pertaining to salvation, I believe the typical Roman Catholic needs to hear the true gospel.

Please do not misunderstand me. I know there are some Roman Catholics attending Roman Catholic churches who are saved and, hence, do not need evangelizing. I realize that some Roman Catholics attending Roman Catholic churches hold to the correct view that salvation is by grace alone through faith alone. But I believe these people come to salvation *in spite of* what Rome teaches on salvation, grace, and faith—not *because of* what Rome teaches. For, as I will demonstrate in this book, in many ways the salvation Rome offers (as documented in the official teachings of the Church) is one that is permeated from beginning to end with the necessity of meritorious works.

This is not to say that evangelicals and Roman Catholics disagree on everything, for clearly they do not. Indeed, Roman Catholics defend numerous Christian doctrines, including the doctrine of the Trinity and the full theistic attributes of God, God as Creator and Sustainer of the universe, the deity of Christ, the virgin birth, the incarnation, the resurrection, Christ's ascension into heaven, His future return in glory, the doctrine of the Holy Spirit (including the Holy Spirit's personality, deity, and involvement in the work of redemption), and other key tenets.[17]

But there are other doctrines that Roman Catholicism gets wrong in the worst sort of way—the most important of which is the nature of the gospel. Reformed theologian Roger Nicole was right when he said that "Protestants believe that much in Catholic theology tends to undermine and compromise that orthodox Christian confession—especially as it relates to the crucial issue of the gospel message."[18] Protestant theologian Harold O. J. Brown, a professor at Trinity Evangelical Divinity School, warned that while Catholicism holds to key fundamental articles of the faith, the Church "so overlays them with extraneous and sometimes false doctrines that the foundations are no longer accessible to the majority of Catholic believers."[19]

The focus of this book does not involve mere peripheral issues over which Christians can feel free to disagree in good conscience. Rather it delves into the critical doctrines that are at the very heart of Christianity. If the "gospel" of Rome is a *different* gospel than that of Scripture, if Mary is *not* the exalted personage Roman Catholics make her out to be, if the pope is *not* the visible representative of Christ on earth who makes "infallible" statements on matters of faith and practice, if the doctrine of the Mass has *no biblical support whatsoever*, then those who place faith in such doctrines have a false hope for the future. They may believe they have been made right with God when they are not right at all.

Because I have Roman Catholic friends and family members, it is not without great consideration that I address these issues. But I am *compelled* to tackle the erroneous tenets of Catholicism because it is my heartfelt conclusion that these doctrinal problems are so serious as to warrant the sixteenth-century Reformation and the *continued* separation on the part of present-day Protestantism. An honest look at the facts reveals that, since the time of the Reformation, the doctrinal chasm has only widened—especially since Rome's decree of papal infallibility in 1870. It has been since that time that a number of aberrant doctrines—including many pertaining to the exaltation of Mary—have been defined by Rome.

It is my love and concern for Roman Catholics that motivates the writing of this book. It is my love and concern for the gospel of Jesus Christ—*a gospel of grace*—that motivates this close scrutiny of Roman Catholicism. May this book equip you to share the message of God's grace with Roman Catholics in your own circle of influence.

How to Use This Book

Each chapter in this book deals with a specific doctrinal issue and includes discussions of the major passages Roman Catholics cite in supporting their theology. Numerous quotations from official Roman Catholic sources are cited to provide a solid, factual base for addressing the issues.

In most chapters you will find suggested "leading questions" you can use in your witnessing encounters. For your convenience, these questions are set apart in the text so you can quickly find the questions you need to make your point.

Keep in mind that the questions are only *representative* of the kinds of issues you might want to bring up regarding specific Bible passages. Be careful not to assume that just because you ask one or more of these questions, your Catholic acquaintance will promptly change his or her view. The questions are not presented as "scripts" with guaranteed results. Some of the questions flex more apologetic muscle than others. There is a wide variety of questions ranging from those that make a minor point to those that make a powerful apologetic statement. Remember, though, that these are simple examples of apologetic argumentation. If used consistently, they can help you effectively demonstrate to the Catholic that many of his or her views are not in agreement with Scripture.

What should you do if your Roman Catholic acquaintance asks a question you cannot answer? Simply say, "That's a good question. I don't know the answer, but I'll look into this matter and we can talk about it the next time I see you." There is no shame in doing this.

Now, you may want to read this book straight through to get a good grasp of Roman Catholic theology and how to refute it. Or you may want to consult individual chapters as needed. Each chapter is essentially self-contained. And since each chapter deals with a distinct area of doctrine with the major passages cited by Roman Catholics, you will find this an easy-to-use reference tool that you can pull off the bookshelf to quickly read up on a particular issue as the occasion arises.

A Few Notes on Method

It is not my goal in this book to simply quote what other Protestants have said about Roman Catholicism. Rather, I intend to quote or cite directly from key representative Roman Catholic sources. One of these—the *Catechism of the Catholic Church*—is an official, concise, and current statement of Roman Catholic doctrine.

This catechism was written under the direction of Joseph Cardinal Ratzinger and was approved by Pope John Paul II in 1992. The pope commented that it "is a statement of the Church's faith and of Catholic doctrine, attested to or illumined by Sacred Scripture, the Apostolic Tradition and the Church's Magisterium [teaching body]. I declare it to be a sure norm for teaching the faith....This catechism is given to them that it may be a sure and authentic reference text for teaching Catholic doctrine."[20] Those who plan to witness often to Roman Catholics would do well to pick up a copy of this book and digest its contents.

It is highly significant that this catechism cites Roman Catholic councils of the past over 1,000 times, especially from the Council of Trent (1545–1563), the First Vatican Council (1869–1870), and the Second Vatican Council (1962–1965). It also cites heavily from pontifical documents (which are considered authoritative by Catholics), from Roman Catholic canon law, from Roman Catholic liturgy (also considered authoritative), and from Thomas Aquinas's *Summa Theologica* (held in very high esteem by Catholics). In view of this, the catechism is an excellent source of information on Catholic beliefs.

Now, as you read *Reasoning from the Scriptures with Catholics*, it is important to keep in mind what this book is not. This is not a book on the history of Roman Catholicism. It is not a book on the Reformation. It is not a book on Martin Luther or John Calvin. It is not a book that seeks to discuss every single doctrine of Roman Catholicism. It is not a book that focuses on areas of agreement between Protestants and Roman Catholics. (There are many fine evangelical Christian books that address these and other aspects of Roman Catholicism, many of which are listed in the Bibliography.) Rather, this book seeks to help you *reason from the Scriptures* with Catholics on the most important issues that separate Roman Catholics from evangelical Christians. It is a witnessing tool to help you show Roman Catholics what the Scriptures teach—especially on issues relating to salvation.

Of course, in a single book there is no way that every single verse that might come up in a discussion with a Roman Catholic can be covered. But this book does provide essential information on the most important verses on which the major Catholic arguments hinge.

So let us proceed. And be assured that my prayers are with you as you take the information in this book and use it to share the gospel of God's grace.

1

Dialoguing with Roman Catholics

"The church is under orders. Evangelistic inactivity is disobedience."
John R. W. Scott

"One of the saddest statistics of our day is that 95 percent of all church members have never led anyone to Christ."
Dr. D. James Kennedy

Y ou can greatly enhance your effectiveness in dialoguing with Roman Catholics by *deciding in advance* to handle your witnessing encounters in a certain way. Here are some helpful suggestions.

Always Prepare by Prayer

I strongly advise you to pray regularly in regard to your witnessing opportunities. Remember, only God in His mighty power can lift the veil of blindness from the human heart (see 2 Corinthians 4:4,6; 3:15-17; John 8:32). Pray fervently for those you witness to and *pray often* (Matthew 7:7-12; Luke 18:1-8; James 5:16).

Prayer is especially important if you have a prearranged appointment with a Roman Catholic acquaintance. In such cases you can pray for the person by name and ask for God's intervention in his or her life. Pray especially that he or she will truly understand the gospel of grace, as opposed to the necessity of meritorious works throughout life.

Develop Personal Relationships

It very well may be that the Catholic you want to witness to is a friend or family member. In that case, you've already got a lot going for you because personal relationships are very important to success in witnessing. If, however, the Catholic you want to witness to is someone you encounter socially, and you don't yet have a personal relationship with him or her, it is important that you try to develop one.

Remember, people like to know that you genuinely care for them, so be interested and be a good listener. (As the saying goes, "People don't care how much you know until they know how much you care.") Keep in mind that you will encourage others to be open and real with you by being open and real yourself. If the person to whom you want to witness has a particular need and there is a way you can reach out in a helpful way, by all means make that a priority.

Do not be in a mad rush to discuss spiritual things, especially if you have the opportunity to work toward developing a personal relationship. When the Lord opens the door for witnessing, however, be ready to walk through it.

The exception to this rule, of course, is if you know for certain that you will never see that particular Catholic again. In that case, you will want to cover as much evangelistic ground as possible, focusing your primary attention on the nature of salvation and the gospel of grace, and by giving a strong personal testimony of what Jesus has done in your life.

Be Kind but Firm

It is *imperative* that evangelical Christians not have a hostile attitude when interacting with Catholic acquaintances on a doctrinal level. After all, as Scripture says, you are to always be ready "to make a defense to everyone who asks you to give an account for the hope that is in you, yet with gentleness and reverence" (1 Peter 3:15). Be comp⁄ driven, not anger-driven.

While being kind and gentle, however, you must also be firm in setting forth and defending the truth of the gospel. Remember, eternal souls are at stake. Just as the first-century Christians were bold in their witness for Christ, so must we be bold witnesses.

Encourage an Examination of Beliefs

When witnessing to a Catholic acquaintance, it is important to encourage him or her to thoroughly examine his or her beliefs. After all, the Bible itself encourages us to do this. Second Corinthians 13:5, for example, exhorts us: "Test yourselves to see if you are in the faith; examine yourselves!" First Thessalonians 5:21 instructs us to test all things and accept only that which is true. Acts 17:10-12 encourages us to follow the example of the Bereans by testing religious claims against the Bible. The Bereans knew the Bible was the only measuring stick for truth and that it alone is to be used in testing religious claims. (Roman Catholics also use "tradition" as an authority. That will be discussed later in this book.)

Inform your Catholic acquaintance that you would like to examine the Scriptures and focus not on what denomination is the best but on what the Scriptures actually say. Show them how Scripture exhorts us to "be diligent to present yourself approved to God as a workman who does not need to be ashamed, handling accurately the word of truth" (2 Timothy 2:15). This will lay a foundation for all that follows.

Gently Persevere in Sharing the Truth

Catholics typically believe they are saved by going through the prescriptions of the Roman Catholic Church. In reality, based on what Scripture says about the nature of salvation, many of them may not be saved at all (see Romans 3:24; 5:1-11; 11:6; Ephesians 2:8,9). For this reason we must keep in mind the words of the apostle Paul in 1 Corinthians 2:14: "A natural man does not accept the things of the Spirit of God; for they are foolishness to him, and he cannot understand them, because they are spiritually appraised." The gospel of God's grace may not make much sense to someone who has been thoroughly schooled in a gospel that involves the necessity of meritorious works throughout life. This calls for prayer, specifically that the Holy Spirit would bear witness to the truth of the gospel of grace in the hearts of those to whom you speak. This also calls for perseverance and patience, which means being willing to cheerfully go over the same thing ten times (if you need to) in order to make something clear.

Do Not Assume All Catholics Believe the Same Thing

It is important to realize that not all Catholics believe the same thing, and not all Catholics know precisely what their Church teaches about certain doctrinal issues. Many Catholics are "cultural Catholics." They have been born into Catholic families and often attend a Catholic church, but they are unaware of some of the official teachings of the Catholic Church.

When reasoning from the Scriptures with Catholics, it is important to base your comments on what the church actually teaches. If it so happens that the Catholic to whom you are speaking says he or she does not believe that particular doctrine, then encourage that person to leave the Roman Catholic Church and join a church where he or she will agree with major doctrines.

Sometimes it can help the flow of conversation not to tell the Roman Catholic what he or she believes, but instead, *ask* about his or her beliefs. Say, "Do you believe...?"

If the answer is "no" to a particular question about their doctrine, you might say, "I'm glad you don't believe that, but what would you do if you found out your church teaches that?" Of course, you should be prepared to back up your claims with documented evidence. A good tool to use on such an occasion would be the recent *Catechism of the Catholic Church*, which often quotes from the Council of Trent, Vatican I, and Vatican II.

Define Your Terms

While Protestants and Roman Catholics agree on a number of doctrines (such as the Trinity, the deity of Christ, the doctrine of the Holy Spirit, and the second coming), there are other doctrines on which they disagree significantly. In discussions of such issues as grace and justification, Roman Catholics use the same words we do but attach entirely different meanings to those words. I call this the "terminology block." Unless you define your terms *biblically* and overcome the terminology block, little true communication will take place. (This book will help you to overcome the terminology block.)

A frustrating reality to be faced in this regard is the fact that Roman Catholics believe their Church's definitions of these words should be trusted because the Catholic Church stands over the Bible. Their mind-set is that their Church's definition is to be preferred because the Church exercises an inerrant authority to properly interpret the Bible for them. Later in the book, I will deal with the authority of Scripture and will help you demonstrate to the Roman Catholic that *Scripture* is the final authority, not the Church.

Take Your Time

The tendency of many evangelicals, when interacting with Roman Catholics on doctrinal issues, is to all-at-once lambaste them with all that is wrong in their belief system: Mariology, prayers to the saints, works-salvation, papal infallibility, tradition, purgatory, and the sacraments. This is what I call "the flame-thrower approach to evangelism." The problem is that the flame-thrower approach rarely yields positive results in terms of leading a person to Christ.

A much better approach is to take your time and not force your Catholic acquaintance to digest more than he or she can take during one sitting. It is better to focus on one or two issues during each discussion than to "get it all out on the table" in a single sitting. (Remember, Jesus told the disciples, "I have many more things to say to you, but you cannot bear them now" (John 16:12). Jesus was sensitive to how much His listeners could digest in a single sitting.

Ask Leading Questions

You will not be able to force your opinion of what a verse means on a Roman Catholic. But if you can help Catholics discover problems in Catholic theology themselves, then you have accomplished a good thing.

One great way of helping a Catholic discover problems in his or her Church's theology is by asking strategic questions based on key verses, all the while remaining tactful and kind. Jesus often asked questions to make a point. He would use questions to draw answers out of His listeners.

The right question, asked in a nondefensive, nonchallenging, unemotional way, may cause your Catholic acquaintance to come face-to-face with a doctrine (such as the biblical teaching on justification) that is completely contrary to what the Catholic Church teaches. By considering such a question, the Catholic is forced to come to a conclusion in his or her own mind.

As I mentioned in the introduction, there are sample questions you might ask Roman Catholics in most chapters. But remember, these questions are not presented as scripts that guarantee an instant spiritual conversion. They are simply examples of apologetic argumentation. If used consistently, questions like these can help you effectively demonstrate to Catholics that some of their views do not line up with Scripture. And if all goes well, the Lord may bless you with the wonderful privilege of leading some Catholics to faith in Christ alone for salvation.

Understand that Family Conflict May Develop

Most Roman Catholics did not become Catholics as a result of examining the theology of evangelical Protestantism and Roman Catholicism, and then deciding that Roman Catholicism had the best theology. Rather, most Catholics are Catholics because they were born into a Catholic family. And, as they grow up and have families of their own, their kids are born into a Catholic family. Catholicism tends to be passed on from generation to generation.

If the Roman Catholic to whom you are speaking ends up trusting in Christ alone for salvation and then leaves the Catholic Church, you need to be aware (and even give a warning) that his or her family, who are likely deeply entrenched in Catholicism, may not only resist but become very angry over this development. James McCarthy, a former Catholic who now has a ministry to Catholics, says, "Often the reason that Catholics react so strongly when a family member converts has more to do with family and culture than it has to do with theology. Having been born Hispanic, or Italian, or Irish, or French, or Filipino, Polish, Austrian, or any one of the other predominately Catholic ethnic groups, Catholicism is 'in their blood.'"[1] It is a part of the culture they inherited from their parents, and grandparents, and so on.

That's why, when a Catholic becomes "born again" and joins an evangelical church, Catholic family members feel that their loved one has virtually defected from the faith. They take it very personally and feel very hurt. A division in the family may result.

Yet, God has told us that, in terms of priority, we must always obey God above man (see Acts 5:29). If there is ever a conflict between what God desires of us and what our family members tell us, we must unhesitatingly yield in obedience to God—even if it leads to disruption in the family. Talk to your Catholic acquaintance about what Jesus Himself said about this:

> He who loves father or mother more than Me is not worthy of Me; and he who loves son or daughter more than Me is not worthy of Me. And he who does not take his cross and follow after Me is not worthy of Me. He who has found his life shall lose it, and he who has lost his life for My sake shall find it (Matthew 10:37-39).

Based on many years of experience, McCarthy says that disruption in the family may eventually lead to other conversions in that family. Once Catholic family members begin to see how their "born-again" loved one is being impacted by a personal relationship with Jesus and is being spiritually transformed with a true love for the Word of God, they may reconsider things.[2] There have been conversions of entire Roman Catholic families in the past—so do not count out that possibility.

You Are a Missionary

A Christian leader once said, "Every heart with Christ is a missionary; every heart without Christ is a mission field." Of course, there are hearts without Christ in both Roman Catholic *and* Protestant churches. We should be concerned about reaching *all* these people. For our present purposes, however, you may consider this book a missionary training manual for reaching Roman Catholics with the wonderful gospel of grace.

2

The Apocrypha—
Does It Belong in the Bible?

"O Bible!...This is the book untainted by any error;
but is pure, unalloyed, perfect truth."[1]
Charles Haddon Spurgeon (1834–1892)

The word *canon* comes from a Greek word that means "measuring stick." Over time, the word came to be used metaphorically of books that were "measured" and thereby recognized as being God's Word. When we talk about the "canon of Scripture" today, we are referring to all the biblical books that collectively constitute God's Word.

Roman Catholics argue that the apocryphal books—seven books and four parts of books of doubtful authenticity and authority*—belong in the canon. I should note that while Protestants call these books "the Apocrypha," Roman Catholics actually refer to them as deuterocanonical (literally,

---

* The Roman Catholic Apocrypha consists of: Tobit, Judith, the Additions to Esther, the Additions to Daniel (the Prayer of Azariah and the Three Young Men, Susanna, and Bel and the Dragon), the Wisdom of Solomon, Ecclesiasticus (also called Sirach), Baruch (also called 1 Baruch), the Letter of Jeremiah, 1 Maccabees, and 2 Maccabees.

"second canon"). This so-called "second canon," however, *does not* have secondary status among Roman Catholics. (For purposes of discussion I will continue to refer to these books as the Apocrypha.)

The Roman Catholic Church decided these apocryphal books belonged in the Bible sometime following the Protestant Reformation. In fact, the Catholic Council of Trent (A.D. 1545–1563) canonized these books some 1,500 years *after* they were written, largely as a result of the Protestant Reformation, under circumstances that are highly suspect.

Martin Luther had criticized the Roman Catholic Church for not having scriptural support for such doctrines as praying for the dead. By canonizing the Apocrypha, which offers support for praying for the dead in 2 Maccabees 12:45,46, the Catholics then had "scriptural" support for this and other distinctively Catholic doctrines.[2] As theologian Wayne Grudem puts it, "It is significant that the Council of Trent was the response of the Roman Catholic Church to the teachings of Martin Luther and the rapidly spreading Protestant Reformation, and the books of the Apocrypha contain support for the Catholic teaching of prayers for the dead and justification by faith plus works, not by faith alone."[3]

Roman Catholics typically argue that the Septuagint (the Greek translation of the Hebrew Old Testament that predates the time of Christ) contained the Apocrypha. This must mean, they reason, that the Apocrypha belongs in the canon. Church fathers such as Iraneaus, Tertullian, and Clement of Alexandria also used the apocryphal books in public worship and accepted them as Scripture. Further, it is argued, the great theologian St. Augustine viewed these books as inspired. (Protestants respond, however, that since all these facts were *already known* in the early centuries of Christianity, the Roman Catholic Church's delay until the sixteenth century to declare the apocryphal books as canonical depletes these arguments of significant force.)

Other arguments offered in favor of the Apocrypha include the notion that the New Testament reflects some of the ideas in the Apocrypha (compare Hebrews 11:35 with 2 Maccabees 7:12). Moreover, there are some early Christian catacomb scenes that portray episodes from the Apocrypha, showing that the early Christian community was familiar with and used the Apocrypha. The Council of Rome (A.D. 382), the Council of Hippo (A.D. 393), and the Council of Carthage (A.D. 397) also accepted the Apocrypha. Finally, some of the books of the Apocrypha were found in Qumran (the Dead Sea community) along with Old Testament canonical books.[4] These factors are said to prove that the apocryphal books belong in the canon.

As noted previously, in Roman Catholic thought the Apocrypha does not have secondary status in terms of belonging in the canon. Indeed, the Council of Trent went so far as to state: "If anyone...should not accept the said books as sacred and canonical, entire with all their parts...and if both knowingly and deliberately he should condemn the aforesaid tradition, let him be anathema."[5] Hence, those who reject the Apocrypha are considered accursed.

Answering Catholic Arguments

Apocryphal Books Do Not Claim to Be Inspired

Unlike the New Testament books, which claimed to be inspired (2 Timothy 3:16; 2 Peter 1:21; 2 Peter 3:16), the apocryphal books *never* make that claim. Moreover, no apocryphal book was written by a true prophet or apostle of God. And no apocryphal book was confirmed by divine miracles—something that happened often among the prophets in the Old Testament and apostles in the New Testament (for example, see 1 Kings 18 and Hebrews 2:4). Further, no apocryphal book contains predictive prophecy, which would have served to confirm divine inspiration.[6]

Ask...

• What does it say to you that not a single apocryphal book claims to have been inspired by God?

• If the apocryphal books are inspired, why weren't the writers of these books confirmed by divine miracles like the Old and New Testament writers?

• If the apocryphal books are inspired, why didn't they contain predictive prophecy like the Old and New Testament books?

In one key apocryphal book—2 Maccabees, from which Roman Catholics draw support for the doctrine of the Mass—the author concedes that it is an abridgement of another man's work and expresses concern as to whether a good job was done or not (see 2 Maccabees 2:23; 15:38). Such would not be the case had this book been truly inspired by God.

New Testament Writers Do Not Quote the Apocrypha

It is a fact that no New Testament writer quoted from any of the apocryphal books as holy Scripture or gave them the slightest authority as inspired books. Jesus and the disciples virtually ignored these books—something that would not have been the case if they had considered them to be inspired. By contrast, there are many quotations by Jesus and the apostles from the canonical books of the Old Testament. (A good example is the Gospel of Matthew, which contains approximately 130 Old Testament citations and allusions.)[7]

Ask...

• What does it suggest to you that the New Testament writers often quoted from the Old Testament, but never quoted from an apocryphal book?

• In view of the fact that the New Testament writers virtually ignored the Apocrypha, do you think they viewed it as Scripture?

Many Church Fathers Denied the Apocrypha

Even though certain church fathers spoke approvingly of the Apocrypha, there were other early church fathers—notably Origin, Jerome, Athanasius, and Cyril of Jerusalem—that denied their inspiration and canonicity. So merely quoting some church fathers in favor of the Apocrypha is not a convincing argument.

Further, as Norman Geisler and Ralph MacKenzie have noted, it is clear that some church fathers used apocryphal books for devotional or preaching purposes, but did not consider them as canonical.[8] One can demonstrate respect for a book without necessarily considering that book canonical.

Early Christian Evidence Argues Against the Apocrypha

While it is true that some early church leaders did quote several of the apocryphal books as Scripture, it is also true that many early church leaders rejected these books. One of the earliest Christian lists of Old Testament books is that of Melito, the bishop of Sardis, who wrote about A.D. 170:

> When I came to the east and reached the place where these things were preached and done, and learnt accurately the books of the Old Testament, I set down the facts and sent them to you. These are their names: five books of Moses, Genesis, Exodus, Numbers, Leviticus, Deuteronomy, Joshua the son of Nun, Judges, Ruth, four books of Kingdoms, two books of Chronicles, the Psalms of David, the Proverbs of Solomon and his Wisdom, Ecclesiastes, the Song of Songs, Job, the prophets Isaiah, Jeremiah, the Twelve in a single book, Daniel, Ezekiel, Ezra.[9]

Notice that Melito affirmed all the Old Testament books except the Book of Esther, but did not mention a single apocryphal book.

Moreover, in A.D. 367 the great champion of orthodoxy Athanasius (a bishop of Alexandria) wrote his *Paschal Letter* in which he listed all the books of our present New Testament canon and all the Old Testament books except Esther. It is true that he mentioned some of the apocryphal books such as the Wisdom of Solomon, the Wisdom of Sirach, Judith, and Tobit. But he said these are "not indeed included in the Canon, but appointed by the Fathers to be read by those who newly join us, and who wish for instruction in the word of godliness."[10]

The Early Jews of Palestine Rejected the Apocrypha

The Jews of Palestine, including the Jewish Council of Jamnia which met in A.D. 90, rejected the Apocrypha as Scripture. This is understandable in view of the fact that there were no Jewish prophets that lived during the 400-year period between the Old and New Testaments. In keeping with this, ancient Jewish historian Flavius Josephus excluded the Apocrypha. And Philo, a Jewish teacher who lived in the first century, quoted from virtually every Old Testament canonical book, but never once quoted from the Apocrypha. H. E. Ryle comments as follows on Philo: "Philo makes no quotations from the Apocrypha; and he gives not the slightest ground for the supposition that the Jews of Alexandria, in his time, were disposed to accept any of the books of the Apocrypha in their Canon of Holy Scripture."[11]

There Are Historical Errors in the Apocrypha

Scholars have noted that, unlike the canonical Scriptures, which have proven to be historically accurate over and over again, the Apocrypha contains clear historical errors. John Ankerberg and John Weldon summarize a few of these:

Tobit contains certain historical and geographical errors such as the assumption that Sennacherib was the son of Shalmaneser (1:15) instead of Sargon II, and that Nineveh was captured by Nebuchadnezzar and Ahasu-erus (14:5) instead of by Nabopolassar and Cyaxares.... Judith cannot possibly be historical because of the glaring errors it contains....[In 2 Maccabees] there are also numerous disarrangements and discrepancies in chronological, historical, and numerical matters in the book, reflecting ignorance or confusion.[12]

Josh McDowell also notes: "Tobit was supposedly alive when Jeroboam staged his revolt in 931 B.C. and was still living at the time of the Assyrian captivity (722 B.C.), yet the Book of Tobit says he lived only 158 years (Tobit 1:3-5; 14:11)."[13]

The reason all this is significant is that historical and archaeological studies have always been the true friend of the canon of the Old and New Testaments, but they are clearly not the friend of apocryphal books. Indeed, historical and archaeological studies have provided solid verification for numerous customs, places, names, and events mentioned in the Bible. Nelson Glueck, a specialist in ancient literature, did an exhaustive study and concluded: "It can be stated categorically that no archaeological discovery has ever controverted a biblical reference."[14] Not so for the Apocrypha.

Of course, this does not mean the apocryphal books are worthless. They are valuable for historical purposes and cultural insights, but they are not inspired and certainly do not belong in the canon. They are clearly man-made documents.[15]

Ask...

• Does God make mistakes?

• Do books inspired by God contain mistakes?

• Did you know that history and archaeology are true friends of the Old and New Testaments because they verify numerous customs, places, names, and events in Bible times?

• Did you know, by contrast, that the apocryphal books contain many historical errors? *(Go over one or two of the errors previously mentioned.)*

• What does that tell you regarding whether the Apocrypha is inspired by God?

The Apocrypha Contains Unbiblical Doctrines

The Apocrypha contains a number of unbiblical doctrines, such as the doctrine of the Mass (2 Maccabees 12:42-45; compare with Hebrews 7:27), the notion that the world was created out of preexistent matter (Wisdom of Solomon; compare with Genesis 1 and Psalm 33:9), the idea that giving alms and other works can make an atonement for sin (Ecclesiasticus [Sirach] 3:3; 3:30; 5:5; 20:28; 35:1-4; 45:16; 45:23; compare with Romans 3:20), the invocation and intercession of the saints (2 Maccabees 15:14; Baruch 3:4; compare with Matthew 6:9), the worship of angels (Tobit 12:12; compare with Colossians 2:18), purgatory and the redemption of souls after death (2 Maccabees 12:42,45; compare with Hebrews 9:27).

Because we know the Old and New Testaments are the Word of God, and because the apocryphal books contain doctrines that contradict the Old and New Testaments, we conclude that the apocryphal books are not the Word of God because, quite simply, *God does not contradict Himself.* If God inspired the Old Testament, the New Testament, *and* the Apocrypha, all three would have to agree with each other. But they do not. The Apocrypha is not inspired.

Ask...

• Since we know that the Old and New Testaments are the Word of God and that the Apocrypha clearly contradicts the Old and New Testaments at numerous points, what can we conclude about the Apocrypha?

The Septuagint Argument Is Flawed

Though it is true that the Septuagint includes the Apocrypha, many Protestant scholars have noted that while the Septuagint was first translated several centuries before the time of Christ, it apparently was not until the fourth century *after* Christ that the Apocrypha was appended to this translation. We know of no Septuagint manuscripts earlier than the fourth century that contain the Apocrypha, suggesting that the Apocrypha was not in the original Septuagint. But even if a first-century manuscript were found with the Apocrypha in the Septuagint, that still does not mean the Apocrypha belongs in the canon.

It is highly revealing that the apostles quoted from the first-century Septuagint, yet there is not a single quote from the Apocrypha in their writings. This could mean one of two things: It could mean that the Apocrypha was simply not in the first-century Septuagint (which is what the historical evidence seems to suggest), or it could mean that if it was in the first-century Septuagint, it was ignored by the apostles because they knew it did not truly belong in the canon of Scripture.

The Catacombs Argument Is Not Convincing

The fact that some scenes from the Apocrypha are portrayed on the walls of catacombs does not mean the apocryphal books are canonical. It simply means that some of the events recorded in apocryphal books were meaningful enough to some people that they drew pictures on the wall.[16] Drawings on walls are hardly a test for canonicity.

There are also numerous events recorded in the Old and New Testament canonical books that *are not* found on catacomb walls, but this does not mean the books are not canonical. In the same way, using reverse logic, the fact that certain scenes from the Apocrypha *are* recorded on catacomb walls does not mean they belong in the canon.

The Church Council Argument Is Not Convincing

As noted above, Roman Catholics often argue that the Council of Rome (A.D. 382), the Council of Hippo (A.D. 393), and the Council of Carthage (A.D. 397) accepted the Apocrypha. This may seem like a strong argument at first sight. But the fact that different Church councils held during different time periods have come to differing conclusions on certain matters proves one thing: Church councils are not infallible. Only God and His Word are infallible. *Human beings and their councils make mistakes.*

Furthermore, some of the councils, such as the local councils of Hippo and Carthage in North Africa, were heavily influenced by Augustine, the most powerful voice of ancient times that accepted the Apocrypha. However, Geisler and MacKenzie have provided strong evidence that shows how ill-founded Augustine's position was. Among other things, they note that Augustine was fully aware that the ancient Jews rejected these apocryphal books.[17] Further, Augustine felt the apocryphal books belonged in the Bible because of their mention "of extreme and wonderful suffering of certain martyrs," which is hardly a criteria for canonicity. Further, Augustine seems to have accepted the apocryphal books as canonical largely based on the fact that these books were contained in the Septuagint of his day. As we have noted, though, there is evidence to suggest that the original Septuagint did not contain the Apocrypha.[18]

Since the reasons for Augustine's acceptance of the Apocrypha are erroneous, and since it was Augustine who swayed some of the early church councils, the conclusions of these councils are just as erroneous as Augustine's.

The Qumran Argument Is Not Convincing

The fact that some apocryphal books were discovered at Qumran does not prove they belong in the canon. If that were true, that would mean *all* the books discovered at Qumran belong in the canon. There were virtually hundreds of fragments of text discovered, including Old Testament books, apocryphal and pseudepigraphal texts, thematic collections of Old Testament passages, and sectarian writings of the Qumran community. Obviously, not all documents found at Qumran are scriptural. The reality is that members of the Qumran community used many of these books for worship purposes without considering them as canonical. There is virtually no evidence that apocryphal books were venerated as Scripture among Qumran inhabitants.

Tests of Canonicity

The issue of the Apocrypha relates directly to the question of canonicity. When the Church formally recognized what books belonged in the canon, there were five primary tests that were applied. Here they are, listed in question format:

1. *Was the book written or backed by a prophet or apostle of God?* This is the single most important test. The reasoning here is that the *Word* of God, which is inspired by the *Spirit* of God for the *people* of God, must be communicated through a *man* of God.[19] Deuteronomy 18:18 informs us that only a prophet of God will speak the Word of God. Second Peter 1:20,21 assures us that Scripture is only written by men of God. In Galatians 1, the apostle Paul argued support for the Book of Galatians by appealing to the fact that he was an authorized messenger of God—an apostle.

2. *Is the book authoritative?* Can it be said of this book as it was said of Jesus, "The people were amazed at his teaching, because he taught them as one who had authority, not as the teachers of the law" (Mark 1:22 NIV)? Does this book ring with the sense of, "Thus saith the Lord"? Is it brimming with divine authority?

3. *Does the book tell the truth about God and doctrine as it is already known by previous revelation?* The Bereans searched the Old Testament Scriptures to see whether Paul's

teaching was true (Acts 17:11). They knew that if Paul's teaching did not agree with the Old Testament canon, it could not be of God. Agreement with all earlier revelation is essential. Paul certainly recognized this, for he said to the Galatians: "But even if we or an angel from heaven should preach a gospel other than the one we preached to you, let him be eternally condemned!" (Galatians 1:8 NIV).

4. *Does the book give evidence of having the power of God?* The reasoning here is that any writing that does not exhibit the transforming power of God in the lives of its readers could not have come from God. Scripture says that the Word of God is "living and active" (Hebrews 4:12). Second Timothy 3:16,17 indicates that God's Word has a transforming effect. If the book in question does not have the power to change a life, then, it is reasoned, the book cannot have come from God.

5. *Was the book accepted by the people of God?* In Old Testament times, Moses' scrolls were placed immediately into the ark of the covenant (Deuteronomy 31:24-26). Joshua's writings were added in the same fashion (Joshua 24:26). In the New Testament, Paul thanked the Thessalonians for receiving the message he preached as the Word of God (1 Thessalonians 2:13). Paul's letters were circulated among the churches (Colossians 4:16; 1 Thessalonians 5:27). It is the norm that God's people—that is, the majority of them and not simply a faction—will initially receive God's Word as such.

Measuring the Apocrypha against these tests shows that the Apocrypha falls far short of the Old and New Testaments. The books were not written by prophets or apostles of God. The books do not ring with the sense of "thus saith the Lord." The books contradict doctrines revealed in the pages of the Old and New Testaments. While some church fathers used the books for devotional purposes, the books nevertheless fail to have the transforming effect of the Old and New Testaments (as many church fathers admitted). And the books, for the most part, were not accepted on a broad scale by the people of God—at least not until 1500 years later when the Catholic Council of Trent pronounced them canonical.

Unlike the Apocrypha, many of the New Testament books were recognized as Scripture during the general time they were written. It is highly revealing that in 1 Timothy 5:18, the apostle Paul joined an Old Testament reference and a New Testament reference and called them *both* (collectively) "Scripture": "For the Scripture says, 'You shall not muzzle the ox while he is threshing' [Deuteronomy 25:4], and 'The laborer is worthy of his wages' [Luke 10:7]." Only three years had elapsed between the writing of the Gospel of Luke and the writing of 1 Timothy (Luke was written around A.D. 60; 1 Timothy was written around A.D. 63). Yet, despite this, Paul (himself a Jew, a "Hebrew of Hebrews") does not hesitate to place Luke on the *same level of authority* as the Old Testament Book of Deuteronomy. It would not have been unusual in the context of first-century Judaism for an Old Testament passage to be called Scripture. But for a New Testament book to be called Scripture so soon after it was written says volumes about Paul's view of the authority of contemporary New Testament books.

Further, the writings of the apostle Paul were recognized as Scripture by the apostle Peter (2 Peter 3:15,16). Paul, too, understood that his own writings were inspired by God and therefore authoritative (1 Corinthians 14:37; 1 Thessalonians 2:13). (Paul wrote over half the New Testament.)

As the following chart reveals, the people of God throughout biblical history recognized that the books written by the prophets and apostles were Scripture.[20] All this is highly telling in view of the fact that Roman Catholics often claim that the Catholic Church determined the canon. This simply is not so. *God* determined the canon, and many people living in biblical times recognized that the individual books written by the prophets and apostles were indeed Scripture. While God *determines* the canon, human beings

Biblical Books	Recognized as Scripture in Biblical Times
Writings of Moses	Joshua 1:7; 1 Kings 2:3; 2 Kings 14:6; 2 Chronicles 17:9; Ezra 6:18; Nehemiah 13:1; Jeremiah 8:8; Malachi 4:4
Writings of Later Prophets	Jeremiah 26:18; Ezekiel 14:14,20; Daniel 9:2; Jonah 2:2-9; Micah 4:1-3
Writings of Luke	1 Timothy 5:18 (compare with Deuteronomy 25:4 and Luke 10:7)
Writings of the Apostle Paul	2 Peter 3:15,16
Writings of Peter	Jude 4-12

discover the canon. While God *regulates* the canon, human beings *recognize* the canon.[21]

Hebrews 11:35—A Citation from the Apocrypha?

The Roman Catholic Teaching: In Hebrews 11:35 we read, "Women received back their dead by resurrection; and others were tortured, not accepting their release, in order that they might obtain a better resurrection." Some Roman Catholics argue that this is actually a quotation from 2 Maccabees 7 (an apocryphal book), where seven brothers and their mother were tortured and killed because they would not renounce their faith. Therefore, some Catholics say, the Apocrypha belongs in the canon.

Response: Such a view is incorrect for a number of reasons. First, note that even if this verse alludes to an apocryphal book, it is definitely not a quotation from it. In fact, there is not a single clear quotation in the New Testament of any apocryphal book. This is completely unlike the Old Testament books, for these books are quoted consistently throughout the New Testament.

Also note that even if there were a citation of an apocryphal book in the New Testament, that in itself does not prove the apocryphal book belongs in the canon of Scripture or that it is inspired by God. Indeed, as expositors Robert Jamieson, A. R. Fausset, and David Brown note, "The writer of Second Maccabees *expressly disclaims inspiration*,"[22] (see 2 Maccabees 2:23 and 15:38). Therefore, even if Hebrews 11:35 did allude to 2 Maccabees, the author of Hebrews was not sanctioning the Apocrypha as inspired.

Ask...

- Since the author of 2 Maccabees expressly disclaims inspiration for his book, is it not clear that this book does not qualify as inspired Scripture?

We must keep in mind that the Bible even alludes to pseudepigraphal books (*pseudepigrapha* means "false writings") such as the "Bodily Assumption of Moses" (see Jude 9). Even Roman Catholics reject that book as belonging in the canon. The Bible also quotes from pagan poets and philosophers (see Acts 17:28; Titus 1:12; 1 Corinthians 15:33), but that does not mean these writings are inspired or belong in the canon.

Ask...

- Did you know that the Bible alludes to false writings (Jude 9) and pagan poets and philosophers (Acts 17:28; Titus 1:12; 1 Corinthians 15:33), and yet none of these documents are considered inspired Scripture?

- That being the case, do you think it is legitimate to argue that the Apocrypha is inspired Scripture because of a possible allusion to an apocryphal book in Hebrews 11:35?

3

Sola Scriptura Versus Tradition—
Part 1

"We owe to Scripture the same reverence which we owe to God."[1]
John Calvin

"The source of all our troubles is in not knowing the Scriptures."[2]
Chrysostom

One of the most volatile issues that separates Protestants from Roman Catholics has to do with the issue of *sola scriptura* ("Scripture alone"). Protestants believe that Scripture alone speaks with God's voice and is authoritative in matters of faith and practice, whereas most Roman Catholics believe that both Scripture *and* tradition constitute the Word of God.

Two Viewpoints

Roman Catholics view the relationship of tradition to Scripture differently. Traditionalists such as Ludwig Ott and Henry Denzinger understand tradition and Scripture to be two sources of revelation. God's revelation is passed on partly in written books and partly in unwritten traditions. Some modern Roman Catholics, such as Cardinal Joseph Ratzinger, would by contrast tend to view tradition more as an interpretation of revelation. Let us take a brief look at each of these.

The Traditional Viewpoint

Roman Catholic traditionalists often make reference to the phrase, "sacred deposit of faith." This refers to the body of beliefs and practices entrusted to the pope and bishops by the 12 apostles, who themselves received this body of belief and practices from Jesus Christ. People are admonished to "adhere faithfully to the written and unwritten Word of God. They must love it, make it their careful study, and in it find their spiritual nourishment. Tradition and Sacred Scripture form one sacred deposit of God's word and this is committed to the Church's care."[3]

According to this viewpoint, a body of truth was passed down to the pope and bishops in two ways: tradition *and* the written Word. Tradition refers to oral teachings, oral worship, and the oral prayers of the apostles. The written Word, by contrast, is what we find recorded in the pages of Scripture. Many Catholics believe that written Scripture and oral tradition *together* form the Word of God. Together they constitute the "sacred deposit of faith." As Henry Denzinger put it, "The written source of revelation is the canonical books of both Testaments....Another source of revelation is ecclesiastical tradition."[4]

The metaphor many Roman Catholics use to explain this is that of two streams flowing into the same pool. Two streams—Scripture and tradition—flow into the same pool of divine revelation. One stream is not enough. If we have only one stream and not the other, the Second Vatican Council tells us that we do not have in our possession all that God wants us to know. The Council of Trent likewise said that the Bible alone is not sufficient for faith and morals, thereby making tradition a necessity. These two "streams" of Scripture and tradition together communicate all that God wants us to know. The "Word of God" is not just the Bible;

it also includes tradition. Therefore, both Scripture and tradition must be accepted and honored with equal sentiments of devotion and reverence.[5]

We are told that the reading of Scripture is not—

> the only or the direct rule of a Christian's faith. The direct rule is the teaching of the living Church, and divine tradition is with Scripture the joint source of revelation. A Catholic dogma, therefore, does not need any scriptural text for its warrant; dogmas are believed not because they are contained in the Scriptures, but because they are taught by the Church.[6]

Have you ever wondered where Roman Catholicism derived such doctrines as Mary's immaculate conception, the assumption of Mary, indulgences, and other unique doctrines? We look in vain for such doctrines in the pages of the Bible. But, as previously noted, many Catholics believe the Word of God is not limited to the pages of the Bible. It is from "tradition" that many distinctive Roman Catholic doctrines are primarily derived.

In the traditional viewpoint, there is a body of oral traditions that actually exists, passed on by the apostles to their successors. Tradition has a real existence and real substance. Doctrines such as the bodily assumption of Mary allegedly came directly from the apostles—a "truth" handed down to us generation by generation.

This sacred tradition involves "the handing on of God's Word by the successors of the apostles."[7] The successors of the apostles are enlightened by the Spirit of truth in such a way that they may "faithfully preserve, expound and spread it [tradition] abroad by their preaching."[8]

The Nontraditional Viewpoint

The second primary view of tradition among Roman Catholics basically says that divine revelation is contained *entirely* within the pages of Scripture and *entirely* in tradition.

In this viewpoint, tradition does not contain any revelation from God that is not already found (at least implicitly) in the Scriptures. This means, of course, that such doctrines as the immaculate conception of Mary, Mary's bodily assumption, and papal infallibility are implicitly found in Scripture.

Apologist and exegete James White tells us that tradition in this viewpoint is more of a framework or system of interpreting the Scriptures, as opposed to revelational material that can be examined in historical sources:

> The tradition can be as solid as apostolic *interpretations* of the Bible or as nebulous as a general concept of the understanding of the Church over time. Different authors give different spins to the concept. But in any case, the oral tradition does not contain any revelation that is not to be found, *at least implicitly*, in the Scriptures.[9]

Conclusion

Whichever of the two viewpoints a Roman Catholic holds to, it is clear that the Protestant view of *sola scriptura* is altogether rejected. Let us now consider *sola scriptura* in more detail.

The Catholic Rejection of Sola Scriptura

There are at least three key arguments Roman Catholics offer in rejection of *sola scriptura* and in favor of the need for tradition.

1. *Not even the Bible argues for the doctrine of sola scriptura.* As Roman Catholic apologist Peter Kreeft put it, "If we believe only what the Scripture teaches, we will not believe *sola scriptura*, for Scripture does not teach *sola scriptura*."[10] In keeping with this, it is argued that the early church did not even have the New Testament and depended on oral tradition. Since the early church was open to tradition, so we should be open to it.

2. *The Bible teaches the authority of tradition.* Roman Catholics note that the apostle Paul wrote, "So then, brethren, stand firm and hold to the traditions which you were taught, whether by word of mouth or by letter from us" (2 Thessalonians 2:15). And, "Now we command you, brethren, in the name of our Lord Jesus Christ, that you keep aloof from every brother who leads an unruly life and not according to the tradition which you received from us" (2 Thessalonians 3:6). Further, it is argued that the apostle John actually preferred oral tradition: "I had many things to write to you, but I am not willing to write them to you with pen and ink" (3 John 13).

3. *The Bible cannot be correctly interpreted without tradition.* Roman Catholics often argue that tradition is for the highest good of the church, for without such tradition, we end up with division (multiple denominations), which is an "intolerable scandal" in view of the fact that Christ called the church to unity. The Bible *alone,* without tradition, is not "a safe guide as to what we are to believe."[11]

Answering Roman Catholics

Protestants Respect Tradition, Not Exalt It

Those of us who hold to *sola scriptura* do not say there never was a time when God's Word was spoken. Quite obviously there was such a time. Yet we also hold that the Scriptures are God's final and full revelation to humankind. The oral traditions once communicated by the apostles have been committed to apostolic writing for all generations to come. All that God intends us to have is found within the Scriptures. Nothing outside the pages of Scripture is needed.

That is not to say that Protestants view tradition as being worthless. Protestants respect "tradition" in the form of confessions and council pronouncements, but they do not accept traditions as being "apostolic," or as being God's revelation, or as something that has an authority equal to that of Scripture. Most Protestants have high regard for the teachings of the early fathers, though obviously they do not believe they are infallible. Protestants do not believe that any form of tradition is infallible like Scripture is. Theologian Loraine Boettner summarizes the Protestant viewpoint this way:

> We do not reject all tradition, but rather make judicious use of it in so far as it accords with Scripture and is founded on truth. We should, for instance, treat with respect and study with care the confessions and council pronouncements of the various churches, particularly those of the ancient church and of Reformation days. We should also give careful attention to the confessions and council decisions of the present-day churches, scrutinizing most carefully of course those of the denomination to which we belong. But we do not give any church the right to formulate new doctrine or to make decisions contrary to the teaching of Scripture. The history of the church at large shows all too clearly that church leaders and church councils can and do make mistakes, some of them serious. Consequently their decisions should have no authority except as they are based on Scripture.
>
> Protestants...keep these standards strictly subordinate to Scripture, and in that they are ever ready to re-examine them for that purpose. In other words they insist that in the life of the church Scripture is primary and the denominational standards are subordinate or secondary. Thus they use their traditions with one controlling caution: they continually ask if this or that aspect of their belief and practice is true to the Bible. They subject every statement of tradition to that test, and they are willing to change any element that fails to meet that test.[12]

The Inspiration and Authority of Scripture— A Clear Contrast with Tradition

The Greek word for inspiration in the Bible, *theopnustos*, literally means "God-breathed." Because Scripture is breathed out by God—because it *originates* from Him—it is true and inerrant.

Biblical inspiration may be defined as God's superintending of the human authors so that, using their own individual personalities (and even their writing styles), they composed and recorded *without error* His revelation to humankind in the words of the original autographs. Benjamin B. Warfield, a prince of theologians, explains that

> the original documents of the Bible were written by men, who, though permitted to exercise their own personalities and literary talents, yet wrote under the control and guidance of the Spirit of God, the result being in every word of the original documents a perfect and errorless recording of the exact message which God desired to give to man.[13]

The writers of Scripture were not mere writing machines. God did not use them like keys on a typewriter to mechanically reproduce His message. Nor did He dictate the words page by page. The biblical evidence makes it clear that each writer had a style of his own:

> One need only compare the powerful style of Isaiah with the mournful tone of Jeremiah in the Old Testament. In the New Testament, Luke manifests a marked medical interest, James is distinctly practical, Paul is theological and polemical, and John has an obvious simplicity. God has communicated through a multiplicity of human personalities, with their respective literary characteristics.[14]

Second Peter 1:21 (NIV) provides a key insight regarding the human-divine interchange in the process of inspiration. This verse informs us that "prophecy [or Scripture] never had its origin in the will of man, but men spoke from God as they were carried along by the Holy Spirit." The phrase "carried along" in this verse literally means "forcefully borne along." Even though human beings were used in the process of writing down God's Word, the human wills of the authors were not the originators of God's message. God did not permit the will of sinful human beings to misdirect or erroneously record His message. Rather, as Norman Geisler and William Nix put it, "God *moved* and the prophet *mouthed* these truths; God *revealed* and man *recorded* His word."[15]

Interestingly, the Greek word for "carried along," *pheromenoi,* in 2 Peter 1:21 is the same as that found in Acts 27:15-17. In this passage the experienced sailors could not navigate the ship because the wind was so strong. The ship was being "driven," "directed," and "carried along" by the wind. This is similar to the Spirit's driving, directing, and carrying the human authors of the Bible. The word is a strong one, indicating the Spirit's complete superintendence of the human authors. Yet, just as the sailors were active on the ship (though the wind, not the sailors, ultimately controlled the ship's movement), so the human authors were active in writing as the Spirit directed.

In keeping with this, theologian Charles C. Ryrie tells us that God's work of inspiration meant using the human authors

> in research (Luke 1:1-4), permitting them to express intense feeling (Romans 9:1-3), transmitting direct revelation (Deuteronomy 9:10), giving authoritative commands (1 Corinthians 7:10), expressing opinions (1 Corinthians 7:40), but always guided and guarded by the Holy Spirit (2 Peter 1:21) so that the product can be said to have been breathed out by God (2 Timothy 3:16).[16]

The Holy Spirit of God is truly the divine author of Scripture. Though He used erring humans as penmen, He superintended them as they wrote, keeping them from all error and omission.[17] The Scriptures, in the original autographs, possess the quality of freedom from error. In all their teachings they are in perfect accord with the truth. In 1980, the International Council of Biblical Inerrancy affirmed that inspiration involves a divine superintendence which preserved the writers in their word choices from using words that would falsify or distort the message of Scripture....Evangelical Christians have wanted to avoid the notion that biblical writers were passive instruments like pens in the hands of God, yet at the same time they affirm that the net result of the process of inspiration would be the same....Inspiration, however God brought it about, results in the *net effect* that every word of Scripture carries with it the weight of God's authority.[18]

It is fascinating to observe that many Old Testament passages quoted in the New Testament are said to have the Holy Spirit or God as their author, even though a human prophet actually uttered the words in the Old Testament. The words spoken by the human prophets thus carried divine authority.

Acts 1:16 is highly significant in this regard, for we read: "Brothers, the Scripture had to be fulfilled which *the Holy Spirit spoke long ago through the mouth of David*

Old Testament Designation	*New Testament Designation*
The psalmist said (Psalm 95:7)	The Holy Spirit said (Hebrews 3:7)
The psalmist said (Psalm 45:6)	God said (Hebrews 1:8)
The psalmist said (Psalm 102:25-27)	God said (Hebrews 1:10-12)
Isaiah said (Isaiah 7:14)	The Lord spoke by the prophet (Matthew 1:22,23)
Hosea said (Hosea 11:1)	The Lord spoke by the prophet (Matthew 2:15)
Eliphaz's words (Job 5:13)	God's Word (1 Corinthians 3:19)[19]

concerning Judas, who served as guide for those who arrested Jesus" (NIV, emphasis added). Though David (and other biblical writers) were used in the process of communicating God's words, it is clear that the Holy Spirit was in charge of the process so that no human error or opinion entered into the picture (compare with Acts 4:24,25; Jeremiah 1:9; Zechariah 7:12).

In 2 Timothy 3:16 (NIV) we read, "All Scripture is God-breathed and is useful for teaching, rebuking, correcting and training in righteousness." The Greek form of "God-breathed" (or "inspired") in this verse is passive. This means the Bible is the *result* of the "breath of God." If the form were active, the verse would be saying that all the Bible breathes or exudes God. But here we are told that God *breathed out* something, namely, the Scriptures. The origin of the Bible—both Old and New Testaments—is thus seen to be God.

The apostle Paul certainly understood that his own writings were inspired by God and therefore authoritative. In 1 Corinthians 2:13 (NIV) Paul said he spoke "not in words taught us by human wisdom but in words taught by the Spirit, expressing spiritual truths in spiritual words." In this passage Paul affirmed that his words were authoritative because they were rooted not in fallible men but infallible God (the Holy Spirit). The Holy Spirit is the Spirit of *truth* who was promised to the apostles to teach and guide them into all the truth (see John 16:13).

Later, in 1 Corinthians 14:37 (NIV), Paul said, "If anybody thinks he is a prophet or spiritually gifted, let him acknowledge that what I am writing to you is the Lord's command." In 1 Thessalonians 2:13 (NIV), Paul likewise said, "And we also thank God continually because, when you received the word of God, which you heard from us, you accepted it not as the word of men, but as it actually is, the word of God, which is at work in you who believe." Again, the reason why Paul's words were authoritative is that they were rooted in

God, not in man. God used Paul as His instrument to communicate *His* word to man.

I include this section on the inspiration and authority of Scripture with a view to demonstrating the obvious contrast between written Scripture and oral tradition. The Bible teaches that Scripture alone is the supreme and infallible authority for the church and the individual believer (1 Corinthians 2:13; 1 Thessalonians 2:13; 2 Timothy 3:16,17; 2 Peter 1:21). Again, this is not to say that creeds and tradition are unimportant, but the Bible alone is our final authority. Creeds and tradition are man-made.

Scripture has final authority because it is a direct revelation from God and carries the very authority of God Himself (Galatians 1:12). What the Bible says, God says. The Scriptures are the final court of appeal on all doctrinal and moral matters. This is what Protestants call *sola scriptura* ("Scripture alone"). All that we must believe as Christians is found within the pages of Scripture. We need no other source, and indeed there is no other source that is authoritative and binding upon the Christian. The Bible alone is sufficient as our sole guide for matters of faith and practice.

Jesus said, "Scripture cannot be broken" (John 10:35 NIV). He never said "tradition cannot be broken." Jesus also said, "I tell you the truth, until heaven and earth disappear, not the smallest letter, not the least stroke of a pen, will by any means disappear from the Law until everything is accomplished" (Matthew 5:18 NIV). He said, "It is easier for heaven and earth to disappear than for the least stroke of a pen to drop out of the Law" (Luke 16:17 NIV).

Jesus used Scripture as the final court of appeal in every matter under dispute. To the Sadducees He said, "You are in error because you do not know the Scriptures or the power of God" (Matthew 22:29 NIV). He told some Pharisees that they invalidated the Word of God by their tradition which has been handed down (Mark 7:13). Jesus informed them, "Neglecting the commandment of God, you hold to the tradition of men" (Mark 7:8). To the devil, Jesus consistently responded, "It is written..." (Matthew 4:4-10). Following Jesus' lead, Scripture alone must be our supreme and final authority.

In Colossians 2:8 the apostle Paul warns, "See to it that no one takes you captive through philosophy and empty deception, *according to the tradition of men*, according to the elementary principles of the world, rather than according to Christ" (emphasis added). Based on the context, we know that the "tradition of men" seeking to influence the church at Colossae was rooted in Jewish legalism and Greek philosophy, both of which were antithetical to Christianity. Paul warns the Colossians against such tradition. Indeed, any tradition that conflicts with the absolute Word of God as contained in Scripture is to be rejected. *Scripture is supreme over tradition.*

Ask...

• Would you please read aloud Mark 7:8 and 7:13, where Jesus is speaking to some Pharisees?

• What is Jesus' attitude toward tradition here?

• Would you please read aloud Colossians 2:8?

• According to this verse, is it possible for human traditions to lead people astray?

It is interesting to note in passing that some Roman Catholics support the legitimacy of tradition based upon what they have learned from tradition. Tradition is thus self-validating. James McCarthy rightly notes that this is nothing but arguing in a circle: "We know that tradition is true and legitimate, because tradition tells us so."[20]

Addressing Specific Roman Catholic Arguments
Did the Roman Catholic Church Give Us the Bible?

One often hears that it was the Roman Catholic Church that gave us the Bible. This simply is not true. As I noted in the previous chapter, the canon of Scripture was being established in the very days that the Bible was being written, before the Roman Catholic Church was even in existence. Luke's Gospel was recognized as Scripture within three years of its writing (see 1 Timothy 5:18; Luke 10:7; Deuteronomy 25:4). Paul's writings were also recognized as Scripture (2 Peter 3:16; 1 Corinthians 14:37; 1 Thessalonians 2:13). Let us not forget that God *determines* the canon, but human beings *discover* the canon. God *regulates* the canon, but human beings *recognize* the canon.[21]

As F. F. Bruce puts it, the New Testament canon was not demarcated by the arbitrary decree of any Church council: "When at last a Church Council—the Synod of Carthage in A.D. 397—listed the twenty-seven books of the New Testament, it did not confer upon them any authority which they did not already possess, but simply recorded their previously established canonicity."[22]

An Explicit Statement of Sola Scriptura in the Bible Is Not Necessary

A doctrine does not have to be taught *explicitly* in Scripture in order for that doctrine to be recognized as true. The doctrine of the Trinity is an example. Scripture does not come right out and say "God is a Trinity." But the Bible does implicitly teach this doctrine by telling us that there is one God (Deuteronomy 6:4), and that the Father, the Son, and the Holy Spirit are each persons who are called God (Matthew 3:16,17; 28:19). Likewise, while the doctrine of *sola scriptura* may not be explicitly taught in Scripture, it most certainly is implicitly taught.[23] There are a number of arguments that may be offered in support of this.

The Lord Jesus used the Scriptures as His final court of appeal. As noted above, Jesus said, "Scripture cannot be broken" (John 10:35). To the devil, Jesus consistently responded, "It is written..." (Matthew 4:4-10). Jesus affirmed the Bible's divine inspiration (Matthew 22:43), its indestructibility (Matthew 5:17,18), its infallibility (John 10:35), its final authority (Matthew 4:4,7,10), its historicity (Matthew 12:40; 24:37), its scientific accuracy (Matthew 19:2-5), and its factual inerrancy (John 17:17; Matthew 22:29).

The apostle Paul affirmed the full adequacy of Scripture in 2 Timothy 3:16,17. In this passage we read, "All Scripture is inspired by God and profitable for teaching, for reproof, for correction, for training in righteousness; that the man of God may be adequate, equipped for every good work." The context for understanding the full significance of this passage is verse 15, where Paul tells Timothy that "from childhood you have known the sacred writings *which are able to give you the wisdom* that leads to salvation through faith which is in Christ Jesus" (emphasis added). Jewish boys formally began studying the Old Testament Scriptures when they were five years of age. Timothy had been taught the Scriptures by his mother and grandmother beginning at this age. Clearly, verse 15 indicates that the Scriptures alone are sufficient to provide the necessary wisdom that leads to salvation through faith in Christ. The Scriptures alone are the source of spiritual knowledge.

Ask...

- According to 2 Timothy 3:15, were the Scriptures alone sufficient in providing Timothy what he needed to know to be saved?

- If the Scriptures alone were sufficient for Timothy, then aren't the Scriptures alone sufficient for us?

Verses 16 and 17 then tell us that all Scripture is "profitable for teaching, for reproof, for correction, for training in righteousness; that the man of God may be adequate, equipped for every good work." This verse does not say that Scripture as interpreted by the Roman Catholic Magisterium (teaching office) is "profitable for teaching, for reproof," and so forth. Nor does it say that Scripture and tradition are "profitable for teaching, for reproof," and so forth. *It is Scripture alone that does these things.* And the reason Scripture can do these things is that "all Scripture is inspired by God" (verse 16). As noted earlier, the word *inspired* means "God-breathed." Scripture is sufficient because it finds its source in God.

It is noteworthy that the word *adequate* (in the phrase "that the man of God may be adequate") means "complete, capable, fully furnished, proficient in the sense of being able to meet all demands."[24] Scripture alone makes a person complete, capable, and proficient. Scripture furnishes all that a person must know to be saved and to grow in grace.

All Apostolic Tradition on Faith and Practice Is in the New Testament

All of the apostolic traditions relating to faith and practice are recorded for us in the pages of the New Testament. This, of course, does not mean that every single thing Jesus or the apostles said is recorded in the New Testament (see John 20:30; 21:25). But virtually all of the apostolic teaching necessary for faith and practice that God wanted communicated to His people is found within the New Testament (as 2 Timothy 3:15-17 indicates).[25]

A look at the biblical record makes it more than clear that God's will was for His revelations to be written down and preserved for coming generations. "Moses wrote down all the words of the LORD" (Exodus 24:4). Joshua too "wrote these words in the book of the law of God" (Joshua 24:26). Samuel "told the people the ordinances of the kingdom, and wrote them in the book and placed it before the LORD" (1 Samuel 10:25). The Lord instructed Isaiah, "Take for yourself a large tablet and write on it in ordinary letters..." (Isaiah 8:1). Isaiah was told, "Now go, write it on a tablet before them and inscribe it on a scroll, that it may serve in the time to come as a witness forever" (Isaiah 30:8).

Dutch theologian Abraham Kuyper has suggested four advantages of written revelation as opposed to oral tradition: 1) Written revelation is durable and not susceptible to errors of memory, and accidental corruptions are minimized; 2) it can be universally disseminated; 3) it has the attribute of fixedness and purity; and 4) it is given a finality and normativeness which other forms of communication cannot attain.[26]

Rome's Claim that the Bible Cannot Be Interpreted Without Tradition Contains a Fatal Flaw

The Roman Catholic Church often claims that the Bible cannot be interpreted rightly without tradition. The big problem with this claim is that once Rome [Vatican City] gives a definitive explanation of a Bible passage via tradition, Rome's explanation must then be interpreted, and in many cases Rome's explanations are more complicated than the Bible passage.[27]

What this means is that Rome has just pushed the problem back one generation. Now, instead of needing help interpreting the Bible, we need help interpreting the tradition that is supposed to make the Bible clearer.

Protestants, of course, believe that the Bible is sufficiently clear. This is a doctrine called *perspicuity*. This does not mean that every single verse in the Bible is equally clear or easy to understand. Rather, it means that the main teachings of the Bible are quite clear. As the old saying goes, the main things are the plain things, and the plain things are the main things.

There is one other point that bears mentioning at this juncture. Church history reveals that there are clear contradictions in the many traditions of Rome. Abelard (A.D. 1079–1142) recognized hundreds of such contradictions.

For example, some church fathers accepted the immaculate conception of Mary, while others did not.[28] What this means is that tradition is not infallible, nor is it authoritative.

Ask...

• Did you know there are many contradictions in the traditions of the Catholic Church? *(For example, some Church fathers accepted the immaculate conception of Mary, while others did not.)*

• Since there are many contradictions in the traditions of Rome, doesn't that mean they are not infallible?

Scripture Sets Parameters Beyond Which We Are Not Free to Go

God in Scripture has set definite parameters for us that we are compelled to obey. The apostle Paul, for example, exhorted the Corinthians "not to exceed what is written" (1 Corinthians 4:6). In Deuteronomy 4:2 we are commanded: "You shall not add to the word which I am commanding you, nor take away from it, that you may keep the commandments of the LORD your God which I command you."

Proverbs 30:5,6 instructs us: "Every word of God is tested; He is a shield to those who take refuge in Him. Do not add to His words lest He reprove you, and you be proved a liar." Revelation 22:18,19 likewise tells us, "I testify to everyone who hears the words of the prophecy of this book: if anyone adds to them, God shall add to him the plagues which are written in this book; and if anyone takes away from the words of the book of this prophecy, God shall take away his part from the tree of life and from the holy city, which are written in this book."

I believe that the Roman Catholic exaltation of tradition violates the intent and spirit of the above commandments. It is not wrong to respect tradition, but it is wrong to attribute the same authority to tradition that is attributed to Scripture. One has its source in God, the other in man.

Jesus Promised to Guide the Apostles, Not Apostolic Successors

In the Upper Room discourse, Jesus gave some very important instructions to the apostles. Among other things, He said, "The Helper, the Holy Spirit, whom the Father will send in My name, He will teach *you* all things, and bring to *your* remembrance *all* that I said to you" (John 14:26, emphasis added).

Norman Geisler and Ralph MacKenzie rightly note the importance of "you" and "your" in this verse. Jesus told the apostles and *them alone* that the Holy Spirit would guide them into all truth. This is not a promise made in regard to any alleged apostolic successors passing on tradition from generation to generation. The Holy Spirit's ministry was to remind the apostles of "*all* that I said *to you.*" The "all" covers everything. There is no need for tradition.[29]

Ask...

• Would you please read aloud from John 14:26?

• When Jesus makes reference to "you" and "your" in this verse, who is He referring to? *(The apostles.)*

• There is no mention of apostolic successors, right?

• So this verse is saying that the Holy Spirit would guide *the apostles alone* into "all" truth, right?

In the next chapter, "Sola Scriptura Versus Tradition— Part 2," I will turn our attention to specific Bible verses that typically come up in the debate over *sola scriptura* versus tradition. It will be seen that every verse that Roman Catholics cite in favor of tradition has been misinterpreted in some way.

4

Sola Scriptura Versus Tradition—Part 2

The Scriptures "are God preaching, God talking,
God telling, God instructing, God setting before us
the right way to think and speak about Him."[1]
J. I. Packer

In the previous chapter we examined a number of arguments offered by the Roman Catholic Church in support of tradition. In the present chapter, we will continue our examination, with a focus on specific verses that typically come up in discussions on this issue. We begin with a standard Roman Catholic "proof text," Matthew 2:23, which Roman Catholics say is based upon tradition.

Matthew 2:23—Was Tradition Handed Down by the Prophets?

The Roman Catholic Teaching: Matthew 2:23 tells us that Jesus "came and resided in a city called Nazareth, that what was spoken through the prophets might be fulfilled, 'He shall be called a Nazarene.'" Roman Catholics often argue that this statement is not found in any Old Testament verse, but is nevertheless said to have come from the prophets. That can only mean one thing: It must have been passed down generation to generation through oral tradition. That being the case, this would be an example of God's Word being passed on via oral tradition and not through written Scripture.[2]

Response: It is a tremendous leap in logic to go from an undocumented prophetic quote to the existence of some supposed oral tradition, for which there is virtually no historical evidence whatsoever. There are several possible explanations that make good sense and do not require a dependence on tradition.

Many exegetes believe the primary meaning of Jesus being called a Nazarene has to do with His despised character. As a backdrop, Nazareth was considered a place of vice in biblical times. "Nazareth had become a military camp town with which all manner of sin and corruption were associated. The Nazarenes were particularly despised by the rest of the Jews."[3] This prompted Nathaniel to say, "Can anything good come out of Nazareth?" (John 1:46).

In view of this, being called a Nazarene back in those days was considered extremely scornful and amounted to being called a despised person. And indeed, the Messiah was prophesied to be a despised character. It may be, then, that Matthew was not intending to say that some Old Testament prophet specifically foretold that the Messiah would live in Nazareth, but rather that the Old Testament prophets collectively foretold that He would be a despised character (Psalm 69:8,20,21; Isaiah 11:1; 49:7; 53:2-8). Matthew emphasizes this theme elsewhere in his Gospel (Matthew 8:20; 11:16-19; 15:7,8). Seen in this light, Matthew gives us the substance of a number of Old Testament verses, not a direct quotation from a single prophet.[4]

Notice that Matthew made reference to "prophets" (plural), which would seem to indicate that he was drawing his information from more than one prophet, instead of seeking to quote a single verse from a single prophet.[5] In view of the plural term *prophets*, "we should not expect to find any given verse, but simply a general truth found in many prophets to correspond to His Nazarene-like character."[6]

Ask...

- Did you know that *Nazarene* was a term of scorn back in biblical times, indicating "one who is despised"?

- Since numerous Old Testament passages indicate that the Messiah would be a despised character, can you see the possibility that Matthew's use of *Nazarene* in reference to the Messiah was intended to give the substance of many Old Testament prophecies and not a direct quote from a single prophet?

Other evangelical scholars, while conceding the viability and likelihood of the above interpretation, suggest another possible alternative. They note that Jewish writers, including the likes of Matthew, who himself was seeking to reach a Jewish audience with the gospel of Jesus Christ, often felt free to conflate and paraphrase citations from the Old Testament.[7] Hence, it may be that Matthew in this verse is conflating several Old Testament verses together instead of quoting a single verse.[8] The problem with this viewpoint is that it is not clear just what Old Testament verses Matthew may have had in mind.

Some scholars suggest Matthew may have simply been alluding to the messianic prophecy in Isaiah 11:1: "Then a shoot will spring from the stem of Jesse, and a branch from his roots will bear fruit." The Hebrew word for "branch" is *netser*, which sounds quite similar to Nazarene. Expositor Craig Keener suggests that "this text could be a play on the Hebrew word *netser*, 'branch,' a title for the Messiah (Jeremiah 23:5; Zechariah 3:8; 6:12; cf. Isaiah 11:1)."[9] It may be that Matthew used such a wordplay to make the point that Jesus at one and the same time is both from Nazareth and is the *Netser*—the promised Branch from the stock of Jesse, the descendant of David, the promised anointed King of God.[10] (Personally, I think this viewpoint is a bit of a stretch.)

Yet another possibility is that the reference to Jesus as a Nazarene might be a wordplay involving the word *Nazirite*. The Nazirites were a class of people dedicated to God (see Numbers 6:1–21).[11] They would often take a vow of separation unto the Lord. Jesus was certainly separated unto God in an absolute sense. The weakness of this view, however, is that there is no reference in Scripture to Jesus ever taking a Nazirite vow.

I believe the best option is to interpret *Nazarene* as a term of scorn and derision. Matthew's intent was likely to indicate that the Old Testament prophets (plural) foretold that the Messiah would be a despised character (Psalm 22:6-8,13; 69:8,20,21; Isaiah 11:1; 49:7; 53:2,3,8; Daniel 9:26). Seen in this light, there is no need to assume that tradition was the source of Matthew's comment.

Ask...

• Does citing Matthew 2:23 in support of tradition really seem legitimate to you, in view of the fact that there are a number of viable interpretations of this verse that do not require any dependence on tradition?

Matthew 23:2,3—The "Chair of Moses" a Proof of Oral Tradition?

The Roman Catholic Teaching: In Matthew 23:2,3 we find Jesus saying to the crowds and to His disciples, "The scribes and the Pharisees have seated themselves in the chair of Moses; therefore all that they tell you, do and observe, but do not do according to their deeds; for they say things, and do not do them."

Roman Catholic apologists often argue that the "chair of Moses" on which the scribes and Pharisees were said to sit is not found anywhere in Old Testament Scripture, and hence Jesus' reference to the term supports the idea of a separate oral tradition. It is also argued that in ancient Israel an authoritative teaching office was passed on by Moses to his successors—through Joshua, the elders, the prophets, and the Sanhedrin.[12] Hence, these words of Jesus support the existence and authority of oral tradition. That same tradition carries on in the successors of the apostles—the Roman popes who speak "from the chair."[13]

Response: Simply because Jesus speaks of a "chair of Moses" does not in itself prove the existence or authority of some oral tradition. That is reading way too much into this text, and in fact is a viewpoint that makes vast and unwarranted assumptions.

Even if Jesus were making some reference to oral tradition here (which is by no means a given), He would not thereby be giving credence to the Roman Catholic view of a continuing authoritative tradition being handed down by apostolic successors. If Jesus was referring to tradition in this verse, He did so only because the tradition *in that one case* contained a true statement (about the existence of the "chair of Moses") that bore mentioning. He was not thereby saying that tradition in itself is authoritative or on an equal par with written revelation, or that an oral tradition was passed on generation by generation to those who sit in this chair. Jesus merely alluded to the *existence* of this chair, and the fact that the scribes and Pharisees have seated themselves in this chair.* No oral tradition is mentioned or implied.

---

* Note that the text says that the scribes and Pharisees are said to "have seated *themselves*" in the chair of Moses. In view of Jesus' condemnation of the Pharisees throughout the rest of Matthew 23, more than a few scholars have suggested that the Pharisees *improperly* "seated themselves" in this chair.

It is worth noting that Jesus in this very same Gospel of Matthew told the Pharisees and teachers of the law, "You invalidated the word of God for the sake of your tradition" (Matthew 15:6). In this verse there is no doubt that Jesus places the Word of God above tradition, and indicates that tradition can be wrong and lead people astray. Jesus points to the Word of God as the final court of appeal.

Ask... ————————————————————

• Since Jesus in this same Gospel of Matthew indicates that tradition can be wrong and lead people astray—and since He places God's Word over tradition (Matthew 15:6)—is it not unwise to argue for the authority of tradition from Matthew 23:2,3?

As I have noted elsewhere, this should not be taken to mean that tradition is necessarily bad or is always wrong. Protestants do respect tradition and even find it historically helpful. If a particular tradition contains an accurate statement, then for Jesus (or anyone else) to quote it is not wrong. If Jesus did cite tradition in Matthew 23 (which, again, is by no means a given), He would have done so only for this reason.[14]

As for what Jesus actually meant by the term "chair of Moses," it is apparently the place in the synagogue where the teacher of the law would sit during the Scripture reading. *The Wycliffe Encyclopedia* tells us:

> This chair in a synagogue was a symbol of the legal authority of Moses which the scribes and Pharisees felt they inherited as teachers of Jewish law. It was the seat for the most distinguished elder, and was next to the ark of the Torah in the synagogue at Dura Europos....Such chairs of solid stone have been found in synagogue ruins at Chorazin and Hammath.[15]

Now, that such chairs of authority existed in ancient synagogues proves only that the Jews in these synagogues recognized a seat of authority from which the teacher of the law would read God's Scripture. But it most certainly does not prove that an oral tradition was passed down generation by generation from Moses to others who would sit in that place of authority. There is virtually no biblical, historical, or archaeological support for such a view.

Apologist James White informs us that historically this "chair of Moses" came into use *far after* the time of Moses, for synagogue worship itself emerged far after the time of Moses. Old Testament scholar Merrill F. Unger places the emergence of synagogue worship in postexilic times.[16] This would mean there is no way the "chair of Moses" can be traced via oral tradition back to the time of Moses. It simply did not exist back then.[17] So reference to Moses's seat hardly constitutes proof of tradition that is handed down generation by generation.

Ask... _____

- Did you know that synagogue worship first emerged in postexilic times, long after the time of Moses?

- Since historically the "chair of Moses" in the synagogue came into use far after the actual time of Moses, is it not clear that reference to this chair cannot be cited in support of an oral tradition that goes back to Moses?

John 20:30,31—Is the New Testament Incomplete?

The Roman Catholic Teaching: In John 20:30,31 we read, "Many other signs therefore Jesus also performed in the presence of the disciples, which are not written in this book; but these have been written that you may believe that Jesus is the Christ, the Son of God; and that believing you may have life in His name." It is sometimes argued that this passage indicates that the New Testament is incomplete and there is therefore a need for tradition.[18]

Response: All this passage is saying is that while Jesus' ministry was characterized by miracles from beginning to end, it is not necessary to record each one in order to establish that Jesus is in fact the promised Messiah. It is interesting to observe that some 35 different miracles are recorded in the four Gospels, but John selected only seven for special consideration so that people might come to believe that Jesus is the Christ, the promised Messiah.[19] The account in John's Gospel is fully sufficient, under the inspiration of the Holy Spirit, to communicate the true identity of Jesus to the people.

This relates to the fact that the miracles in John's Gospel are called "signs." They are called signs because signs always *signify* something. In the case of Jesus, the miracles were signs in the sense that they signified that He was the promised Messiah. Indeed, these miraculous signs were specifically predicted of the Messiah in the Old Testament (see Isaiah 29:18; 35:4-6).

The point of John 20:30,31, then, is that enough signs were included in the Gospel of John to prove beyond any doubt that Jesus is in fact the promised Messiah. It was not necessary to provide an overkill of evidence by including every single miracle. John was satisfied to provide *massive* evidence for Jesus' identity instead of *overwhelming* evidence. This being the case, it is illegitimate to cite this verse in proof of the need for tradition with the charge that the New Testament is incomplete.

Ask... ———————————————————

- Did you know that miracles are always called signs in John's Gospel, because they signify Christ's true identity as the Messiah?

- Does it make sense to you that John did not want to overwhelm his readers by detailing every single miracle of Jesus, but rather chose to present seven pivotal miracles as more than enough proof of Jesus' identity?

• Since John's Gospel was inspired by the Holy Spirit, is it not clear that the exact miracles God wanted included were in fact included, and hence a charge of "incompleteness" is unwarranted?

John 21:25—Is the New Testament Incomplete?

The Roman Catholic Teaching: In John 21:25 we read, "And there are also many other things which Jesus did, which if they were written in detail, I suppose that even the world itself would not contain the books which were written." It is sometimes argued from this verse that the New Testament is incomplete, and there is therefore a need for tradition. Karl Keating says that "the Bible actually denies that it is the complete rule of faith. John tells us that not everything concerning Christ's work is in Scripture (John 21:25)."[20]

Response: John's only point in this verse is that Jesus' ministry was so wonderful, so miraculous, so beyond the ability of human words to fully capture that the Gospel account he wrote reflects only a portion of the wonder of Jesus. John's sense is that he had but dipped a cup in the ocean of wonder that is Jesus Christ. Someone has calculated that one can read the accounts of Jesus in the Gospels in about three hours. If all that Jesus said and did during His full three-year ministry were considered, then surely John's expression is reasonable.

Inasmuch as John's Gospel was directly inspired by the Holy Spirit, however, we know for sure that what is communicated in this Gospel is exactly what God wanted communicated. *Sola scriptura* does not claim that what is in the Bible is exhaustive; it only claims that what is in the Bible is fully sufficient. Everything that God wanted us to have in terms of His revelation to man is found within the pages of Scripture. We need nothing further. Hence, to use this verse in support of tradition—arguing that the New Testament is incomplete—is unwarranted.

Ask...

- Since John's Gospel was inspired by the Holy Spirit, is it not clear that the exact information God wanted included was in fact included, and hence a charge of incompleteness is unwarranted?

Galatians 1:14—Was Paul Zealous for Tradition?

The Roman Catholic Teaching: In Galatians 1:14 the apostle Paul affirmed to his readers in Galatia, "I was advancing in Judaism beyond many of my contemporaries among my countrymen, being more extremely zealous for my ancestral traditions." Frankly, this is not a verse that Roman Catholics typically cite in favor of tradition. But I think it is a good verse to bring up when they raise the issue because they so often cite the apostle Paul in support of tradition.

Response: In this verse Paul is speaking of the time prior to his conversion to Jesus Christ. The traditions of which he speaks relate to his Pharisaic upbringing. He had been schooled in the beliefs of the Pharisees. He had spent much time studying the law of Moses and the accompanying rabbinical traditions.

In the context of Galatians 1:14, Paul is dealing with Jewish legalistic foes who were deceiving some of the Galatians by trying to mix legalism into the gospel of grace. Paul declares that he himself had once been a foremost protagonist of the Jewish religion (holding to all the Pharisaic traditions), but he had *left* it for something better: a salvation based on faith in Christ and rooted in God's grace.

By referring to tradition in this verse, Paul is not thereby indicating a continuing belief on his part in tradition, or that he believed tradition had any authority on a level with the Word of God. Indeed, Paul taught that Scripture alone was inspired and was completely sufficient in itself to give us all we need for faith and practice (2 Timothy 3:15-17). Paul's reference to tradition was a reference to his former life as a Pharisee (a life he left behind), not to his present life as an apostle of God who wrote over half of the New Testament.

1 Corinthians 10:4—Christ "the Rock," Rooted in Tradition?

The Roman Catholic Teaching: In 1 Corinthians 10:1-4 the apostle Paul spoke of the wilderness sojourn following Israel's exodus from Egypt:

> For I do not want you to be unaware, brethren, that our fathers were all under the cloud, and all passed through the sea; and all were baptized into Moses in the cloud and in the sea; and all ate the same spiritual food; and all drank the same spiritual drink, for *they were drinking from a spiritual rock which followed them; and the rock was Christ* [emphasis added].

This verse explicitly states that Christ the Rock followed the ancient Israelites during their sojourn experience. But the Old Testament text says nothing of the physical rock that the Israelites drank from as having *moved* (Exodus 17:1-7; Numbers 20:2-13). So where did the idea come from?

Roman Catholics note that there was a rabbinical tradition indicating that the rock followed the Israelites during their journey. It is also noted that another tradition—one given by Philo—equates this rock with preexistent wisdom. The apostle Paul allegedly drew on this tradition and equated this "wisdom" with Christ Himself. Hence, the fact that Paul drew on tradition shows that it was viewed as authoritative, just as it is viewed as authoritative by Roman Catholics today.[21]

Response: As a well-trained Jew, Paul was certainly well acquainted with a variety of Jewish traditions and sources, as well as with Greek philosophy and mythology. But this does not mean that any of the sources or traditions Paul alluded to are inspired or authoritative. As noted earlier, Paul viewed Scripture alone as inspired and fully sufficient for all we need for faith and practice (2 Timothy 3:15-17).

Let us also be clear on the fact that Paul as an apostle of God, who wrote 1 Corinthians under the inspiration of the Holy Spirit, *corrected tradition.* It was not just a "rock" that followed the Israelites (as Jewish tradition noted), and it was not just "preexistent wisdom" that followed the Israelites (as the tradition from Philo noted); rather, it was *Jesus Christ the Son of God* that followed the Israelites. Expositors Robert Jamieson, A. R. Fausset, and David Brown comment:

> Not the literal rock (or its water) "followed" them...as if Paul sanctioned the Jews' tradition (Rabbi Solomon on Numbers 20:2) that the rock itself, or at least the stream from it, followed the Israelites from place to place (compare Deuteronomy 9:21). But Christ, the "Spiritual Rock" (Psalm 78:20,35; Deuteronomy 32:4,15,18,30,31,37; Isaiah 28:16; 1 Peter 2:6), accompanied them (Exodus 33:15).[22]

If we learn anything here, it is that *Scripture is in authority over tradition.* And when there is a conflict between the two, we should follow Scripture and not tradition.

Ask...

- Since Paul in 1 Corinthians 10:4 corrected both the rabbinical and Philo traditions, pointing out the true identity of the "rock," is it not clear that Paul's apostolic words as recorded in Scripture take precedence over tradition?

---

1 Corinthians 11:2—Are We to Hold Firmly to Traditions?

The Roman Catholic Teaching: In 1 Corinthians 11:2 we read, "Now I praise you because you remember me in everything, and hold firmly to the traditions, just as I delivered them to you." Roman Catholics often cite this verse to demonstrate how the apostle Paul held tradition in high regard. It is argued that we today should have the same attitude Paul did.[23]

Response: This is reading more into the verse than is warranted. This verse simply refers to information that Paul personally and directly handed down to the Corinthian believers with whom he had spent time. As an apostle, Paul communicated God's truth to the Corinthians in person, face-to-face. As the *International Critical Commentary* points out, as yet there were no written Gospels for Paul to appeal to, and hence such face-to-face transmission of information was necessary up until that information could be permanently recorded in written form.[24] Paul most certainly was not giving justification for a continuing line of oral information passed down from apostles to Roman Catholic bishops. He makes reference *only* to the apostolic teachings that he had personally delivered to the Corinthians.

As noted earlier, Paul viewed the Scriptures as God's final and full revelation to humankind (2 Timothy 3:15-17). The oral traditions once communicated by the apostle Paul have been committed to apostolic writing for all generations to come. *All* that God intends us to have is found within the Scriptures. Nothing outside the pages of Scripture is needed.

1 Corinthians 11:23—Tradition "Delivered"?

The Roman Catholic Teaching: In 1 Corinthians 11:23 we read, "For I received from the Lord that which I also delivered to you, that the Lord Jesus in the night in which He was betrayed took bread." Roman Catholics tell us that the phrase "delivered to you" speaks of tradition.[25]

Response: This verse can only be used to support the fact that apostolic teachings were for a time orally transmitted. It is reading something into the verse to draw the sweeping conclusion that Paul was saying that oral tradition would continue for thousands of years into the future through a line of Roman Catholic bishops. As noted above, the apostolic teachings were communicated orally *only* until the time when they could be put into writing. Once those writings were complete, oral transmission ceased.

This is in keeping with something Paul said in 2 Thessalonians 2:5: "Do you not remember that while I was still with you, I was telling you these things?" From this we can clearly see that the apostles would often repeat *in written form* what was formerly communicated *in oral form*. All the oral traditions once handed down by the apostles were eventually committed to writing, after which time the oral traditions became obsolete and unneeded.

Ask...

- Would you please read aloud 2 Thessalonians 2:5?

- Based on this verse, is it not clear that the apostles would often repeat in written form what was formerly communicated in oral form?

- Can you see that once the apostolic teachings were recorded in written form, the oral teachings were no longer needed?

---

2 Thessalonians 2:15—Holding Firm to Traditions?

The Roman Catholic Teaching: In 2 Thessalonians 2:15 we read, "So then, brethren, stand firm and hold to the traditions which you were taught, whether by word of mouth or by letter from us." Roman Catholics often cite this verse to show that the apostle Paul believed in the authority of tradition:

> The faith does not end with the apostles; it only begins from them its tradition through history until Jesus comes again (see Matthew 28:20). Paul makes it clear that he only hands on what he has received (see 1 Corinthians 15:1-3;

2 Thessalonians 2:15). Those who receive the teaching are to preserve it carefully (see 1 Timothy 6:12; 2 Timothy 1:14; 3:14).[26]

Pope Paul VI said:

And so the apostolic preaching, which is expressed in a special way in the inspired books, was to be preserved by an unending succession of preachers until the end of time. Therefore the Apostles, handing on what they themselves had received, warn the faithful to hold fast to the traditions which they have learned either by word of mouth or by letter (see 2 Thessalonians 2:15).[27]

Response: At first sight, this verse might seem to support the Roman Catholic position. But notice the critically important words, "from *us*" (that is, *the apostles*). Paul was talking to people he had personally taught *as an apostle of God*.

The Greek word for "traditions" (*paradosis*) simply refers to "that which has been passed down." Paul had earlier passed down some apostolic teachings about the second coming of Christ to the Thessalonian Christians (the context of 2 Thessalonians makes this clear), and Paul reminds them in this verse to hold firm to those teachings.[28]

As noted earlier, the apostles for a time communicated their teachings orally until those teachings could be permanently recorded in written form. Once the apostles committed their teachings to written form and then died (so they could no longer exercise their living authority as apostles), the written Scriptures alone are our final authority for matters of faith and practice (2 Timothy 3:15-17).

Bible expositors Jamieson, Fausset, and Brown write:

Inspired tradition, in Paul's sense, is not a supplementary oral tradition completing *our* written Word, but it is identical with the written Word *now* complete; then the latter [written Word] not being complete, the tradition was necessarily in part oral, in part written, and continued so until, the latter [written Word] being complete before the death of St. John, the last apostle, the former [oral tradition] was no longer needed. Scripture is, according to Paul, the complete and sufficient rule in all that appertains to making "the man of God *perfect, thoroughly furnished* unto *all* good works" (2 Timothy 3:16,17).[29]

Ask...

• Can you see that once apostolic teachings were permanently recorded in written form, the oral teachings were no longer needed?

2 Thessalonians 3:6—Live According to Tradition?

The Roman Catholic Teaching: In 2 Thessalonians 3:6 we read, "Now we command you, brethren, in the name of our Lord Jesus Christ, that you keep aloof from every brother who leads an unruly life and not according to the tradition which you received from us." Roman Catholics often cite this verse in support of their view of the authority of tradition.[30]

Response: Again, as noted above, *tradition* (Greek: *paradosis*) in this verse simply refers to what the apostle Paul had orally passed down to the Thessalonian believers—that is, *oral teaching direct from the mouth of an apostle.* Specifically, in context, the "tradition" of which Paul spoke relates to the importance of living a productive and disciplined life, instead of living in an unruly way. Eventually, this oral teaching was committed to writing so that the oral teaching was rendered obsolete. Once committed to writing, there was no further need for tradition.

2 Timothy 2:2—Entrust Tradition to Faithful Men?

The Roman Catholic Teaching: In 2 Timothy 2:2 we read, "And the things which you have heard from me in the presence of many witnesses, these entrust to faithful men, who will be able to teach others also." Roman Catholics often argue that this verse supports the idea of a separate oral tradition. Catholic theologian Ludwig Ott comments that "the full truth of Revelation is contained in the doctrine of the Apostles which is preserved unfalsified through the uninterrupted succession of the bishops."[31]

Response: The Roman Catholic view assumes that what Paul taught was different from what Paul wrote in his Epistles. The fact is, the teaching that Paul gave to Timothy was no different than the teaching contained in Paul's Epistles: Romans, Galatians, and the like. I know this is redundant, but I must repeat it again: Oral teachings from the apostles were necessary for a time until they could be committed to writing, and once they were in written form, there was no further need for the oral teachings. Paul viewed Scripture alone as having final authority (2 Timothy 3:15-17).

2 Timothy 3:8—"Jannes and Jambres," Rooted in Tradition?

The Roman Catholic Teaching: In 2 Timothy 3:8 we read, "And just as Jannes and Jambres opposed Moses, so these men also oppose the truth, men of depraved mind, rejected as regards the faith." Roman Catholic theologians sometimes argue that the apostle Paul must have drawn on tradition to gain the names of the two magicians that opposed Moses, for this information is not found in the pages of the Old Testament (Exodus 7).[32] Hence, Paul expounded on Christian doctrine based on tradition (just as Roman Catholics do today).[33]

Response: Evangelical Christians agree that the reference to Jannes and Jambres in 2 Timothy 3:8 apparently draws not on the Old Testament but on a fairly widespread Jewish legend about two of Pharaoh's magicians who competed against Moses and lost (Exodus 7:11; 9:11). This legend appears in Pseudo-Philo, the Dead Sea Scrolls, the Talmud, Targums, and various rabbinical writings. Even pagan accounts—Pliny the Elder (A.D. 23-79) and Apuleius (circa A.D. 130)—record these individuals as magicians of Moses' time. The Pythagorean philosopher Numenius (second century A.D.) also speaks of these two.[34]

Evangelicals deny that the mere drawing of this fact from tradition necessarily means that tradition is inspired or authoritative. If Paul was referring to tradition in this verse, he did so only because the tradition *in this case* contained a true statement that bore mentioning. He was not thereby saying that tradition in itself is authoritative or on an equal par with written revelation. The Holy Spirit so superintended Paul and his writing that he was led to select this true fact from uninspired tradition and include it in the inspired writing of 2 Timothy.

Let us be clear: *The inclusion in a biblical book of a true fact from a tradition does not thus mean that the tradition itself is inspired.* It simply means that the tradition includes a true fact!

Ask...

• Can you see that the inclusion in Scripture of a true fact from tradition does not necessarily mean that tradition is inspired or authoritative, but rather that the tradition simply includes a true fact?

3 John 13—Did John Prefer Tradition?

The Roman Catholic Teaching: In 3 John 13 we read, "I had many things to write to you, but I am not willing to write them to you with pen and ink." Roman Catholics often argue from this verse that John much preferred oral tradition to written Scripture.[35]

Response: All John was doing in this verse was expressing his desire to have some personal face-to-face contact as opposed to just writing a letter. Indeed, that is what John says in the very next verse: "I hope to see you shortly, and we shall speak face to face" (3 John 1:14). Roman Catholics are reading way too much into this verse.

Ask...

- Would you please read aloud from 3 John 13 *and* 14?

- Contextually, is it not clear that all John was saying is that he desired some personal face-to-face contact, as opposed to just writing a letter?

- Seen in this light, do you really think it was John's intent to argue for tradition in this verse?

5

Papal Infallibility and the Teaching Authority of the Church— Part 1

"Simon Peter, the Rock, very often looked
more like a sandpile than a rock."[1]
John Powell

Roman Catholics allege that St. Peter's Basilica in Vatican City was built above Peter's tomb. They believe Peter took up residence in Rome in A.D. 42 and remained there until his martyrdom in A.D. 67. Indeed, "his very primacy led Peter to settle in Rome, as the place from which the primacy that had its principle in him could best be exercised."[2]

Catholics claim Peter was the first bishop, or pope, of Rome. He allegedly ruled the universal church from that city, and, according to Catholics, whoever succeeds Peter as the bishop of Rome also succeeds him as pope.

Catholic scholars realize that Scripture nowhere explicitly states that Peter went to Rome. But they argue that tradition on this point is unmistakable. As well, they believe that in the light of tradition, certain New Testament passages seem to confirm that Peter may have ended up in Rome.[3] (I will discuss some of these verses in the next chapter.)

The seat of power in the Roman Catholic Church is the pope—"the Supreme Pontiff." He is said to be the Vicar of Christ on earth. *Vicar* literally means "one serving as a substitute or agent." The pope as "Vicar of Christ" acts *for* and *in the place of* Christ. As the successor of Peter, the pope exercises authority over the 3250 bishops in the Church. The *Catechism of the Catholic Church* tells us that the pope has "full, supreme, and universal power over the whole Church, a power which he can always exercise unhindered."[4]

The pope is assisted by top advisers and administrators called cardinals who oversee the *Roman Curia*—the administrative and judicial offices of the Vatican.[5] If the pope should die, it would be the task of this group of cardinals to elect a new pope.

Below the pope and cardinals are the archbishops, who preside over one or more dioceses in a given territory. They are typically addressed as, "Your Excellency." Among other things, they have the authority to call bishops to provincial councils and to act as first judge of appeal over a decision of one of the bishops.

The bishops themselves are viewed as the successors of Christ's apostles. According to the Second Vatican Council, the bishops "have by divine institution taken the place of the apostles as pastors of the Church, in such wise that whoever listens to them is listening to Christ and whoever despises them despises Christ and him who sent Christ."[6]

The Essential Catholic Handbook tells us that bishops have three kinds of power in the church which they inherited from the apostles: sanctifying power, ruling power, and teaching power.[7] Sanctifying power is that power by which the bishops via their prayers, works, teachings, and sacraments (which infuse grace) make parishioners spiritually well-nourished and holy. Ruling power has to do with shepherding and governing God's people in individual churches and collectively in the Church worldwide. Teaching power is that exclusive power involving the proper interpreting of

God's revelation and teaching it with authority.[8] These powers are not exercised independently by the bishops, but under the guidance and authority of the pope, the supreme pontiff.

Below the pope, cardinals, archbishops, and bishops are the priests, who serve in individual parish churches. Their primary task is to administer the sacraments (especially the Mass and Penance) and pastor the flock of God.

The Infallibility of the Pope

As we will see throughout the rest of this book, many of the distinctive Roman Catholic doctrines have come from the allegedly infallible teachings of the popes. Catholics believe that when the pope speaks *ex cathedra* (from the Latin, meaning "from the chair") on issues pertaining to faith and morals, he is infallible. Indeed, we are told, the Spirit of truth (that is, the Holy Spirit) guarantees that when the pope declares that he is teaching infallibly as Christ's representative and visible head of the Church on matters of faith and practice, he cannot lead the Church into error.[9]

Avery Dulles defines the pope's infallibility as "immunity from error, that is, protection against either passive or active deception."[10] This means that when speaking on matters of faith and morals, the pope can neither deceive nor be deceived. When not speaking ex cathedra, however, it is possible that the pope could be fallible in something he says or teaches.

As defined by the First Vatican Council,

> The Roman Pontiff, when he speaks ex cathedra—that is, when in discharge of the office of pastor and teacher of all Christians, by virtue of his supreme apostolic authority, he defines a doctrine regarding faith or morals to be held by the universal Church, by the divine assistance promised to him in Blessed Peter, is possessed of that infallibility with which the divine Redeemer willed that his Church should be endowed in defining doctrine regarding faith or morals; and therefore such definitions

are irreformable of themselves and not in virtue of consent of the Church.[11]

The Second Vatican Council put it this way:

> The Roman Pontiff...enjoys this infallibility in virtue of his office, when, as supreme pastor and teacher of all the faithful...he proclaims in an absolute decision a doctrine pertaining to faith or morals. For that reason his definitions are said to be irreformable by their very nature and not by reason of the assent of the Church, in as much as they were made with the assistance of the Holy Spirit promised to him in the person of blessed Peter himself; and as a consequence they are in no way in need of the approval of others, and do not admit of appeal to any other tribunal. For in such a case the Roman Pontiff does not utter a pronouncement as a private person, but rather does he expound and defend the teaching of the Catholic faith as the supreme teacher of the universal Church, in whom the Church's charism of infallibility is present in a singular way.[12]

Episcopal Infallibility

Not only is the pope infallible when he speaks ex cathedra on matters of faith and practice, the bishops too are infallible when they speak "with one voice"—that is, when all the bishops agree on a doctrine. They are assured freedom from error "provided they are in union with the Bishop of Rome and their teaching is subject to his authority."[13] The scope of their infallibility, like that of the pope, "includes not only revealed truths but any teaching, even historical facts, principles of philosophy, or norms of the natural law that are in any way connected with divine revelation."[14]

The Catholic Catechism puts it this way:

> Individual bishops do not enjoy the prerogative of infallibility. Nevertheless, when, in the course of their authentic teaching on faith or morals, they agree on one position to

be held as definitive, they are proclaiming infallibly the teaching of Christ. This happens when, though scattered throughout the world, they observe the bond of fellowship tying them to each other and to Peter's successor. This occurs more obviously when, united in an ecumenical council, they are the teachers and judges of faith and morals for the universal Church, and an obedient adherence must be given to their definitions of faith.[15]

Such a view is understandable in view of the Catholic teaching on apostolic succession. This refers to "the uninterrupted handing on" of episcopal power and authority from the apostles to contemporary bishops.[16] This transfer of episcopal power is effected whenever a validly ordained Catholic bishop ordains a successor by the laying on of hands. We are told that "those ordained as bishops have continued to fulfill the roles of the apostles, and have been continually in communion with the Apostolic See, that is, with the Bishop of Rome."[17]

The *Catechism of the Catholic Church* likewise tells us that in order that the gospel might always be preserved in the Church, the apostles left bishops as their successors: "They gave them their own position of teaching authority."[18] In fact, we are told, "the apostolic preaching, which is expressed in a special way in the inspired books, was to be preserved in a continuous line of succession until the end of time."[19] In view of this apostolic succession, the bishops are said to speak infallibly when they speak with one voice on a matter.

The Teaching Magisterium

The teaching Magisterium is an outgrowth of the idea that the bishops are "infallible" when they speak on faith and morals with one voice. The Magisterium (rooted in the Latin word for "master") is a body made up of the bishops and the pope. It functions as the authoritative teaching body of the Church that safeguards doctrines. The purpose of this body is to ensure that the faithful do not go doctrinally astray. It alone has the right to interpret and judge the correct meaning of God's Word. The *Catechism of the Catholic Church* tells us that the task of giving an authentic interpretation of the Word of God, whether in its written form or in the form of tradition, "has been entrusted to the living teaching office of the Church alone."[20] It is believed that God protects this body from teaching falsehood in any way.

Sometimes Roman Catholics argue in favor of the Magisterium by saying it is the only means of preserving true unity in the Church. Without the Magisterium, there would be doctrinal chaos in the Church. Without the Magisterium, denominations emerge, each seeking to interpret the Bible as it sees fit. The only way to maintain doctrinal unity is for the Magisterium to be at the helm.

In the book *Dogmatic Theology for the Laity*, we read that "the teaching office of the Church is more important than the Bible; only an infallible Church can interpret the true meaning of Sacred Scripture; no one can do this for himself."[21]

Answering Roman Catholics

Peter Was Not a Supreme Pontiff

Scripture gives no indication that Peter was supreme over all the other disciples. In fact, the four Gospels indicate that no apostle held a supreme position in New Testament times. All the New Testament verses that speak of Peter are virtually silent regarding any alleged supremacy on his part.

It is noteworthy that in Luke 22:24-30, just prior to the time of Christ's arrest and crucifixion, some of the disciples got into an argument regarding who among them would be considered the greatest. One must wonder why the disciples would continue to even ask this question if the issue had been settled, with Peter having emerged as God's choice for some supreme position.[22] The very fact that such discussions took place shows that no apostle had attained a supreme position during Jesus' three-year ministry. Jesus treated each of the disciples with an equal level of respect and trust.

Ask... _____

- If Peter was supreme, why did the disciples continue to debate among themselves who would be considered the greatest (Luke 22:24-30)?

_____

Further, there is not a single epistle in the New Testament where we find any evidence of Peter being called a "pope," nor is there any mention of a papacy. Instead, we find all the disciples working together on a seemingly equal level of authority.

James White suggests that if indeed Peter were in a supreme position of power, he would have said something in his second epistle to the effect that his readers should be sure to follow his successor in Rome.[23] After all, Peter was getting on in years and would have supported the papacy had such a papacy existed. But Peter did no such thing because there was no such papacy.

Another argument we can make note of is the fact that the apostle Paul affirmed in 2 Corinthians 12:11 that he was not inferior to any of the other apostles. Paul would not have said this had a papacy been in existence. It is also highly revealing that while Peter is prominent in the first 12 chapters of the Book of Acts, the apostle Paul is the prominent figure in chapters 13–28. This would not make sense if Peter were the pope. Further, when Paul lists the authority structure in the early church in 1 Corinthians 12:28, there is no mention of a pope: "And God has appointed in the church, first apostles, second prophets, third teachers" (1 Corinthians 12:28).[24]

Ask... _____

- How could the apostle Paul affirm he was not inferior to any other apostle in 2 Corinthians 12:11 if Peter had risen to a position of supremacy?

- If Peter had risen to a position of supremacy, why is the apostle Paul the prominent figure in Acts 13–28?

- If God intended that there be a papacy, why didn't He include it in the authority structure of the church as outlined in 1 Corinthians 12:28—which includes apostles, prophets, and teachers?

Further, in the Book of Acts we find a detailed history of the early church, and there is no mention or even a hint of the existence of a papacy. Nor is there the slightest hint of Petrine supremacy. Instead, we find verses that indicate that Peter was not in a supreme position. For example, we read that the apostles "sent" Peter and John to Samaria after they heard about God's work in Samaria (Acts 8:14). (Peter would have done the sending had he been supreme.) As well, Peter certainly plays no supreme role in the Jerusalem Council (see Acts 15:1-35), for he is portrayed as one among a number of apostles. Instead, James seems to be the person of dominance there (see verses 13-35).

Ask...

- If Peter was supreme, wouldn't he be the one sending others instead of being sent by others to Samaria (Acts 8:14)?

- If Peter was supreme, why does it seem that James was the dominant person at the Jerusalem Council (Acts 15:13-35)?

Another thing that clearly emerges from the pages of the New Testament is that Peter was not infallible. The apostle Paul in the Book of Galatians provides us this key example:

When Cephas [Peter] came to Antioch, I opposed him to his face, because he stood condemned. For prior to the coming of certain men from James, he used to eat with the Gentiles; but when they came, he began to withdraw and hold himself aloof, fearing the party of the circumcision. And the rest of the Jews joined him in hypocrisy, with the result that even Barnabas was carried away by their hypocrisy. But when I saw that they were not straightforward about the truth of the gospel, I said to Cephas in the presence of all, "If you, being a Jew, live like the Gentiles and not like the Jews, how is it that you compel the Gentiles to live like Jews?" (Galatians 2:11-14).

Peter was clearly not immune from error. He made a mistake—*and in a matter of faith, at that.* Peter also shows an attitude of hypocrisy in his behavior (something hardly fitting for a "supreme pontiff").

Note also that if Peter were considered a supreme pontiff during this time, the apostle Paul would have been way out of line in publicly correcting Peter like he did. The fact that Paul corrected Peter shows quite clearly that Peter was not considered supreme in any way.

Ask...

• Doesn't the fact that the apostle Paul publicly corrected Peter on a matter of faith and practice demonstrate that Peter himself was not viewed as supreme (Galatians 2:11-14)?

We might further note that the very idea that Peter ended up going to Rome toward the end of his life is extremely problematic. We know from church history that Irenaeus's list of the 12 bishops of Rome did not include Peter's name. (Irenaeus lived from A.D. 130–200, and he certainly would have been aware of all the bishops who lived in the first century.) That would have been an incredible omission if indeed Peter had been a bishop in Rome.

Further, scholars have noted that Peter ministered heavily among the Jews of his time (Galatians 2:7,8). In view of this, it would have been strange for Peter to move on to

Rome, since that city was not a center of Judaism. The first 15 chapters of the Book of Acts show that Peter was in Jerusalem, Judea, Samaria, Galilee, and Antioch. There is never any mention of Rome.

Another very important factor is that the apostle Paul, in his Epistle to the Romans (written about A.D. 58), greets some 26 people by name (see Romans 16:1-16). *Peter is not one of them.* It seems inconceivable that Paul would have failed to mention a greeting to Peter if Peter had indeed been headquartered in Rome (since A.D. 42, as Roman Catholics claim).

Ask...

• If Peter ended up in Rome, why didn't the apostle Paul mention a greeting to Peter in his letter to the Romans (see Romans 1:7; 16:1-16)?

It is also highly significant that in all of the Epistles written by the apostle Paul while he was in prison in Rome—including Ephesians, Philippians, Colossians, and Philemon—there is never any mention of a visit from Peter. If Peter had been headquartered in Rome, it would be unthinkable that Peter would not have visited Paul. It would also be unthinkable for Peter to have visited him and Paul not to have mentioned it in one or more of the Epistles (see 2 Timothy 4:16).

Ask...

• If Peter ended up in Rome, why didn't he ever visit the apostle Paul while Paul was imprisoned in Rome? *(There is no mention of a visit by Peter in any of the Epistles Paul wrote from Rome.)*

Conclusion: From a biblical perspective, it seems highly unlikely that Peter ended up in Rome.

The Scripture Is Infallible, Not the Pope

In claiming to be infallible when speaking on matters of faith and morals, the pope claims for himself something that even the apostles did not. The apostle Paul is an example. In the Book of Galatians, Paul warned against the danger of a false gospel and said, "But even though we, or an angel from heaven, should preach to you a gospel contrary to that which we have preached to you, let him be accursed" (Galatians 1:8). The gospel that Paul preached is permanently recorded *in written form* in his Epistles. And if anything conflicts with that written Scripture, it is to be rejected. Scripture alone is infallible and hence authoritative (John 10:35).

When in Acts 17:11 the Bereans tested Paul's truth claims against the Old Testament Scriptures, Paul did not chasten them but rather commended them. Paul's attitude is encapsulated in this admonition: "Examine everything carefully; hold fast to that which is good" (1 Thessalonians 5:21).

We should follow this advice in regard to the truth claims of the pope. His teachings should be measured against the teachings of Scripture. And in doing so it becomes clear, at least in many cases, that the pope's teaching is patently unbiblical.

I will deal with some specific doctrinal examples of this later in the book, but as a way of illustrating the fallibility of the pope, consider the Galileo debacle. Galileo was a scientist who was also a believing Christian and had a high regard for Scripture. When Galileo, using a telescope, posited the theory that the sun, not the earth, was the center of the solar system, this rocked the boat with the pope and the Roman Catholic Church, which held to the theological position of an earth-centered system. Galileo was promptly summoned by an Inquisition in 1632, was tried, and was pronounced "vehemently suspected of heresy."[25] From that point forward, he was forced to repeat the seven penitential psalms once a week for three years, and was held under house arrest until his death in 1642.[26] This episode clearly undermines the Roman Catholic view on the infallibility of the pope.

It is not surprising that Roman Catholic scholars have tried to weasel out of this situation by various means, including the suggestion that the pope was not speaking ex cathedra on this occasion.[27] The truth is that the pope was a finite human being who was prone to mistakes as all other human beings are. Only God has infinite understanding and makes no mistakes. That is why His Word is infallible (John 10:35)—*it comes straight from Him* (2 Timothy 3:16). Scripture never promised that there would be successors to Peter who would be divinely protected from error when speaking ex cathedra. That is a man-made doctrine.

We might also mention the sad reality of "antipopes" in Roman Catholicism's history. This refers to the fact that there have been times in Catholic history in which there has been more than one pope at a time. (Those interested in this aspect of Roman Catholic history should consult historical works on the Great Schism between A.D. 1378 and 1417 when there were rival popes at Arignon and Rome.) In fact, scholars tell us: "There have been about thirty-five antipopes in the history of the church."[28] When there are two popes at once, the Roman Catholic is left in a dilemma: Which pope is the Vicar of Christ on earth? Which one is the phony? Which one makes infallible statements on morals and faith when he speaks ex cathedra?[29] While many Roman Catholics ignore this issue, it is something that has never been satisfactorily answered, and which deals a hard blow to the claim of infallibility.

Ask...

- How do you explain the fact that there have been 35 occasions in which there has been more than one pope at a time in the Roman Catholic Church?

- Doesn't this undermine the Roman Catholic view on infallibility?

A further problem for the Roman Catholic view of infallibility is the fact that some of the Church's popes have taught heresy. One example would be Pope Honorius I (A.D. 625–638), who was soundly condemned by the Sixth General Council for teaching the monothelite heresy (the teaching that there was only one will in Christ).[30] *How can an infallible pope teach fallible heresy?* It does not make sense. I have not seen any satisfactory explanation by Roman Catholic apologists on this issue. To say that the pope was not attempting to make an infallible pronouncement on this occasion is not a satisfactory explanation. The reality is that the pope—Christ's alleged vicar on earth—doctrinally misled people.[31]

Ask... _____

• If the pope is infallible, how can it be that Pope Honorius I (A.D. 625–638) was condemned for teaching heresy by the Sixth General Council?

_____

The Apostles Were Totally Unique

Related to this whole issue of alleged apostolic succession is the important scriptural fact that the apostles were totally unique, and they did not pass on anything to a line of successors. The uniqueness of the apostles is seen in the unique miraculous powers they possessed. The apostles were handpicked by God and were given special, unmistakable "signs of an apostle" (2 Corinthians 12:12). These sign gifts included the ability to raise people from the dead on command (Matthew 10:8), heal incurable diseases (Matthew 10:8; John 9:1-7), and perform immediate exorcisms (Matthew 10:8; Acts 16:16-18). On one occasion an apostle pronounced a supernatural death sentence on two people who had "lied to the Holy Spirit," and they immediately dropped over dead (Acts 5:1-11).

Significantly, these miraculous powers ceased during the lives of the apostles. We read in Hebrews 2:3,4, "After it was at the first spoken through the Lord, it was confirmed to us [apostles] by those who heard, God also bearing witness with them, both by signs and wonders and by various miracles and by gifts of the Holy Spirit according to His own will" (insert added).

While the apostles and their miraculous confirmations have passed away, their authoritative teachings remain in authority in the pages of holy Scripture. "The authority of apostolic *writings* has replaced the authority of the first-century apostolic *writers*."[32]

Related to this, we read in Jude 3: "Contend earnestly for the faith which was once for all delivered to the saints." In the Greek text, the definite article *(the)* preceding *faith* points to the one and only faith; there is no other. "The faith" refers to the apostolic body of truth that became regulative upon the church (see Acts 6:7; Galatians 1:23; 1 Timothy 4:1).[33] Bauer, Arndt, and Gingrich, in their highly regarded *Greek Lexicon*, tell us that *faith* in this verse refers to "that which is believed, a body of faith or belief, a doctrine."[34] This "faith" or body of doctrine was *once for all* handed down to the saints by the *unique* apostles of God, and their message was confirmed by mighty miracles.

The word translated "once for all" (Greek: *apax*) refers to something that has been done for all time, something that never needs repeating. The revelatory process was finished after this "faith" had "once for all" been delivered by the apostles. Note also that the word *delivered* (an aorist passive participle) here indicates an act that was completed in the past with no continuing element.

Scripture indicates that the church is built on the foundation of the prophets and apostles (Ephesians 2:20). Of course, once a foundation is built, no further foundation is needed. And because no further foundation is needed, there is no need for apostolic successors. The Bible clearly teaches that apostles and prophets were foundational gifts, and there is not a shred of biblical proof that there were to be successors to the apostles in the Roman Catholic Church.

We Do Not Need a Magisterium

Contrary to the idea that we must submit our understanding of God's Word to an organization (the Magisterium), individual believers are exhorted and instructed by Scripture to test things for themselves (1 Thessalonians 5:21; 1 John 4:1). They are to be like the Bereans, who examined what the apostle Paul said in light of the Word of God, to make sure that Paul's teachings were in line with Scripture (Acts 17:11; see also Galatians 1:8). (Note that the Bereans were not priests; they were laypeople living in Berea.)

Scripture alone is our spiritual guide, and the Holy Spirit alone is our teacher (John 14:18,26). In keeping with the doctrine of the priesthood of believers, each believer himself can study the Scriptures and come to a conviction, under the leading of the Holy Spirit, as to what the text means.

As noted earlier in the book, Protestants believe that the Bible is clear *(perspicuous)*. This is not to say that every verse and every doctrine in the Bible is equally clear, but the main verses and the main doctrines *are* clear. In the common vernacular of our day, "In the Bible the main things are the plain things and the plain things are the main things."[35] An example of a "plain thing" that is a "main thing" is that salvation comes by faith in Christ. Close to 200 references in the New Testament make this main, plain point (John 3:16 is one among these references).

A big problem for the Roman Catholic view is that even the teachings of the Magisterium need interpreting. As one scholar put it, "If an infallible teaching Magisterium is needed to overcome the conflicting interpretations of Scripture, why is it that even these supposedly infallible decisive declarations of the Magisterium are also subject to conflicting interpretations?"[36] The fact of the matter is that there are statements by the Magisterium on important issues like Mary, tradition, and justification that have been interpreted *differently* through the years by Roman Catholics.

Ask...

- If an infallible teaching Magisterium is needed to overcome the conflicting interpretations of Scripture, how are we supposed to overcome the conflicting interpretations among Roman Catholics (by, for example, Jesuits, Franciscans, and Dominicans) regarding what the pronouncements of the Magisterium mean?

As for the claim that the Magisterium is needed to ensure unity in the church, I must point out that in reality the Roman Catholic Church has been characterized by significant *disunity* in recent years. As James McCarthy notes, one of the reasons the Church published the new *Catechism of the Catholic Church* was to draw the Church back to doctrinal unity. Debated issues include such critically important doctrines as the authority of the pope, the Trinity, and the Eucharist.[37]

This freedom to interpret the Scriptures—something that relates to what we call the "priesthood of the believer"—is clearly a biblical doctrine (Acts 17:11). But it is important not to misunderstand what is being said here. Protestants who believe in the priesthood of the believer also believe that God has given to the church pastors and teachers, and we should all learn from them. We can also learn from writings of the past (for example, the church fathers). We do not advocate a doctrinal free-for-all.

We are to handle the Word of God rightly (2 Corinthians 4:2; 2 Peter 3:16). But it is *we* who do the handling—not the Roman Catholic Magisterium. And when we listen to a teacher or a pastor, or read something written by a church father, we always test truth claims against the infallible Word of God (1 Thessalonians 5:21; Acts 17:11).

6

Papal Infallibility and the Teaching Authority of the Church— Part 2

"They have become so certain of the infallibility of the councils and doctors that they have now established the edict, publicly seen, that if we do not accept what they say, we are put under the ban. Now, let us take a spear in hand and make a hole in their shield."[1]
Martin Luther

In the previous chapter we examined a number of arguments offered by the Roman Catholic Church in support of papal infallibility and the teaching authority of the Church. In the present chapter, we will continue our examination, with a focus on specific verses that typically come up in discussions on this issue. We begin with a standard Roman Catholic argument for the supremacy of Peter in Matthew 10:2-4.

Matthew 10:2-4; Mark 3:16-19; Luke 6:14-16—Does the Fact that Peter's Name Is Listed First Point to His Primacy?

The Roman Catholic Teaching: In Matthew 10:2-4 we read: "Now the names of the twelve apostles are these: The first, Simon, who is called Peter, and Andrew his brother; and James the son of Zebedee, and John his brother; Philip and Bartholomew; Thomas and Matthew the tax-gatherer; James the son of Alphaeus, and Thaddaeus; Simon the Zealot, and Judas Iscariot, the one who betrayed Him." It is sometimes argued by Roman Catholics that since Peter is named first, he must have ascended to primacy: "His name always appeared first in the listing of the Apostles (Mark 3:16)."[2]

Response: This is reading far more into the text than is warranted. It is true that Peter played a dominant role in the early church. No Protestant denies that. Peter may have even become the spokesman and representative of the 12 during Jesus' three-year ministry.[3] At the same time, however, let us be careful to note that Peter viewed himself as one among many who shepherded the flock of God. He referred to himself as a "fellow elder" (1 Peter 5:1). Note also that it was James who exercised primacy and not Peter at the Council of Jerusalem (Acts 15:1-21).

Some people may note that Peter wrote two New Testament books and hence his role was central. That is true. But the apostle Paul wrote 13 books in the New Testament. So the fact that Peter wrote a small portion of the New Testament is no indication of a rise to primacy.

Ask... _____

- If Peter was supreme above the other apostles, why did he refer to himself as a "fellow elder" (1 Peter 5:1)?

- If Peter was supreme, why was James apparently in charge at the Council of Jerusalem instead of Peter (Acts 15:1-21)?

- If Peter was supreme, why did he write far fewer New Testament books than did the apostle Paul?

_____

Matthew 16:18—Is Peter the "Rock" Upon Which the Church Is Built?

The Roman Catholic Teaching: Matthew 16:18 is probably one of the most disputed Bible texts between Roman

Catholics and Protestants. To provide the proper context, I will quote verses 13 through 18:

> Now when Jesus came into the district of Caesarea Philippi, He began asking His disciples, saying, "Who do people say that the Son of Man is?" And they said, "Some say John the Baptist; and others, Elijah; but still others, Jeremiah, or one of the prophets." He said to them, "But who do you say that I am?" And Simon Peter answered and said, "Thou art the Christ, the Son of the living God." And Jesus answered and said to him, "Blessed are you, Simon Barjona, because flesh and blood did not reveal this to you, but My Father who is in heaven. And I also say to you that you are Peter, and upon this rock I will build My church; and the gates of Hades shall not overpower it."

Roman Catholic authorities often say this passage supports their view of papal infallibility. They say Peter is the rock upon which Christ built the church:

> His original name was Simon, but Jesus gave him the name "Peter," which is Greek, or "Cephas," which is the Aramaic equivalent. "Peter" and "Cephas" mean "the rock" (John 1:42). Such a name was appropriate to the strong character of the man, but the name became a supremely significant metaphor when Christ later made the dramatic assignment: "You are Peter and on this rock I will build my Church" (Matthew 16:18). There could be no question about the recognition of Peter's leadership.[4]

Response: There are a number of factors in the Greek text that argue against this interpretation. First, whenever Peter is referred to in this passage (Matthew 16), it is in the second person ("you"), but "this rock" is in the third person (verse 18). Moreover, "Peter" (*petros*) is a masculine singular term, and "rock" (*petra*) is a feminine singular term. Hence, they do not have the same referent. Jesus did not say to Peter,

"You are *Petros* and on this *Petros* I will build my church." Jesus said, "You are *Petros* (Peter), and upon this *petra*, I will build my church." It would seem that, in context, *petra* here refers to Peter's confession of faith that Jesus is the Christ.

Ask...

* Since Peter in Matthew 16:18 is referred to in the second person ("you"), but "this rock" is in the third person, does it not seem clear that Peter is not the "rock" upon which the church would be built?

It is critical to note that the entire context of Matthew 16:13-20 is all about Jesus, not Peter.[5] Indeed, the key issue of discussion is Jesus' identity. Jesus asked the disciples about who the people say He is (verse 13). Peter then declared correctly that Jesus is the Christ (verse 16). Then in verse 20, to prevent a premature disclosure of His identity, Jesus warned them not to tell anyone that He was the Christ. *Throughout this entire passage Jesus is the theme, not Peter.*

Many Catholics respond by suggesting that Jesus spoke these words to Peter in the Aramaic language: "You are *Kepha*, and upon this *kepha* I will build my Church." Unlike the Greek (where two different words are used: *petros* and *petra*), the Aramaic uses one word (*kepha*), and hence Peter must be the "rock" of which Christ spoke:

> The word for Peter and for rock in the original Aramaic is one and the same; this renders it evident that the various attempts to explain the term "rock" as having reference not to Peter himself but to something else are misinterpretations. It is Peter who is the rock of the Church.[6]

Protestants respond that all of this is mere conjecture. We do not know what Jesus might have said in Aramaic. The Catholic must be reminded that what we have in our possession are Greek New Testament manuscripts which use two distinct words: *petros* and *petra*. And since Scripture is inspired by the Holy Spirit, the exact words God wanted in Matthew 16:18 were placed into this verse by divine superintendence.

Ask...

- As a matter of policy, do you think it is wiser to base doctrine on the original Greek manuscripts of the New Testament, or on conjecture as to what Jesus might have said in Aramaic?

- If Scripture is inspired by the Holy Spirit, as Scripture itself indicates (2 Timothy 3:16,17), then do you think the Holy Spirit made a mistake in His word choice in Matthew 16:18?

Ephesians 2:20 (NIV) affirms that the church is "built on the foundation of the apostles and prophets, with Christ Jesus himself as the chief cornerstone." Two things are clear from this: First, *all* the apostles, not just Peter, are the foundation of the church; second, the only one who was given a place of uniqueness or prominence was Christ, the capstone. Indeed, Peter himself referred to Christ as "the cornerstone" of the church (1 Peter 2:7), and the rest of believers as "living stones" (verse 5) in the superstructure of the church. Colossians 1:17,18 affirms that Christ alone is the head of the church. Christ is called a rock in Romans 9:33 and in 1 Corinthians 10:4. Both the immediate context of Matthew 16:18 and the broader context of all of Scripture point away from Peter being "the rock." We must not forget, "No man can lay a foundation other than the one which is laid, which is Jesus Christ" (1 Corinthians 3:11).

Ask...

- Since the church is built on the foundation of the prophets and apostles (plural), doesn't this indicate that the church was not built on Peter alone (singular)?

- Since Christ is referred to by Peter as "the cornerstone" of the church (1 Peter 2:7), doesn't Christ alone occupy the place of prominence?

- How do you interpret 1 Corinthians 3:11?

What is more, the same authority Jesus gave to Peter (Matthew 16:18) is later given to *all* the apostles (Matthew 18:18). This indicates that Peter is not unique.

Matthew 16:18—Does the Survival of the Church Depend on Apostolic Succession?

The Roman Catholic Teaching: In Matthew 16:18 we read of the church, "The gates of Hades shall not overpower it." Some Roman Catholics reason that in order for this verse to be true, it would be necessary to have a continuation of a line of authority on earth—which means the apostles would have to pass on their power to bishops as successors. Without this succession of bishops, the church would be in danger of succumbing.[7]

Response: Roman Catholics are reading something into the text that simply is not there. Apostolic succession is not even remotely alluded to. The fact is, the "gates of Hades" do not prevail against the church because of the divine power of Jesus Christ, not because of any alleged apostolic succession. The church is owned by Jesus, since He purchased it with His own blood (Acts 20:28)—and what He owns, He protects.

Ask...

- Does it make sense to you that since Christ Himself *built* the church (Matthew 16:18), *purchased* the church with His blood (Acts 20:28), and is the *head* over the church (Ephesians 5:23), that He Himself will *protect* the church?

- Do you think that Christ as almighty God is capable of protecting the church without the assistance of finite human beings (apostolic successors)?

• Do you think it is stretching it a bit to say that the fulfillment of Jesus' promise in this verse requires apostolic successors?

There are many expositors who apply this verse to the impending death of Christ, and there is some warrant for this interpretation. The Jews of New Testament times would have understood the "gates of Hades" to refer to physical death. Bible scholar Craig Keener notes that the "gates of Hades" in the Old Testament (Job 38:17; Psalm 9:13) and subsequent Jewish tradition referred to the realm and power of death.[8] This being so, Jesus may have been informing the disciples that His impending death on the cross would not prevent or stand in the way of His work of building the church.[9] Contextually, just a few verses later (Matthew 16:21), Jesus spoke of His death. It may be, then, that He was anticipating His death and His victory over death through the resurrection, after which He would be the head of the church and build it through the ages (Ephesians 5:23; Matthew 16:18).

Another possible interpretation, held by some evangelicals, is that death in any form will not silence the church—the death of Jesus, the death of the apostles, the death of Christians anywhere. By Christ's divine power, the church will be sustained forever. But so-called apostolic successors are nowhere in view in this verse.

Matthew 16:19—Does the Fact That Peter Was Given the Keys of the Kingdom Indicate His Primacy?

The Roman Catholic Teaching: In Matthew 16:19 we read Jesus' words to Peter: "I will give you the keys of the kingdom of heaven; and whatever you shall bind on earth shall be bound in heaven, and whatever you shall loose on earth shall be loosed in heaven." Roman Catholics believe this verse proves the primacy of Peter over the church, and by extension, proves the primacy of the pope (Peter's successor) over the church.[10] Indeed,

> When [Peter] acknowledged Christ as the Son of God, our Lord declared that such knowledge was a revelation from God, and on account of his open confession of the truth, Christ promised to build His Church upon him, the Rock, and to entrust to him His entire household, namely, all His followers. This is the symbolism of the keys (Matthew 16:18,19).[11]

The primacy of the pope, based on this verse, was declared at the First Vatican Council (1870):

> Peter, the Prince and Chief of the Apostles, the pillar of faith and foundation of the Catholic Church, received the keys of the kingdom from our Lord Jesus Christ, the Savior and Redeemer of mankind, and lives, presides, and judges, to this day and always, in his successors the Bishops of the Holy See of Rome which was founded by him and consecrated by his blood. Whence, whoever succeeds to Peter in this See, does by the institution of Christ himself obtain the primacy of Peter over the whole Church. The Roman Pontiff possesses the primacy over the whole world, and that Roman Pontiff is the successor of Blessed Peter, Prince of the Apostles, and is true Vicar of Christ, and Head of the whole Church, and Father and Teacher of all Christians; and that full power was given to him in Blessed Peter to feed, rule, and govern the Universal Church by Jesus Christ our Lord.[12]

The Second Vatican Council likewise stated: "The Lord made Peter alone the rock-foundation and the holder of the keys of the Church (cf. Matthew 16:18,19), and constituted him shepherd of his whole flock (cf. John 21:15 ff.)."[13]

Ludwig Ott, Roman Catholic theologian, says that the keys to which Jesus refers represent "supreme authority on earth over the earthly empire of God. The person who possesses the power of the keys has the full power of allowing a person to enter the empire of God or to exclude him from it [and]...the power to forgive sins must also be included in the power of the keys."[14] This power was allegedly given to Peter and lives on in each of Peter's successors (the popes).

Response: The context of this verse relates to witnessing and evangelism by the apostles. All this verse is saying is that the apostles were given the power to grant or deny access into the kingdom of God *based on how people respond to the gospel message.* Those who respond favorably to the gospel are "granted" access, while those who choose not to believe the gospel and refuse to believe in Jesus are "denied" access to the kingdom of God.

We must keep in mind that the terms *bind* and *loose* were Jewish idioms indicating that what is announced on earth has already been determined in heaven. To *bind* meant to forbid, refuse, or prohibit; to *loose* meant to permit or allow. We can announce the prohibition or allowance of certain things on earth because heaven (or God) has already made an announcement on these matters. The Greek construction of the latter half of Matthew 16:19 makes this clear, for there we have two perfect passive participles in periphrastic construction. (The perfect tense indicates an action that was completed in the past but has continuing results.) The proper translation is, "Whatsoever you bind upon earth *shall have already been bound in heaven,* and whatsoever you loose upon the earth *shall have already been loosed in heaven."* Hence, again, Christians can announce the prohibition or allowance of certain things on earth because heaven has already made an announcement on these matters.

Theologian Robert Gromacki has researched the historical backdrop of these terms among the ancient Jews and helps us to understand just how a Jew would have understood the meaning of Jesus' words in the first century:

> What is the power of *binding* and *loosing?* These disciples immediately recognized the background of its meaning. If you were a Jew, living at the time of Christ, and you had done something that you thought could be a violation of the Mosaic Law, you would have taken your problem to

the ruling elders. They would have debated your case; then they would have come to one of two conclusions. They would have either bound or loosed you. If they had *bound* you, this meant that you had violated the Mosaic Law and that you were obligated to pay the penalty—sacrifice and/or restitution. If they had *loosed* you, this meant that you had not violated the Mosaic Law. No sacrifice was necessary. These ruling elders were simply declaring *what had already been legislated* by Moses.[15]

In the same way, *binding* in the context of Matthew 16:19 refers to prohibiting entry into God's kingdom to those who reject the apostolic witness of Jesus Christ. *Loosing* refers to granting entry into God's kingdom among those who accept that witness (see John 20:23; Acts 2:38-41). The apostles could prohibit entry (bind) or grant entry (loose) into God's kingdom only because heaven has already declared that entry into the kingdom hinged on accepting the apostolic witness regarding Jesus Christ.

As we read through the Book of Acts, it is clear that Peter and the apostles did indeed "grant access" into the kingdom of God to various people. Indeed, there were Jews (Acts 2:14-36), Samaritans (8:4-25), and Gentiles (9:32–10:48) who were granted access to the kingdom of God *based on their positive response to the gospel*. What we do not see in the Book of Acts is Peter rising to a position of supremacy and exercising authority over all others. The history recorded in the Book of Acts completely stands against the Roman Catholic interpretation.

Ask... _____

- Do you know of a single verse in the Book of Acts where Peter is seen as exalted to a position of supremacy? (*There is none.*)

- Catholics may respond that they do not need support from the Bible since tradition points to Peter's supremacy. Or they may say, "We Catholics wrote the Bible. We don't need it to prove Peter's supremacy." (If these kinds of issues come up, see the discussion of "Sola Scriptura Versus Tradition" in chapters 3 and 4.)

This understanding of binding and loosing is in perfect keeping with a correct understanding of the "keys of the kingdom" mentioned in this same verse. Theologian Wayne Grudem helps us to understand what these keys refer to:

> Elsewhere in the New Testament a key always implies *authority to open a door and give entrance to a place or realm.* Jesus says, "Woe to you lawyers! for you have taken away the key of knowledge; you did not enter your-selves, and you hindered those who were entering" (Luke 11:52). Moreover, Jesus says in Revelation 1:18, "I have the keys of Death and Hades," implying that he has the authority to grant entrance and exit from those realms. (Cf. also Revelation 3:7; 9:1; 20:1; also the messianic pre-diction in Isa. 22:22.)
>
> The "keys of the kingdom of heaven" therefore repre-sent at least the authority to preach the gospel of Christ (cf. Matt. 16:16) and thus to open the door of the kingdom of heaven and allow people to enter.
>
> Peter first used this authority by preaching the gospel at Pentecost (Acts 2:14-42). But the other apostles also were given this authority in a primary sense (they wrote the gospel in permanent form in the New Testament). And all believers have this "key" in a secondary sense, for they can all share the gospel with others, and thereby open the kingdom of heaven to those who will enter it.[16]

Ask...

- Does the fact that God gave the same authority to the other apostles as He gave to Peter in terms of "binding" and "loosing" (Matthew 18:18) help you see that Peter was not exalted above the others?

In view of the above facts, it is evident that Matthew 16:18,19 provides no support for the Roman Catholic eleva-tion of Peter. As Robert Jamieson, A. R. Fausset, and David Brown note, "One thing is clear, that not in all the New Testament is there the vestige of any authority either claimed or exercised by Peter, or conceded to him, above the rest of the apostles—a thing conclusive against the Romish claims in behalf of that apostle."[17]

Matthew 23:9,10—Should We Think of the Pope as a Spiritual "Father"?

The Roman Catholic Teaching: Jesus said, "Do not call anyone on earth your father; for One is your Father, He who is in heaven" (Matthew 23:9,10). Despite this verse, the pope says (based on tradition) that it is fine for people to make ref-erence to him as "Holy Father."[18]

Response: As a backdrop to understanding Jesus' words in Matthew 23:9,10, I should note that among the ancient Jews, particularly the Pharisees, the rabbis of the time were often respectfully referred to as "Abba" or "papa." It was a title of great honor. The former rabbis who had died were often collectively referred to as "the fathers." They were considered the source of wisdom among the Jews. The rab-bis in turn would address their disciples as their children. The word *father* among the ancient Jews came to denote "authority, eminence, superiority, a right to command, and a claim to particular respect."[19]

Jesus' primary point in Matthew 23:9 would seem to be that only God should be in the place of holy reverence and unquestioned obedience. Only God truly deserves the title "Father" in this highly exalted sense. Only God is "Holy Father." Only God is truly the wise One who cares for us as His beloved children, in contrast to the Pharisees who often led their followers into spiritual bondage.

I believe the same point applies to the pope. Indeed, the pope has set himself up in a far more exalted position as "Holy

Father" than any Pharisee ever did. If what Jesus said holds true for the Pharisees, it certainly must hold true for the pope.

I want to be careful not to imply, however, that merely being a spiritual father is wrong. In the New Testament the apostle Paul was a spiritual father to young Timothy (1 Corinthians 4:15), and referred to Timothy as "my dear son" (2 Timothy 1:2 NIV). Jesus is using the term *father* in Matthew 23:9,10 in a much more exalted sense—a sense requiring holy reverence and unquestioned obedience.

Matthew 28:20—Did Jesus Teach Apostolic Succession in the Great Commission?

The Roman Catholic Teaching: In the last part of Jesus' Great Commission, He said, "Lo, I am with you always, even to the end of the age" (Matthew 28:20). Roman Catholics reason that if Jesus promised to be with the apostles to the end of the age, that would mean there would have to be successors to the apostles who would be around until the end of the age—and hence this proves the doctrine of apostolic succession. "This same norm of apostolic doctrine endures in the successors of him upon whom the Lord imposed the care of the whole sheepfold [John 21:15 ff.], whom He promised He would not fail even to the end of the world [Matthew 28:20]."[20] Indeed, "the faith does not end with the apostles; it only begins from them its tradition through history until Jesus comes again (see Matthew 28:20)."[21]

Response: Roman Catholics are reading too much into Jesus' words. This verse does not even remotely allude to apostolic succession. Jesus is simply promising His followers that He would be with them always. Keep in mind the context: *making disciples.* As the disciples themselves made other disciples, the new disciples would then go forward and make further disciples, and then those disciples would go forward and make even further disciples, and so on. As this process continues until the end of the age, Christ promised that He would be with them.

In promising to be with His disciples throughout the ages, Jesus is acting in keeping with one of His names— *Immanuel*, which means "God with us" (Matthew 1:23). Jesus affirmed that whenever two or three gather in His name, "there I am in their midst" (Matthew 18:20). All this is consistent with similar promises God Himself made throughout Old Testament times to be with His people (Genesis 26:24; 28:15; Exodus 3:12; Joshua 1:5,9; Judges 6:12,16; 2 Samuel 7:3; Isaiah 41:10; 43:5; Haggai 1:13). As is true in Matthew 28:20, in none of these verses is there the slightest hint of apostolic succession.

Ask... _____

(First go over the above facts and explain what is meant by "making disciples.")

• Can you see that the promise of Christ in Matthew 28:20 to be with His disciples throughout the ages is consistent with God's wonderful promises to His people throughout Scripture, and does not require or imply apostolic succession?

Luke 22:31,32—Does Christ's Prayer for Peter Point to Peter's Infallibility as a Pope?

The Roman Catholic Teaching: In Luke 22:31,32 we read Jesus' words to Peter: "Simon, Simon, behold, Satan has demanded permission to sift you like wheat; but I have prayed for you, that your faith may not fail; and you, when once you have turned again, strengthen your brothers." Roman Catholic theologians believe that this prayer by Christ ensures the infallibility of Peter and his successors in protecting the faith. We read in Denzinger's *The Sources of Catholic Dogma*: "St. Peter always remains unimpaired by any error, according to the divine promise of our Lord the Savior made to the chief of his disciples: 'I have prayed for thee, that thy faith fail not.'"[22]

Response: This verse has nothing to do with papal infallibility. Indeed, Christ's words relate only to the one issue of Peter's denial of Christ (Luke 22:34). There is nothing in the verse to even remotely suggest that Christ was making some veiled promise relating to the infallibility of Peter. All we have here is the Lord Jesus praying for Peter's restoration after his impending fall. Jesus prayed that Peter's faith would not fail following his dismal failure as a disciple. Jesus' prayer for Peter is in keeping with His general intercessory ministry for all believers (Romans 8:34; Hebrews 7:25; see also John 17:15).

John 21:15-17—Did Jesus Elevate Peter to a Place of Supremacy?

The Roman Catholic Teaching: In John 21:15-17 we read:

> So when they had finished breakfast, Jesus said to Simon Peter, "Simon, son of John, do you love Me more than these?" He said to Him, "Yes, Lord; You know that I love You." He said to him, "Tend My lambs." He said to him again a second time, "Simon, son of John, do you love Me?" He said to Him, "Yes, Lord; You know that I love You." He said to him, "Shepherd My sheep." He said to him the third time, "Simon, son of John, do you love Me?" Peter was grieved because He said to him the third time, "Do you love Me?" And he said to Him, "Lord, You know all things; You know that I love You." Jesus said to him, "Tend My sheep."

Roman Catholic theologians often argue that Christ's instruction to Peter to "tend My lambs" and "shepherd My sheep" proves that Jesus was putting Peter in a position of authority over the church. Indeed, the word *shepherd* is particularly a term of authority. We read in the *Manual of Dogmatic Theology*: "Since this authority is given only to Peter, then Peter holds the true primacy through which he performs the offices of the supreme pastor of Christ's church."[23]

Response: We do not find any hint in this passage that Jesus was elevating Peter to a position of supremacy. Rather, Jesus exacts a threefold confession of love from Peter to make up for his threefold denial of Christ. The Lord is simply restoring a fallen apostle. Christ was seeking Peter's restoration. The only reason Peter was singled out here is that he is the single apostle that denied Christ. Jesus was not exalting Peter above the other apostles here, but bringing him up to their level![24]

Ask...

- What grievous act of Peter motivated Jesus' words to him? *(Denying Christ three times.)*

- In view of this act, what was Jesus' goal in speaking to Peter? *(To restore Peter.)*

- Is it not clear that the only reason Peter was singled out here is that he is the single apostle that denied Christ?

Elsewhere in Scripture we see that the other apostles too are called to feed and watch out for the "sheep" of the church (see Acts 20:28). This indicates that Peter was not given some unique calling over and against the other apostles.

Peter himself wrote:

Therefore, I exhort the elders among you, as your *fellow elder* and witness of the sufferings of Christ, and a partaker also of the glory that is to be revealed, *shepherd the flock of God among you*, exercising oversight not under compulsion, but voluntarily, according to the will of God; and not for sordid gain, but with eagerness; nor yet as lording it over those allotted to your charge, but proving to be examples to the flock. And when the Chief Shepherd appears, you will receive the unfading crown of glory (1 Peter 5:1-4, emphasis added).

Notice two things here: 1) Peter indicates that others besides himself shepherd the flock of God, thereby showing that he is not unique; 2) Peter refers to himself as a "fellow elder," thereby putting himself on the same level as other elders. Peter did not view himself as supreme.

Ask...

* Since other elders besides Peter shepherd the flock of God, is it not clear that Peter does not see himself in a position of supremacy (1 Peter 5:1-4)?

John 20:23—Do Roman Catholic Priests Have the Power to Forgive Sins?

The Roman Catholic Teaching: In John 20:23 we read, "If you forgive the sins of any, their sins have been forgiven them; if you retain the sins of any, they have been retained." Roman Catholic authority Ludwig Ott tells us on the basis of this text that "the Church has received from Christ the power of remitting sins committed after Baptism."[25] Moreover, "with these words Jesus transferred to the Apostles the mission which He Himself had received from the Father....As He Himself had forgiven sins on earth...He now invested the Apostles also with the power to forgive sins."[26]

Response: This verse is translated more literally from the Greek: "Those whose sins you forgive *have already been* forgiven; those whose sins you do not forgive *have not been* forgiven." The verse does not carry the idea that we have the power to forgive sins in ourselves, but that we are proclaiming what heaven has already proclaimed.

There is no dispute that the disciples to whom Christ was speaking were given the power to pronounce the forgiveness and/or retaining of sins. But all this means is that they were given the authority to declare what God does in regard to salvation when a person either accepts or rejects Jesus Christ as Savior. Remember, only God can actually forgive sin (Mark 2:7; Luke 7:48,49). The disciples (and, by extension, all believers) only have the prerogative of announcing to other people that if they trust in Christ, their sins will be forgiven; if they reject Christ as Savior, their sins will not be forgiven. We have the authority to make that declaration because God Himself has already declared it in heaven. As His representatives, we declare to other people what He has already declared.

That this view is correct is clear from the fact that in the Book of Acts we never witness the apostles themselves explicitly forgiving other people's sins. Rather, we witness the apostles proclaiming God's forgiveness of sin in their preaching (for example, Acts 5:31; 10:43; 13:38; 26:18).

Ask...

• In the Book of Acts can you find a single example of an apostle forgiving someone of his or her sins ("I absolve you...")? (*The answer is no.*)

Note also that there is not a clue in the text of Scripture to the effect that only validly ordained priests were to possess the power to forgive sin. In our book *When Cultists Ask*, Norman Geisler and I point out:

> All the early believers, including laypersons, proclaimed the gospel by which sins are forgiven (Romans 1:16; 1 Corinthians 15:1-4). This ministry of forgiveness and reconciliation was not limited to any special class known as "priests" or "clergy" (2 Corinthians 3–5).
>
> Even Philip, who was only a deacon (Acts 6:5) and not an elder or priest (in the Roman Catholic sense), preached the gospel to the Samaritans. This resulted in the conversion of many of them (8:1-12), which involved the forgiveness of their sins (13:38). The apostles later came, not to convert them, but to give them the special "gift of the Holy Spirit" (cf. 2:38; 8:18) and an outward ("he saw,"

8:18) manifestation (i.e., tongues, cf. 2:1-4) that accompanied this special gift (cf. 1:5; 2:38; 10:44-46).[27]

Acts 12:17—Did Peter End Up Going to Rome?

The Roman Catholic Teaching: In Acts 12:17 we read that following Peter's release from prison, "he departed and went to another place." It is suggested by some Roman Catholics that "it is possible that [the place mentioned in Acts 12:17] was Rome."[28]

Response: This viewpoint is highly speculative. In terms of chronology, Peter's going to "another place" in Acts 12:17 would have been around A.D. 42–45. Yet we know for a fact that Peter attended the Jerusalem Council in A.D. 49 (see Acts 15:7). While Catholics suggest that Peter may have gone to Rome, he could have just as easily gone to Bethany, or Caesarea, or Capernaum, all of which were more easily accessible to Jerusalem than Rome.

We also know that Peter was in Antioch some time prior to A.D. 49–52 (Galatians 2:11), and before A.D. 56 it is possible he may have been in the city of Corinth since there was a "party of Peter" there (1 Corinthians 1:12).[29] Furthermore, as Bible scholar E. Shuyler English has noted, "Paul, who disdained to 'build upon another man's foundation' (Romans 15:20), would scarcely have written a treatise such as the Epistle to the Romans had Peter been in Rome as bishop for about fourteen years."[30]

2 Timothy 2:2—A Proof for Apostolic Succession?

The Roman Catholic Teaching: In 2 Timothy 2:2 we read, "And the things which you have heard from me in the presence of many witnesses, these entrust to faithful men, who will be able to teach others also." Some Roman Catholics say that the idea of entrusting doctrine to faithful men to be passed onto others supports apostolic succession.[31]

Response: Roman Catholics are reading something into this verse that is not there. There is virtually no mention of apostolic succession here. Paul is simply talking about the same kind of discipleship discussed in Matthew 28:19,20. As Timothy was discipled by Paul, so Timothy was to disciple others and pass onto them the truths of Scripture, so that these men too could pass on to others what they had learned. The process continues on and on down through the ages, *but this is not apostolic succession.*

7

Forensic Justification Versus Meritorious Justification—Part 1
The Roman Catholic View

"Idolatry is not only the adoration of images...but also trust
in one's own righteousness, works, and merits."[1]
Martin Luther

One of the greater challenges in engaging in discussions
with Roman Catholics involves the issue of salvation.
Often when you ask them what they believe to be the basis
of salvation, they will mention Christ and His death on the
cross, they will mention faith, and they will mention the
need for grace, but they will also throw into the mix a life of
meritorious works and participation in the various sacramental rituals of the Roman Catholic Church.

Certainly Catholics deny that their Church teaches a
works salvation. They will talk about how salvation is impossible apart from the grace of God. But though things start out
by grace in the Roman Catholic system of salvation, as we
will see in this chapter, works do indeed get mixed into the
picture. By virtue of the fact that a life of meritorious works
is necessary to gain final salvation, it is clear that in reality
the Roman Catholic view of salvation is works-oriented.

Salvation may involve grace and faith, but it is not by grace alone (*sola gratia*) or by faith alone (*sola fide*).

In the present chapter, I will focus heavy attention on the Roman Catholic view of justification, and a number of other issues closely related to it. I approach this subject with some hesitation in view of the fact that a proper treatment of it would require an entire book, not just a few chapters. Abbreviated treatments always run the risk of not presenting "the whole picture." My goal, however, will be to avoid sacrificing accuracy for the sake of brevity. I think you will come to agree with me that this is one of the most important issues we have to deal with while engaging in discussions with Roman Catholics.

Justification in Roman Catholicism

Grace, faith, *and* works come into play in the Roman Catholic view of justification. It starts out with grace—with what Roman Catholics call "first actual grace." This grace is "first" in the sense that it is God who initially reaches out to a person and gives the grace that will enable the individual to seek God, to have faith,* and to prepare his or her soul for baptism and justification. "First actual grace" leads a person to this doctrinal acceptance. It is "actual" in the sense that good acts are the goal. This grace does not have an automatic influence, but rather the person must decide for or against it. One must respond to it for it to become effectual. He or she must cooperate and yield to its influence. If someone cooperates with this grace, that person will end up performing "salutary acts." This performing of good works is believed to prepare a person's soul for baptism and justification. As the Council of Trent put it, when someone is "proposing to receive baptism, they are moved to begin a new life and to keep God's commandments."[2] If someone rejects this grace and ends up dying, he is lost.

---

* Faith involves an acceptance of the major doctrines of the Roman Catholic Church as taught in the creeds.

When a person is finally baptized, according to Roman Catholics, original sin is removed from his or her soul, and in its place sanctifying grace is infused. It is at this point that the person experiences "initial justification." No one can merit or earn this grace, and hence this initial aspect of justification is said to be by grace. When the soul is infused with this sanctifying grace of God, inherent righteousness becomes one of the soul's characteristics.

Here is the backdrop to initial justification: When Adam and Eve fell into sin, they lost the divine life God had bestowed upon them through sanctifying grace. Since then, every human being born into the world has been born without this divine life or sanctifying grace. According to the Catholic *Encyclopedic Dictionary of the Bible*:

> On account of his sin Adam lost the gifts God had given him: sanctifying grace; the right to heaven; freedom from death and suffering; enjoyment of the Garden of Paradise; perfect submission of all his passions to the control of reason....Since Adam was not only the first man but had been appointed by God the head of the human race, his sin (not Eve's) had serious consequences on all his descendants. They are all born without the gifts Adam had, which would have been theirs had Adam not sinned. This privation of sanctifying grace and other gifts possessed by Adam before his fall is called original sin (Rom. 5:19).[3]

This means that for a person to be saved, there must be a restoration of sanctifying grace. At the moment of baptism, this is exactly what happens. Sanctifying grace is infused into the person and the spiritually dead person becomes spiritually alive. The actual amount of sanctifying grace that is infused into the soul hinges on the person's prebaptismal preparations. (Someone who fully cooperates with "first actual grace" prior to baptism will end up with more sanctifying grace than a lesser committed person.)

The spiritual transformation that takes place at baptism is often referred to as "justification" by Roman Catholics. The reasoning goes like this: At baptism the guilt that comes from original sin is removed, and the person is infused with sanctifying grace. Hence, because of what this grace accomplishes, it is often called justifying grace. Justification involves both the removal of sin and a transition from that state devoid of sanctifying grace to a state of grace.

Hence, baptism is not an optional matter for the Roman Catholic. The Council of Trent emphatically stated that "if anyone shall say that baptism is optional, that is, not necessary for salvation: let him be anathema."[4]

Following this initial justification which occurs at baptism, there is a second aspect of justification that occurs throughout life as the person continues to cooperate with God's grace and progresses in good works, thereby meriting further grace that is necessary for him or her to enter eternal life. This means that the person must sustain his new relationship with God and continue cooperating with God's grace to gain full and final justification, being cautious along the way not to commit a mortal sin (a conscious, deliberate, serious sin), which has the effect of erasing grace from the soul. The believer will only know for certain that he or she is finally justified at the end of the process (that is, when he or she dies). In the meantime, his or her constant duty is to cooperate as much as possible with the grace of God, so that continued meritorious works can be performed.

The *Catechism of the Catholic Church* tells us:

> Since the initiative belongs to God in the order of grace, *no one can merit the initial grace* of forgiveness and justification, at the beginning of conversion. Moved by the Holy Spirit and by charity, *we can then merit* for ourselves and for others the graces needed for our sanctification, for the increase of grace and charity, and for the attainment of eternal life.[5]

Hence, when you hear a Roman Catholic say "We believe in justification by grace," it is important not to forget that he or she is speaking of the first aspect of justification—that is, "initial justification." Further, they argue, the good works one must engage in to prepare for baptism result from the influence of first actual grace. Hence, *grace does play a role.* But salvation is not by *grace alone.* The second aspect of justification definitely involves meritorious works, including such things as loving one's neighbor, obeying God's commandments, praying, fasting, and the like.

If you ask the average Roman Catholic what is involved in salvation, he or she will likely give you a works scenario. The person will affirm that God's grace made it all possible, and faith is necessary, and Christ certainly provided the basis of our salvation by dying on the cross. But the Catholic will also say that *we must now do our part and engage in good works.*[6]

Hence, while justification is said to begin by God's grace, it is backloaded with lots of things that a person must do. Taken in its totality, this amounts to a works system of salvation. Salvation in Roman Catholicism does involve grace and faith, but it is not by *grace alone* or by *faith alone*, as the Reformers taught. Grace alone is not sufficient without human works to yield final and full justification. While Catholics acknowledge the *necessity* of grace, they do not acknowledge the *exclusivity* of grace.

One of the more disturbing aspects of Roman Catholic theology is the teaching that the grace of justification can be gained and lost and gained and lost, on and on. It is a *conditional* justification. Catholics believe that committing a mortal sin virtually erases sanctifying/justifying grace from the soul. For a person who commits such a sin, the only remedy is to become "rejustified" through the sacrament of penance.* "Those who through sin have forfeited the received grace of

---

* I will address the issue of mortal sin and the sacrament of penance in greater detail in chapter 12.

justification can again be justified when, moved by God, they exert themselves to obtain through the sacrament of penance the recovery, by the merits of Christ, of the grace lost."[7]

It is much like a roller-coaster system of salvation. One hour you are justified (in a state of grace), the next hour you can lose all justification as a result of committing a mortal sin (and grace is erased), and the next hour you can be justified all over again as a result of going to confession, participating in the sacrament of penance (at which time grace is restored).

Roman Catholicism confuses and merges justification and sanctification. Catholics believe that someone's increasing level of righteousness eventually enables the person to gain final justification. The goal of the individual Roman Catholic is to continue to cooperate with God's grace and grow in sanctification (righteousness) and good works, and participate in the various Roman Catholic sacraments, with a view to attaining final justification before God. What all this means is that in Roman Catholicism, *good works precede final justification.* Justification is conditioned upon good works. As Pope John Paul II put it, "a good life is the *condition* of salvation."[8]

In keeping with this, Roman Catholics believe that a person's level of justification can be increased throughout life. The Council of Trent said that if anyone says that justification "is not preserved and also not *increased* before God through good works, but that those works are merely the fruits and signs of justification obtained, but not the cause of its increase, let him be anathema."[9] The council also affirmed: "If anyone says that the sinner is justified by faith alone, meaning that nothing else is required to cooperate in order to obtain the grace of justification, let him be anathema."[10] Indeed, we are told, "no one ought to flatter himself with faith alone, thinking that by faith alone he is made an heir and will obtain the inheritance."[11] Further, "if anyone says that a man who is justified and however perfect is not bound to observe the commandments of God and the Church, but only to believe, as if the Gospel were a bare and absolute promise of eternal life without the condition of observing the commandments, let him be anathema."[12]

Obviously, since justification involves a process whereby meritorious works are required, different people find themselves on different levels on the road of justification. Some people are more successful than others in their merit-earning activities. Catholic theologian Ludwig Ott commented:

> As the Reformers wrongly regarded justification as a merely external imputation of Christ's justice,* they were obliged also to hold that justification is identical in all men. The Council of Trent, however, declared that the measure of the grace of justification received varies in the individual person who is justified, according to the measure of God's free distribution and to the disposition and the co-operation of the recipient himself.[13]

To make sure he is where he should be on the road of justification, the Roman Catholic must cooperate with the grace of God in producing meritorious works. As noted previously, in Roman Catholicism justification involves an infusion of grace into a person's soul that enables him or her through the power of that grace to do good works. These works are meritorious in God's sight. *Eternal life is said to be merited by the good works that are performed by the person in the state of grace.*

Roman Catholics argue that outside that state of grace, any works we might perform are not meritorious. Since it is God who infuses us with the grace that enables us to do good and therefore meritorious works, Roman Catholics say their view of salvation is not works-oriented. (I will evaluate this

---

* Justification in Protestant theology refers to God's forensic declaration that the person has been restored to a state of righteousness on the basis of belief and trust in the work of Christ rather than on the basis of his or her own accomplishment.

claim in the next two chapters and demonstrate that grace and meritorious works are mutually exclusive.)

In Roman Catholic theology, "merit" has definite merit for the person in a state of grace. Cooperating with God's grace and doing good works merits a reward (heaven) from God. Throughout a person's life this merit is accumulated. But, as noted above, should the Catholic commit a mortal sin, then all merit and grace are thereby forfeited. Yet, if the person then participates in the sacrament of penance, lost merit and grace are thereby restored.

Roman Catholic theology teaches that some people are so good and righteous and full of merit that they end up being "canonized" as saints. Roman Catholics today often ask these saints in heaven to intercede on their behalf before God. Their prayers are viewed as powerfully effective since the saints have built up so many merits during their time on earth.

According to Catholic theology, there is a storehouse of merit deposited by the saints on which other people can draw for help. These saints have allegedly done more good deeds than necessary for their own salvation and have put "money in the bank of heaven" on which others in need can draw. By engaging in prayers and good deeds on behalf of the dead in purgatory, Catholics can shorten the stay of their dead loved ones in purgatory as they draw on this huge treasury of merit. (I will address this issue in greater detail in chapter 13.)

No Assurance of Salvation

It is not surprising that in Roman Catholic theology there is no assurance of salvation. Indeed, apart from a special revelation given to someone regarding assurance, it is only *following the moment of death* that people find out for sure whether or not they have attained eternal life.[14] For it is at this moment that the Catholic faces what is called the "particular judgment" when God determines his or her destiny.

What is the basis of the judgment? In a capsule, the whole thing hinges on whether you have sanctifying grace in your soul at the moment of your death. If you have such grace in your soul at that moment, then you have managed to preserve grace until the end and can look forward to eternal life. (Even then, though, you will probably have to spend time in purgatory before being granted entrance to heaven. Even if the guilt of your sins is forgiven via the sacrament of penance, the temporal punishment for those sins remains. These punishments must be expiated by works either in this life, or following death in purgatory. More on this later in the book.) If your soul is devoid of such grace at the moment of death—something that could happen if you commit a mortal sin (which erases grace) and you fail to go to a priest in time for the sacrament of penance (which restores grace)—*then you are damned forever.*

The lack of assurance in Roman Catholic theology is more than evident in this statement from the Council of Trent:

> If one considers his own weakness and his defective disposition, he may well be fearful and anxious as to the state of grace, as nobody knows with the certainty of faith, which permits of no error, that he has achieved the grace of God.[15]

What About Infant Baptism?

About 16 million infants and youngsters (under seven years of age) are baptized annually in the Roman Catholic Church. As noted above, Roman Catholics believe that as a result of baptism, original sin is removed from the soul and sanctifying grace is infused. Hence, Catholics believe their kids, once baptized, are in a state of salvation. They assume their kids are right with God by virtue of being baptized.

Catholics cite Jesus' words in John 3:5: "Unless one is born of water and the Spirit, he cannot enter into the kingdom of God." During the sacrament of baptism, the priest touches the water and asks God to send the Holy Spirit upon the water, and proclaims that all who are buried with Christ in the death of baptism are also raised to newness of life.[16] Following the baptism of the infant, and having then been clothed in a white baptismal garment, the infant is told by the priest that he or she has become a new creation, and that he or she has been clothed in Christ.[17]

What is the reasoning behind all this? In Roman Catholic doctrine, the infant must be baptized in order to remedy the spiritual disease of original sin, which has its roots in Adam's sin in the Garden of Eden. Because of Adam's sin, the entire human race was affected. Every infant is born with the stain of original sin and is hence alienated from God. Getting baptized takes care of this problem. A baptized infant is viewed as guiltless before God. He is "set free" from original sin. Further, Roman Catholics believe that as a result of baptism the infant is now born again, is given the gift of divine life, is made a partaker of eternal life, is made a member of Christ's body, and is made a temple of the Holy Spirit.

Now, I must be careful here, because I want to fairly represent the Catholic view. Simply because the guilt of original sin is removed at baptism, and simply because that baby is "initially justified," does not mean that that baby has now once-for-all attained eternal salvation. (For example, as he matures past the age of accountability and subsequently sins, he can lose the grace he received at baptism.) In the Roman Catholic system of theology, baptism is basically a first step on the road to salvation. It is the beginning point. It gets the ball in motion, so to speak. But there is more—much more—that must be done throughout life. (More on all this later in the book.)

How does this relate to the death of infants who have not reached the age of accountability? Infants who have been baptized in the Roman Catholic Church before reaching the age of accountability do not have to go to purgatory. They go straight to heaven at the moment of death, and there they enjoy the "beatific vision." (This refers to the essential happiness of heaven that is involved in seeing the very essence of God—unsurpassably beautiful and good.) These infants do not suffer in purgatory because they have accrued no guilt (since they have not reached the age of accountability) and hence deserve no temporal punishment.

An infant that dies before the parents bring him or her in for baptism is viewed as being not bad enough to go to hell, but neither can he or she go to heaven since baptism is required for entrance into heaven. Some Roman Catholic theologians have suggested that there must be an in-between place—*limbo*—to which unbaptized infants go at the moment of death. There they do not enjoy the glorious benefits and wonders of heaven, but neither do they suffer the pain and suffering of hell. This belief in "limbo" is not an official dogma of the church, but few priests and Roman Catholic theologians deny it either.[18]

8

Forensic Justification Versus Meritorious Justification—Part 2
Answering Roman Catholics

"Now the article of justification...is this: that by faith only in Christ, and without works, we are pronounced righteous and saved."[1]
Martin Luther

In the previous chapter we examined the Roman Catholic view of justification and various related issues. In the present chapter, we will seek to provide a general Protestant response regarding these issues. Then, in the next chapter, specific Bible verses related to salvation and justification will be examined in detail.

The Protestant View of Justification

In contrast to the Roman Catholic view, Protestants view justification as a singular and instantaneous event in which God declares the believing sinner to be righteous. Justification viewed in this way is a judicial term in which God makes a legal declaration. It is not based on performance or good works. It involves God's pardoning of sinners and declaring them absolutely righteous at the moment they trust in Christ for salvation (Romans 3:25,28,30; 8:33,34; Galatians 4:21–5:12; 1 John 1:7–2:2).

Here is the theological backdrop: Humankind's dilemma of "falling short of God's glory" (Romans 3:23) pointed to the need for a solution. Man's sin—his utter unrighteousness—was such that there was no way of his coming into a relationship with God on his own. Humankind was guilty before a holy God, and this guilt of sin put a barrier between man and God.

The solution is found in *justification*. Negatively, this word means that a person is once-for-all pronounced not guilty before God. Positively, the word means that a person is once-for-all pronounced righteous before God. The very righteousness of Christ is imputed to the believer's life. (To impute means "to credit," "to attribute," or "to transfer." Christ's righteousness is *credited* to the believer's life.) From the moment that someone places faith in Christ the Savior, God sees that person through the lens of Christ's righteousness.

The Protestant view is often referred to as "forensic justification." *Forensic* comes from a Latin word meaning "forum." This word has its roots in the fact that in the ancient Roman forum, a court could meet and make judicial or legal declarations. Forensic justification, then, involves God's judicial declaration of the believer's righteousness before Him. The believer is legally acquitted of all guilt, and the very righteousness of Christ is imputed to his account. Henceforth, when God sees the believer, He sees him in all the righteousness of Christ.

Note that this declaration is something external to man. It does not hinge on man's personal level of righteousness. It does not hinge on anything that man does. It hinges solely on God's declaration. It is a once-for-all judicial pronouncement that happens the moment a sinner places faith in Christ. Even while the person is yet a sinner and is experientially not righteous, he is nevertheless righteous *in God's sight* because of forensic justification.

This view of justification has support from the Old Testament. For example, in Deuteronomy 25:1 we read of judges who "*justify the righteous* and condemn the wicked" (emphasis added). The word *justify* here clearly means "declare to be righteous" just as *condemn* means "declare to be guilty." The word is used in a forensic sense here and elsewhere in the Old Testament (see, for example, Job 27:5 and Proverbs 17:15). And when the apostle Paul (an Old Testament scholar par excellence) used the word *justify* in the Book of Romans, he did so against this Old Testament backdrop.[2]

As noted above, at the moment someone places personal faith in Christ, God makes an incalculable "deposit" of righteousness into that individual's personal spiritual bank account. It is a once-for-all act on God's part. It is irrevocable. It is a done deal. It cannot be lost. God's pronouncement is final. And this final pronouncement on God's part insures that the believing sinner will never receive just punishment for the sins committed during life. This is the wonderful gift of salvation.

Romans 3:24 (NIV) tells us that God's declaration of righteousness is given to believers "freely by his grace." The word *grace* literally means "unmerited favor." It is because of God's unmerited favor that believers can freely be declared righteous before God. This righteousness cannot be earned.

This does not mean, however, that God's declaration of righteousness has no objective basis. God did not subjectively decide to overlook man's sin or wink at his unrighteousness. Jesus died on the cross for us. He died in our stead. He paid for our sins. Jesus ransomed us from death by His own death on the cross (2 Corinthians 5:21).

There has been a great exchange. As the great Reformer Martin Luther said, "Lord Jesus, You are my righteousness, I am Your sin. You have taken upon Yourself what is mine and given me what is Yours. You have become what You were not so that I might become what I was not."[3]

A key blessing that results from being declared righteous is that we now have peace with God (Romans 5:1). The

Father sees believers through the lens of Jesus Christ. And because there is peace between the Father and Jesus Christ, there is also peace between the Father and believers, since believers are "in Christ."

If someone were to look through a piece of red glass, everything would appear red. If that person were to look through a piece of blue glass, everything would appear blue. If he or she were to look through a piece of yellow glass, everything would appear yellow, and so on.

Likewise, when we believe in Jesus Christ as our Savior, God looks at us *through the Lord Jesus Christ*. He sees us in all the white holiness of His Son. Our sins are imputed to the account of Christ and Christ's righteousness is imputed to our account. For this reason, the Scriptures indicate that there is now no condemnation—literally, *no punishment*—for those who are in Christ Jesus (Romans 8:1).

Evangelical Protestants believe in justification *by faith in Christ alone* (Romans 4; Galatians 3:6-14). God justifies "the one who has faith in Jesus" (Romans 3:26). Indeed, "We maintain that a man is justified by faith apart from works of the Law" (Romans 3:28). "Abraham believed God, and it was reckoned to him as righteousness" (Romans 4:3). "Having been justified by faith, we have peace with God through our Lord Jesus Christ" (Romans 5:1).

Good works, however, are a *by-product* of salvation (Matthew 7:15-23; 1 Timothy 5:10,25). Good works result from the changed purpose for living that salvation brings (1 Corinthians 3:10-15). We are not saved *by* our works, but *in order to do* good works. We do works not to *get* salvation, but because we have *already gotten* it. Works are a *consequence* of justification, not a *condition* for it.

Scripture indicates that following the single, instantaneous act of justification, a moral transformation begins at that point in the life of the believer—a process we call sanctification. (See Appendix D for more on the issue of sanctification.) In Protestantism, sanctification flows from justification, whereas in Roman Catholicism, justification flows from sanctification (righteousness). Catholicism has it backward.

The Wonder of God's Grace

As noted above, *grace* literally means "unmerited favor." The very meaning of the word goes against Roman Catholic theology, for it refers to the undeserved, unearned favor of God. Romans 5:1-11 tells us that God gives His incredible grace to those who actually deserve the opposite—that is, condemnation.

Significantly, the Bible makes virtually no reference whatsoever to "sanctifying grace." In the Bible, grace is quite simply *grace*—and it refers to the unmerited favor of God. "Unmerited" means it cannot be worked for. But Catholicism nevertheless teaches that people must do meritorious works to earn grace. If grace is not free, though, it is not truly grace. "If it is by grace, it is no longer on the basis of works, otherwise grace is no longer grace" (Romans 11:6).

Further, the idea that God's grace is repeatedly communicated to His people through seven sacraments has no biblical basis either. We will look in vain for a reference to "seven sacraments" in the Bible. God's grace is given to us not through ritualistic ceremonies, but straight from God to all who believe in the Person of Jesus Christ: "Therefore having been justified by faith, we have peace with God through our Lord Jesus Christ, through whom also we have obtained our introduction by faith into this grace in which we stand; and we exult in hope of the glory of God" (Romans 5:1,2).

Eternal life, according to Scripture, cannot be earned. Verse after verse in Scripture indicates that eternal life is a free gift that comes as a result of believing in the Savior, Jesus Christ. Jesus said: "Truly, truly, I say to you, he who believes *has* eternal life" (John 6:47, emphasis added). "The *free gift of God* is eternal life in Christ Jesus our Lord" (Romans 6:23, emphasis added). "I will give to the one who thirsts from the spring of the water of life *without cost*" (Revelation 21:6, emphasis added).

Merit plays no role in obtaining eternal life. From a biblical perspective, opting for the merit system can only be bad, since all of us "merit" one thing—eternal death: "For the wages of sin is death, but the free gift of God is eternal life in Christ Jesus our Lord" (Romans 6:23).

We simply cannot do good works to earn favor with God. Rather, our favor with God comes only as a result of placing faith in Christ, after which time the Father sees us as being "in Christ." Experientially we may still be quite imperfect. But the Father sees us as having the very perfection of Christ since we are "in Christ." As a result of our relationship with Christ, and as a result of walking in dependence on the Spirit, good works are increasingly produced in our lives. Good works, as noted earlier, are the *result* of our relationship with Christ, not the *source* of it.

One of my favorite passages in the Bible is Psalm 130:3,4 (NIV): "If you, O LORD, kept a record of sins, O Lord, who could stand? But with you there is forgiveness." This passage is brimming with grace. The phrase "kept a record" was an accounting term among the ancients. It refers to keeping an itemized account.

The point of the psalmist is that if we think God is keeping a detailed, itemized account of all our sins, there would be no way for us to have a relationship with Him. It would be impossible. The good news is that God does not keep such an itemized account but rather forgives those who trust in Christ.

True grace is sometimes hard for people to grasp. After all, our society is performance-oriented. Good grades in school depend on how well we perform in school. Climbing up the corporate ladder at work depends on how well we perform at work. Nothing of any real worth is a "free ticket" in our society. But God's gift of salvation is a grace-gift. *It is free!* We cannot attain it by a good performance. Ephesians

2:8,9 affirms, "By grace you have been saved through faith; and that not of yourselves, it is the gift of God; not as a result of works, that no one should boast." Titus 3:5 tells us that God "saved us, not on the basis of deeds which we have done in righteousness, but according to His mercy."

By contrast, Romans 3:20 says that "by the works of the Law no flesh will be justified [or declared righteous] in His sight" (insert added). In Galatians 2:16 the apostle Paul tells us that "a man is not justified by the works of the Law but through faith in Christ Jesus."

Gifts cannot be worked for—*only wages* can be worked for. As Romans 4:4,5 (NIV) tells us, "When a man works, his wages are not credited to him as a gift, but as an obligation. However, to the man who does not work but trusts God who justifies the wicked, his faith is credited as righteousness." Since salvation is a free gift, *it cannot be earned.*

The person who seeks salvation through self-effort is like the man who, in attempting to sail across the Atlantic Ocean, found his sailboat becalmed for days with no wind. Finally, frustrated by his lack of progress, he tried to make his stalled sailboat move by pushing against the mast. Through strenuous effort, he succeeded in making the boat rock back and forth, and thereby created a few small waves on the otherwise smooth sea. Seeing the waves and feeling the rocking of the boat, he assumed he was making progress and so continued his efforts. However, though he exerted himself a great deal, he actually got nowhere.[4]

So it is with trying to work for our salvation. Our efforts to save ourselves are both futile and exhausting. No matter how hard we try, it is no use. The source of salvation lies in God's grace alone, not in exertions of willpower, or in efforts of discipline, or any other self-effort. *Salvation is a free gift!*

Does "Merit" Have Any Merit?

When Protestants say the Roman Catholic system of salvation is works-oriented, they are not saying Catholics give no place to Christ and His atonement. Nor are they saying Catholics give virtually no place to grace. What they are saying is that in Roman Catholic theology, the work of *Christ alone* does not save. The fact that works are a part of the equation—*such that without those works there would be no final justification*—ultimately makes the Roman Catholic view of salvation works-oriented.

In an effort to deal with verses that argue against works salvation, some Roman Catholic scholars have made an artificial distinction between "works" and "works of the law." "Works of the law" are not necessary for salvation, it is argued, while "works" *are* necessary. This distinction is a false one. Indeed, the verses in the New Testament where the apostle Paul addresses the issue of works cannot be limited to "works of the law," but rather simply deal with "works." Any way you look at it, the apostle Paul argues against any kind of works (see Romans 2:14; 3:21-24; Ephesians 2:8,9).

When the jailer asked the apostle Paul how to be saved, Paul did not say: "Well, you better write all this down: You need to be a member of the Roman Catholic Church, get baptized, never commit a mortal sin, participate in seven sacraments throughout life, recite the rosary, perform lots of meritorious works, and when you die, spend some time in the flames of purgatory—and then you'll be saved." Rather, Paul answered simply: "Believe in the Lord Jesus, and you shall be saved" (Acts 16:31).

The Roman Catholic position seems to assume that human beings can actually *do* things that make them acceptable to God, but such an idea goes against the entire grain of Scripture. We are told that "no one is good except God alone" (Mark 10:18). We are told that "all our righteous deeds are like a filthy garment" (Isaiah 64:6). In view of this, God's grace—God's unmerited favor—is our only chance for salvation (Ephesians 2:8,9). Based on God's grace, all who believe in Jesus become recipients of eternal life (John 3:16; Luke 10:20).

While Protestants reject the Roman Catholic doctrine of merit, Protestants do recognize the biblical doctrine of the judgment seat of Christ, before which every Christian must one day appear. At that judgment, Christians will indeed receive rewards for their faithfulness on earth, or suffer the loss of rewards for a lack of faithfulness on earth.

We read in 2 Corinthians 5:10, "For we must all appear before the judgment seat of Christ, that each one may be recompensed for his deeds in the body, according to what he has done, whether good or bad." And in Romans 14:10,12 we read, "We shall all stand before the judgment seat of God.... Each one of us shall give account of himself to God." This reward, however, has nothing to do with whether or not someone is saved. Rather, the reward has to do with people who are *already* saved, and will in the future be judged and rewarded by God based on their level of faithfulness and commitment during their time on earth.

Baptism Not a Requirement for Salvation

Baptism is surely important, and it should be among the first acts of obedience to God following a person's conversion to Christ (by faith alone). But baptism is not a *requirement* for salvation. Nor is it a cause of justification.

As a preface to my brief comments on this issue, I want to note that there are certain Protestant denominations (such as Lutherans and Anglicans) that hold to a form of baptismal regeneration. Hence, I am not trying to unfairly single out Roman Catholics on this issue. (I should note, though, that Roman Catholicism is unique in saying that baptism is the way adults receive "initial justification.") The following comments are certainly applicable to both Roman Catholics and those Protestants who hold to baptismal regeneration, but they are especially relevant to the Roman Catholic position since Catholicism proclaims this doctrine infallibly.[5]

There are several scriptural factors that lead me to the conclusion that baptism is not necessary for salvation. I realize an entire book could be written on this issue. My comments here are intended only as brief summary. First, when Jesus was crucified between two thieves, one of them placed faith in Christ right there on the cross. Jesus immediately said to him, "I tell you the truth, today you will be with me in paradise" (Luke 23:43 NIV). The thief had no opportunity to jump down from the cross and get baptized, but was nevertheless saved.

Second, in Acts 10 we find Cornelius, a devout Gentile, exercising faith in Christ and becoming saved. Yet the account in Acts 10 makes it patently clear that Cornelius was saved *prior* to being baptized in water. After all, the moment Cornelius believed in Christ, the gift of the Holy Spirit was poured out on him (Acts 10:45). The fact that the Holy Spirit came upon Cornelius prior to being baptized in water shows that he was saved prior to his baptism.

Third, in 1 Corinthians 1:17 the apostle Paul said, "For Christ did not send me to baptize, but to preach the gospel." Here a distinction is made between the gospel and being baptized. We are told elsewhere that it is the gospel that brings salvation (1 Corinthians 15:2). And baptism is not a part of that gospel. So baptism is not necessary for salvation. Nevertheless, we should still get baptized (*following* our conversion) because God has instructed us to.

We must keep in mind the purpose of baptism. It is not a "cause" of justification. Rather, in the New Testament, baptism is portrayed as a symbol of our death and resurrection with Jesus Christ. As we go down into the water, that motion symbolizes our death with Christ. As we are raised up out of the water, that motion symbolizes our resurrection and new life with Christ. Baptism is symbolic, and in New Testament days it was a way of making public someone's identification with Jesus Christ.

In a way, baptism is like a wedding ring: They both symbolize transactions. A wedding ring symbolizes marriage, just as baptism symbolizes salvation in Jesus Christ. The mere wearing of a wedding ring does not make a person married any more than being baptized makes someone saved. But both the wedding ring and baptism *symbolize* marriage and a saved state. From a biblical perspective, baptism *follows* salvation by faith (see Acts 2:41; 8:13; 18:8).

Eternal Security in Salvation

Roman Catholics cannot enjoy the security of knowing that they are saved. They hope, but they cannot know for sure. As one Catholic cardinal put it, "Church teaching is that I don't know, at any given moment, what my eternal future will be. I can hope, pray, do my very best—but I still don't know."[6]

Of course, such insecurity makes sense in view of the Roman Catholic view of justification. After all, if someone commits a mortal sin, he or she thereby forfeits all merit and loses all sanctifying grace within the soul. If the individual dies in such a state prior to getting to a priest for the sacrament of penance, that person is damned forever. So, in a very real way, Roman Catholicism teaches eternal *insecurity*.

I realize there are certain Protestant groups (such as the Arminians) who also teach that a person can lose salvation. But I believe the consistent testimony of Scripture is that once a person becomes a part of the family of God, he or she is absolutely secure in that salvation. Scripture affirms: "Much more then, *having now been justified* by His blood, we shall be saved from the wrath of God through Him" (Romans 5:9, emphasis added). We read: "Whom He predestined, these He also called; and whom He called, these He also justified; and whom He justified, these He also glorified" (Romans 8:30). We are promised that "the gifts and the calling of God are irrevocable" (Romans 11:29). Scripture asserts: "God has given us eternal life, and this life is in His Son. He who has the Son has the life; he who does not have the Son of God does not have the life. These things I have written to you who believe in the name of the Son of God, *in order that you may know* that you have eternal life" (1 John 5:11-13, emphasis added).

Ephesians 4:30 indicates that believers are sealed unto the day of redemption by the Holy Spirit (see also Ephesians 1:13). This seal—which indicates ownership, authority, and security—cannot be broken (even by the believer himself). The seal guarantees our entry into heaven.

Besides this, we are told that the Father keeps us in His sovereign hands, and no one can take us out of His hands (John 10:28-30; 13:1). God has us in His firm grip. And that grip will never let us go.

Not only that, but the Lord Jesus Himself regularly intercedes and prays for us (Hebrews 7:25). His work of intercession, as our divine High Priest, is necessary because of our weaknesses, our helplessness, and our immaturity as children of God. He knows our limitations, and He knows the power and the strategy of the foe with whom we have to contend (Satan). He is therefore faithful in making intercession for us. (And His prayers are always answered.)

Of course, the fact that someone is eternally secure does not mean the Christian can get away with anything in terms of personal sin. If the child of God sins and refuses to repent, God brings discipline—sometimes *very severe* discipline—into his or her life to bring about repentance (Hebrews 12:4-11; 1 Corinthians 11:30). Christians will either respond to God's light or they will respond to His heat. Either way, though, they are saved.

It is much like a human family. If my son or daughter does something wrong and refuses to repent, I take disciplinary measures, but I do not kick him or her out of my family. God does not kick us out of His family when we fail to repent, but He does discipline us until we do repent. He loves us far too much to allow us to remain in sin.

9

Forensic Justification Versus Meritorious Justification—Part 3
Reasoning from the Scriptures

"Just as Christian came up to the cross, his burden loosed from off his shoulders and fell from off his back and began to tumble, and so continued to do till it came to the mouth of the sepulcher, where it fell in, and I saw it no more."[1]
John Bunyan

In the previous two chapters we have examined and responded to the Roman Catholic view of justification and related issues. In the present chapter, we complete our look at justification with a focus on the key verses that typically come up in the debate. We begin with James 2:17,26.

James 2:17,26—What Does James Mean When He Says Faith Without Works Is Dead?

The Roman Catholic Teaching: In James 2:17 we read, "Even so faith, if it has no works, is dead, being by itself." Verse 26 likewise says, "For just as the body without the spirit is dead, so also faith without works is dead." Roman Catholics often cite these verses in support of the idea that meritorious works are required for final salvation.[2]

Response: In this passage, James is basically answering the question, "How can someone tell whether or not a person

145

has true faith?" And all that follows in chapter 2 answers this question.

James begins by asking, "What use is it, my brethren, if a man says he has faith, but he has no works? Can that faith save him?" (James 2:14). Notice the oft-neglected little word *says*. Some people have genuine faith; others have an empty profession of faith that is not real. The first group of people who have genuine faith have works to back up the fact that their faith is genuine. Those who make an empty profession of faith show their lack of true faith by the absence of works. So, James answers his question by pointing out that you can tell whether a person has true faith by the test of works.

Martin Luther said it best: James 2 is not teaching that a person is saved by works or by personal merit. Rather, a person is "justified" (declared righteous before God) by faith alone, but *not by a faith that is alone*. In other words, genuine faith will always result in or be accompanied by good works in the saved person's life.

Keep in mind that James is writing to Jewish Christians ("to the twelve tribes"—James 1:1) who were in danger of giving nothing but lip service to Jesus. James's intent, therefore, is to distinguish true faith from false faith. He shows that true faith results in works, which become visible evidences of faith's invisible presence. In other words, good works are the "vital signs" indicating that faith is alive.

Apparently, some of these Jewish Christians had made a false claim of faith. It is this spurious boast of faith that James was condemning. Merely claiming to have faith is insufficient. Genuine faith is evidenced by works. Indeed,

> Workless faith is worthless faith; it is unproductive, sterile, barren, dead! Great claims may be made about a corpse that is supposed to have come to life, but if it does not move, if there are no vital signs, no heartbeat, no perceptible pulse, it is still dead. The false claims are silenced by the evidence.[3]

The fact is, apart from the spirit, the body is dead; it is a lifeless corpse. By analogy, apart from the evidence of good works, faith is dead. It is lifeless and nonproductive. That is what James is teaching in these verses. His focus is on the nature of faith, not on the reward of works.

Ask... _____

- James 2:26 indicates that apart from the spirit, the body is dead, right?

- By analogy, is it not clear that apart from the evidence of good works, faith is dead?

- Can you see from this verse that good works are the "vital signs" indicating that faith is alive?

- So, this verse is talking about the nature of true faith and not the reward of works, right?

- Would you please read aloud from Romans 3:20 and tell me what you think it means?

- Can I share one of my favorite passages with you— Ephesians 2:8,9?

James 2:21—Was Abraham Justified Before God by Works and Not By Faith?

The Roman Catholic Teaching: In James 2:21 we read, "Was not Abraham our father justified by works, when he offered up Isaac his son on the altar?" Roman Catholics often cite this verse with a view to proving that final justification before God is not by faith alone but requires works.[4]

Response: In this verse James is not talking about justification *before God*, but rather justification *before men*. We know this to be true because James stressed that we should "show" (James 2:18) our faith. That is, our faith must be something that can be seen by others in "works" (verses 18-20).

As James McCarthy puts it:

> James wants his readers to understand that if they are going to claim to have faith even as Abraham, then their works of obedience should demonstrate it even as Abraham's obedience demonstrated his faith. It is a man's *actions* that *declare* him to be righteous, not mere talk or a professed faith that is not lived out.[5]

It is critical to recognize that James acknowledged that Abraham was justified before God by faith, not works: "Abraham believed God, and it was reckoned to him as righteousness" (James 2:23). When he spoke of Abraham being "justified by works" earlier in verse 21, he was speaking of what Abraham did *that could be seen by men*; namely, he offered his son Isaac on the altar. Here Abraham proves the reality of his faith by offering up his son. This event with Isaac took place some 30 years after Abraham had first believed in God (at which time he was justified before God).

The apostle Paul in Romans 4:5 speaks about justification before God: "But to the one who does not work, but believes in Him who justifies the ungodly, his faith is reckoned as righteousness." Paul here speaks of Abraham's salvation experience (justification), which is based wholly on faith. This took place back in Genesis 15. At that time God imputed righteousness to Abraham's account.

So how do we relate Paul's teaching to that of James 2:21? Paul in the Book of Romans spoke about the time God justified Abraham once for all, reckoning righteousness to him as a result of his faith in God. Paul spoke of Abraham's justification *before God*. James, by contrast, spoke about something far later—after Abraham had waited many years for the birth of Isaac, and then after Isaac had grown old enough to carry wood up the mountain for a sacrifice. It was at this point—30 years after his justification before God—that Abraham was "shown to be righteous" *before men* by his works. It was in this sense that James says Abraham was "justified by works" when he offered his son Isaac upon the altar (James 2:21).[6]

Put another way, Paul stressed the *root* of justification (faith in God), while James stressed the *fruit* of justification (works before men). But certainly each man acknowledged both doctrines. Paul, for example, taught that we are saved by grace through faith (Ephesians 2:8,9), but then he quickly added, "We are His workmanship, created in Christ Jesus for good works, which God prepared beforehand, that we should walk in them" (verse 10).[7]

Ask...

- Did you know that Paul in the Book of Romans spoke about the time God justified Abraham once for all, reckoning righteousness to him as a result of his faith in God (Romans 4:3)? (*This is when he became "saved."*)

- Did you know that James, by contrast, spoke about something 30 years later—when Abraham was "shown to be righteous" before men by his willingness to sacrifice Isaac (James 2:21)?

- Put another way, can you see that Paul stressed the *root* of justification (faith in God), while James stressed the *fruit* of justification (works before men)?

Philippians 2:12,13—Does Salvation Involve the Performing of Good Works?

The Roman Catholic Teaching: In Philippians 2:12,13 we read: "So then, my beloved, just as you have always obeyed, not as in my presence only, but now much more in my absence, work out your salvation with fear and trembling; for it is God who is at work in you, both to will and to work for His good pleasure." This seems to support the Roman Catholic position that final justification requires meritorious works.[8] We are told, "Eternal salvation is at stake at every moment of one's earthly pilgrimage. Each Christian must work out his or her personal salvation in fear and trembling (see Philippians 2:12)."[9]

Response: As a backdrop, we must keep in mind the particular situation of the church in Philippi. This church was plagued by 1) rivalries and individuals with personal ambition (Philippians 2:3,4; 4:2), 2) the teaching of Judaizers (who said that circumcision was necessary for salvation—3:1-3), 3) perfectionism (the view that one could attain sinless perfection in this life—3:12-14), and 4) the influence of "antinomian libertines" (people who took excessive liberty in how they lived their lives, ignoring or going against God's law—3:18,19).[10] Because of such problems, this church as a unit was in need of "salvation" (that is, salvation in the temporal, experiential sense, not in the eternal sense).

It is critical to recognize that *salvation* in this context is referring to the *community* of believers in Philippi and not to *individual* believers. Salvation is spoken of in a *corporate* sense in this verse. The Philippians were called by the apostle Paul to "keep on working out" (continuously) the "deliverance of the church into a state of Christian maturity."[11]

The Greek word for "work out" (*katergazomai*) is a compound verb that indicates achievement or bringing to a conclusion. Paul was calling the Philippians to solve all the church's problems, thus bringing corporate "salvation" or deliverance to a state of final achievement. Paul would not permit things to continue as they were. The problems must be solved. The Philippians were to "work it out to the finish."[12]

In the phrase "work out your own salvation," the words *your own* are strongly emphatic in the Greek. As Bible scholar H. C. G. Moule notes, "The Apostle is in fact bidding them 'learn to walk alone,' instead of leaning too much on *his* presence and personal influence. 'Do not make me your proxy in spiritual duties which must be your own.'"[13] This was all the more necessary in view of the fact that the apostle Paul was absent from the church (Philippians 2:12).

The Philippians were to accomplish their appointed task with an attitude of "fear and trembling." This does not mean Paul wanted the Philippians to have terror in their hearts as a motivation. Rather, the words *fear and trembling* are an idiomatic expression pointing to great reverence for God and a humble frame of mind. (Many in Philippi were apparently prideful and had little reverence for God.) Such humility and reverence for God would help them overcome the problems they were experiencing in the church (see 1 Corinthians 2:3; 2 Corinthians 7:15; Ephesians 6:5).

Ask... _____

- Would you mind if I shared with you the context of Philippians 2:12? (*Go over the above details.*)

- Can you see that from a contextual and historical point of view, this verse makes great sense when understood as referring to *corporate* salvation of the church in Philippi—a church that had specific problems Paul wanted them to deal with on their own?

- Did you know that the same apostle Paul who wrote Philippians 2:12 also wrote Ephesians 2:8,9—"For by grace you have been saved through faith; and that not of yourselves, it is the gift of God; not as a result of works, that no one should boast"?

_____

Besides the above facts which militate against the Roman Catholic interpretation of Philippians 2:12, it is also significant that in other writings of the apostle Paul, he clearly sets forth what theologians call "eternal security." For example, in Romans 8:29,30 Paul said: "For whom He foreknew, He also predestined to become conformed to the image of His Son...and whom He predestined, these He also called; and whom He called, these He also justified; and whom He justified, these He also glorified." Here we find an unbroken progression from predestination to glorification. And the tense of the word *glorified* (in the Greek) indicates that our future glorification is so certain that it can be said to be already accomplished.

Ask... _____

- Can you see that there is an unbroken chain from predestination to glorification in Romans 8:29,30?

- What do you think this means?

_____

We find more Pauline evidence for eternal security in Ephesians 4:30, where we are told that believers are "sealed" by the Holy Spirit unto the day of redemption. A seal indicates possession and security. "The presence of the Holy Spirit, the seal, is the believer's guarantee of the security of his salvation."[14] The believer is thus assured that he will, in fact, be with God in heaven for all eternity.

Ask... _____

- What do you think it means in Ephesians 4:30 to be "sealed" by the Holy Spirit unto the day of redemption?

_____

Luke 18:18—Did Jesus Teach that a Person Can Do Something to Merit Eternal Life?

The Roman Catholic Teaching: In Luke 18:18 we read of a ruler who came up to Jesus and asked, "Good Teacher, what shall I do to inherit eternal life?" Some Roman Catholics interpret this as supporting the idea that merit is involved in attaining eternal life. After all, the verse implies a person can "do" something to get eternal life. "All the synoptics...present Jesus as affirming the commandments as a necessary condition for entering eternal life (see Matthew 19:16-20; Mark 10:17-19; Luke 18:18-20)."[15] "Jesus teaches that people must keep these commandments to enter eternal life (see Matthew 19:16-18, Mark 10:17-19, Luke 18:18,20)."[16]

Response: We must consider this verse in its full context. The rich young ruler asked Jesus how to inherit eternal life. Jesus then responded by telling him he must follow the commandments of God (verses 19,20). The ruler responded that he had kept the commandments (verse 21). So Jesus informed him he must do one thing more: sell all that he had and give it all to the poor (verse 22). At hearing this, the man became very sad, for he was a man of great wealth.

At first glance, it might seem that Jesus was teaching salvation by works to the rich young ruler. But this was not the case. Scripture is clear that the law does not save (Romans 3:28), but it does condemn (3:19). Jesus was demonstrating to the young man that he stood condemned before the law. The fact that he was unwilling to give his money to the poor was a sure indication that he had not even kept the first great commandment to love God more than anything else (see Matthew 22:36,37).[17]

Furthermore, as Norman Geisler has pointed out, the rich young ruler's question was confused.[18] A person cannot "do" anything to receive an inheritance of any kind—including eternal life. An "inheritance" by its very nature is a gift. Since eternal life is presented throughout Scripture as a gift (Romans 6:23; John 3:36; 5:24; 20:31; 1 John 5:13), a person cannot "do" anything to earn it. The apostle Paul said, "Now when a man works, his wages are not credited to him as a gift, but as an obligation. However, to the man who does not work but trusts God who justifies the wicked, his faith is credited as righteousness" (Romans 4:4,5).

The only "work" by which a person can be saved is "faith." Recall that when Jesus was asked, "What can we do to accomplish the works of God?" Jesus answered, "This is the work of God, that you *believe* in Him whom He has sent" (John 6:29).

Ask... _____

- Would you please read aloud from Romans 3:28?

- What does this verse say about whether or not keeping the law can save a person?

- Would you please read aloud from Romans 6:23?

- What does this verse say about eternal life?

- Did you know that an inheritance by its very nature is a gift and cannot be earned?

- Can you see that the rich young ruler's question was confused, since a man can "do" nothing to "inherit" the free gift of eternal life?

- Would you please read aloud from John 5:24?

- According to this verse, how does one receive this free gift of eternal life?

Matthew 5:12—Was Jesus Teaching that Good Works Build Up Merit?

The Roman Catholic Teaching: In Matthew 5:12 we read, "Rejoice, and be glad, for *your reward in heaven is great*" (emphasis added). Some Roman Catholics believe this verse adds support to their view that meritorious works are required for final salvation.[19]

Response: We must consider this verse in its full context. Beginning with verse 11 we read:

> Blessed are you when men cast insults at you, and persecute you, and say all kinds of evil against you falsely, on account of Me. Rejoice, and be glad, for your reward in heaven is great, for so they persecuted the prophets who were before you (Matthew 5:11,12).

Jesus is not saying in this passage that His followers must endure persecution with a view to meriting heaven. Rather, Jesus is saying that even in the midst of present persecution His followers (who are already "saved" and already definitely headed for heaven) can be happy, knowing full well what the nature of heaven will in fact be.

We know from other Scripture that heaven will be characterized by joy (Revelation 21:1-5), serene rest (Revelation 14:13), absolute righteousness (2 Peter 3:13), a satisfaction of all needs (Revelation 7:16,17), a complete lack of sin and sorrow (Revelation 21:1-4), praise and worship (Revelation 19:1-6), and a reunion with all Christian loved ones (1 Thessalonians 4:13-17). With this as our ultimate destiny, little problems in the present are essentially "no big deal."

Ask...

- If your three-week summer vacation in the Bahamas is just a week away, would that give you a sense of happiness, even in the midst of a tumultuous situation at the workplace this week?

- In the same way, if your ultimate destiny is a wonderful and blissful life in heaven for all eternity, would that give you a sense of happiness, even though life in the present is throwing you some punches?

- *That is all Matthew 5:12 is saying!*

Romans 2:6,7—Did Paul Teach That Heaven Can Be Merited by Good Works?

The Roman Catholic Teaching: In Romans 2:6,7 we read that God "will render to every man according to his deeds: to those who by perseverance in doing good seek for glory and honor and immortality, eternal life." Catholic theologian Ludwig Ott tells us that "St. Paul, who stresses grace so much, also emphasized on the other hand, the meritorious nature of good works performed with grace, by teaching that the reward is in proportion to the works: 'He [God] will render to every man according to his own labor' (Romans 2:6)."[20] We are told that "it is a universally accepted dogma of the Catholic Church that man, in union with the grace of the Holy Spirit, must merit heaven by his good works.... We can actually merit heaven *as our reward*."[21]

Response: Taken in its proper context, this passage does not teach that works—including "works performed with grace"—are a condition for receiving salvation. We first note that in this very Book of Romans, Paul emphatically states that salvation is entirely *apart* from works: "For we maintain that a man is justified by faith apart from works of the Law" (Romans 3:28). "But to the one who does not work, but believes in Him who justifies the ungodly, his faith is reckoned as righteousness" (4:5). Paul's words in Romans 2:6,7 cannot be taken in such a way that they contradict these other clear statements.

In Paul's theology, works are the *result* of salvation, not the *condition* of salvation. Ephesians 2:10 makes it clear that we are saved unto good works. We are saved *by* grace but *for* works. We do not work *for* grace but *from* grace (see Titus 2:11,12; 2 Corinthians 5:14). Good works do not *bring* salvation; they simply *attest* to the salvation that has already been received by faith (Romans 6:23; 10:9,10; 11:6). These works are portrayed as an *evidence* that a person has saving faith.

In the context of Paul's writings, it would seem that Romans 2:6-8 emphasizes that how a person habitually acts or conducts himself in daily life indicates the state of his heart. A person who habitually engages in good works thereby shows that his heart has been regenerated by God (verse 7). A person who habitually engages in bad deeds shows his alienation from God (verse 8).

Ask... _____

- Would you please read aloud from Romans 3:28 and then Romans 4:5?

- What do these verses say about the relationship of works to salvation?

- Since Scripture does not contradict itself, does it make sense to you that however Romans 2:6-8 is interpreted, it must be done so that it agrees with Romans 3:28 and 4:5?

- Did you know that Paul talks about salvation by grace *with no works involved* in Ephesians 2:8,9, and then in verse 10 speaks of works that *follow* this salvation?

- Does it makes sense to you that works are the *result* of salvation, not the *condition* of salvation?

Hebrews 10:35—Can Heaven Be Merited by Works?

The Roman Catholic Teaching: In Hebrews 10:35 we read, "Therefore, do not throw away your confidence, which has a great reward." Some Roman Catholics believe this verse adds support to their view that meritorious works are required for final justification.[22]

Response: The backdrop to this verse is that it was very difficult for Jews of the first century to become Christians. The Jews living in and around the Palestine area were under the authority of the high priest. The high priest had sufficient influence to cause a Jew to lose his job, have his children expelled from synagogue school, inflict persecution, and much more. Many scholars believe that when some Jews became Christians in the first century, the high priest put some heavy-duty pressure (persecution) on them.

This caused some of the Jewish Christians to waver and become a bit "gun-shy" in their Christian lives. They were not as open about their Christian faith. Perhaps they thought that if they kept quiet about their faith and withdrew from external involvement in Christian affairs (like church attendance), the high priest would lighten up on them. Some of them may have contemplated going back to participating in Judaism—back to the temple, the law, and the sacrifices.

The author of the Book of Hebrews saw such an attitude as a retreat from spiritual maturity in Christ. Throughout this epistle, he thus encouraged them to move on to maturity in Christ and stand boldly for Christ in the face of persecution.

The broad context of Hebrews 10 focuses on the finality of Christ's sacrifice on the cross by contrasting it with the lack of finality of the Old Testament system of law and sacrifices (which these Jewish believers had formerly subscribed to). Christ's redemption is superior because it needs no repetition and no supplementation. Therefore, a retreat from commitment to Christ and spiritual maturity in Christ is about the worst thing someone could do.

In Hebrews 10:32 (NIV) these Jewish readers are admonished to "remember those earlier days after you had received the light, when you stood your ground in a great contest in the face of suffering." *They started out great.* The author then mentions in verses 33 and 34 a variety of difficult situations the readers had endured, including public shame, imprisonment, and loss of property. The readers had undergone these experiences with joy, knowing they had a better possession and an abiding one (verse 34). The loss of temporal possessions was insignificant in light of the assurance of possessing heavenly treasures.

It is immediately after this that the author of Hebrews said in verse 35, "Therefore, do not throw away your confidence, which has a great reward." The "reward" points back to the previous verse where reference is made to a better possession and an abiding one (verse 34). And this better and abiding possession is further discussed in the very next chapter where reference is made to "a better country...a heavenly one" (11:16). The author of Hebrews is simply exhorting his readers to stand strong in their confidence, knowing full well that regardless of what persecution they may face in the present, they are headed for a wonderful destiny in heaven.

This backdrop is the reason why the author devotes chapter 11 to faith. In Hebrews 11:1 we read, "Now faith is the assurance of things hoped for, the conviction of things not seen." Right now, in the midst of persecution, someone might be tempted to give up because he or she does not "see" heaven yet. But that person must keep the faith, realizing that faith "is the assurance of things hoped for, the conviction of things not seen." Someone may not see heaven yet, but he or she can rest assured that it is coming.

Contrary to the Roman Catholic view that this verse teaches that meritorious works are required for a destiny in heaven, all this verse is really saying in context is that the very awareness of one's future destiny in heaven should motivate a person in the present to faithfully endure hardship. Jesus is not saying His Jewish followers must endure persecution with a view to meriting heaven.

Exodus 32:30–32—Does Moses' Mediation Point to a Treasury of Merit?

The Roman Catholic Teaching: In this passage, Moses tells the nation of Israel:

> "You yourselves have committed a great sin; and now I am going up to the LORD, perhaps I can make atonement for your sin." Then Moses returned to the LORD, and said, "Alas, this people has committed a great sin, and they have made a god of gold for themselves. But now, if Thou wilt, forgive their sin—and if not, please blot me out from Thy book which Thou hast written!" (Exodus 32:30-32).

Some Roman Catholics believe this verse adds support to their claim of a "treasury of merit" from which those in need can draw by indulgences. (I will discuss indulgences in detail in chapter 13.) We read that "even in the Old Testament the idea of vicarious atonement by innocent persons for guilty is known. The innocent person takes on himself responsibility for the displeasure of God which the guilty person has merited, in order by sacrifice to win again the Divine favor for the latter."[23]

Response: Roman Catholics are reading something into the text that is not there. First, note that there is no mention of—*not even a slight allusion to*—any treasury of merit to which someone can contribute and from which other people can draw. All this passage does is portray Moses being willing to engage in great sacrifice on behalf of his people.

Here is the backdrop: Though the most blatant idolaters in the nation had already been put to death by the sword for their sin of idolatry with the golden calf, Moses knew that the nation as a whole was still guilty before God. The fact is, God had made a covenant with the nation as a whole, and the nation as a whole now bore collective guilt for this breach of the covenant (see Joshua 7).

Moses, therefore, wanted to make things right by seeking to make atonement (literally, "cover" the sin) for the people (Exodus 32:30). Moses seems to have assumed that the penalty for their sin would be death, as is often threatened in the law (28:43). Moses informed God that if He did not forgive the people (removing the death penalty), he wanted to have his name removed from the book God had written (32:32). The question is, "What book was Moses referring to?"

Some scholars suggest that this is the book of life mentioned in Revelation 20:15 and 21:27. The book of life lists only the names of believers. If Moses was referring to this book, then his request amounted to saying that he wanted to forego salvation if God did not forgive the people. Seen in this light, Moses would be portrayed as willing to offer a supreme sacrifice to save his people.

Other scholars have suggested that the book was a census of the people. Many ancient societies kept registers of their citizens (Isaiah 4:3; Jeremiah 22:30; Ezekiel 13:9). If a person was not enrolled in the official register, he or she was not allowed to enjoy the rights and legal protection afforded a citizen. When a person died in that society, his or her name was removed from the register. Seen in this light, perhaps Moses' statement was intended to communicate that he was willing to have his name blotted out of the register of the theocratic nation of Israel and die a premature death (but not forego salvation) if God did not forgive the people.

Whichever view is correct, it is clear from the passage that God rejected Moses's offer and promised to punish the sinners themselves by premature death (Exodus 32:33,34). This indicates that *no human being can atone for the sins of another*. The prophets often spoke of individual responsibility for sins (Jeremiah 31:29,30; Ezekiel 18; 33:10-20). In our book *When Cultists Ask*, Norman Geisler and I note that in terms of Moses and the sinful Israelites,

> what God did accept was Moses' sacrificial desire as an indication of the sincerity of his heart, as God did in the case of Abraham (cf. Genesis 22). But God did not accept any offer to give up a place in God's book for the sins of Israel. God did not accept Moses' life as an atonement for Israel; He merely accepted Moses' *willingness* to be sacrificed for them. Moses never even suffered having his name taken out of God's book, to say nothing of any temporal suffering for Israel's sins. Likewise, the apostle Paul expressed a willingness to go to hell if Israel could be saved (Romans 9:3). This too was an admirable but unfulfillable desire. God never accepted Paul's offer. It was a commendable offer, not actually possible, but nonetheless indicative of Paul's passion for his people.[24]

Clearly, then, this passage provides no support for any so-called "treasury of merit" from which those in need can draw by indulgences. Such an idea is completely foreign to the context.

Ask...

- Would you please read aloud from Ezekiel 18:20?

- What does this verse say about the possibility of one man sacrificing himself for another man's sin?

- Since God rejected Moses' offer and promised to punish the *sinners themselves* by premature death (Exodus 32:33,34), doesn't this too indicate that God will not allow one man to sacrifice himself for another man's sin?

- Doesn't all this imply that the merits of one man cannot benefit another?

(Suggest further study from Jeremiah 31:29,30; Ezekiel 18; and 33:10-20 for more information about how God holds each person responsible for his own sin, and hence the merits of others do not benefit anyone else.)

Verses on the Need for Baptism

Acts 2:38—Is Baptism Necessary for Salvation?

The Roman Catholic Teaching: In Acts 2:38 we read, "And Peter said to them, 'Repent, and let each of you be baptized in the name of Jesus Christ for the forgiveness of your sins; and you shall receive the gift of the Holy Spirit.'" Roman Catholics argue that this verse supports the necessity of baptism for salvation. Indeed, Ludwig Ott, citing this verse, tells us that "baptism has the power both of eradicating sin and of effecting inner sanctification."[25]

Response: Admittedly, this is not an easy verse to interpret. But a basic principle of Bible interpretation is that difficult passages are to be interpreted in light of the easy, clear verses. We should never build a theology on difficult passages.

As a backdrop, the great majority of passages dealing with salvation in the New Testament affirm that salvation is by faith alone. A good example is John 3:16,17 (NIV): "For God so loved the world that he gave his one and only Son, that whoever believes in him shall not perish but have eternal life. For God did not send his Son into the world to condemn the world, but to save the world through him." Even Peter, who is the one who uttered the words in Acts 2:38, elsewhere acknowledges that a person is saved *prior* to baptism. For example, in Acts 10:47 we read Peter's words, "Surely no one can refuse the water for these to be baptized who have received the Holy Spirit just as we did, can he?" Salvation came first for these people (as evidenced in their possession of the Holy Spirit), and baptism followed.

How, then, are we to understand Acts 2:38? A single word in the verse gives us the answer. The verse reads, "Peter replied, 'Repent and be baptized, every one of you, in the name of Jesus Christ *for* the forgiveness of your sins. And you will receive the gift of the Holy Spirit'" (NIV, emphasis added).

Students of the Greek language have often pointed out that the Greek word *for* (*eis*) is a preposition that can indicate *causality* ("in order to attain") or a *result* ("because of"). An example of using *for* in a resultant sense is the sentence, "I'm taking an aspirin for my headache." Obviously, this means I am taking an aspirin as a result of my headache. I am not taking an aspirin in order to attain a headache.

An example of using *for* in a causal sense is the sentence, "I'm going to the office for my paycheck." Obviously, this means I am going to the office in order to attain my paycheck.

In Acts 2:38 the word *for* is used in a resultant sense. The verse might be paraphrased, "Repent, and be baptized every one of you in the name of Jesus Christ *because of* (or *as a result of*) the remission of sins." The verse is not saying, "Repent, and be baptized every one of you in the name of Jesus Christ *in order to attain* the remission of sins."

Properly interpreted, then, this verse indicates that water baptism *follows* the salvation experience, not *causes* the salvation experience.

Ask...

- Did you know that Greek scholars say the word *for* is a preposition that can indicate either *causality* ("in order to attain") or a *result* ("because of")?

- An example of using *for* in a resultant sense is the sentence, "I'm taking an aspirin for [*as a result of*] my headache."

- An example of using *for* in a causal sense is the sentence, "I'm going to the office for [*in order to attain*] my paycheck."

- What would Acts 2:38 be saying if *for* is being used in a resultant sense? ("Repent, and be baptized every one of you in the name of Jesus Christ *as a result of* the remission of sins.")

You might want to remind the Roman Catholic that in this same Book of Acts, when the desperate Philippian jailer asked Paul what he must do to obtain salvation and have eternal life, Paul said nothing about baptism. He merely said, "Believe in the Lord Jesus, and you shall be saved" (Acts 16:31). Simple and to the point!

This is consistent with what we see elsewhere in Scripture. Consider the following:

— John 3:15—"...whoever believes may in Him have eternal life."

— John 5:24—"Truly, truly, I say to you, he who hears My word, and believes Him who sent Me, has eternal life, and does not come into judgment, but has passed out of death into life."

— John 11:25—"Jesus said to her, 'I am the resurrection and the life; he who believes in Me shall live even if he dies.'"

— John 12:46—"I have come as light into the world, that everyone who believes in Me may not remain in darkness."

— John 20:31—"These have been written that you may believe that Jesus is the Christ, the Son of God; and that believing you may have life in His name."

(Note: I won't be repeating here the material from the previous chapter regarding the fact that we are justified *the moment we place faith in Christ*, and that justification is not a process that begins at baptism. You will want to review this earlier material when questions about baptism come up.)

John 3:5—Is Baptism Necessary for Salvation?

The Roman Catholic Teaching: In John 3:5 we read the words of Jesus: "Truly, truly, I say to you, unless one is born of water and the Spirit, he cannot enter into the kingdom of God." Roman Catholics interpret this as meaning that baptism is required for salvation. Indeed, baptism is said to confer the grace of justification.[26] "The universal necessity of this 'rebirth' through Baptism is emphasized by Our Lord: 'Unless a man be born again of water and the Spirit, he cannot enter into the kingdom of God' (John 3:5)."[27] Indeed, "Baptism, the door to life and to the kingdom of God, is the first sacrament of the New Law offered by Christ to all men that they might have eternal life (John 3:5)."[28]

Response: I begin with the observation that there are so many verses in John's Gospel that indicate belief in Christ as the sole condition for salvation that John would have to have been dishonest if in fact *both* belief in Christ *and* baptism were necessary for salvation (see John 5:24; 6:35; 7:38; 8:24; 9:35; 10:38; 11:26; 12:44-48; 20:31). However John 3:5 is interpreted, it must be in keeping with all these other verses.

Critical to a proper understanding of John 3:1-5 is verse 6: "That which is born of the flesh is flesh, and that which is born of the Spirit is spirit." Flesh can only reproduce itself as flesh, and flesh cannot pass muster with God (see Romans 8:8). The law of reproduction is "after its kind" (see Genesis 1). So, likewise, the Spirit produces spirit.

In Nicodemus' case, we find a Pharisee who would have been trusting in his physical descent from Abraham for entrance into the Messiah's kingdom. The Jews believed that because they were physically related to Abraham, they were in a specially privileged position before God. Christ, however, denied such a possibility. Parents can transmit to their children only the nature that they themselves possess. Since each parent's nature, because of Adam's sin, is sinful, each parent transmits a sinful nature to the child. And what is sinful cannot enter the kingdom of God (verse 5). The only way someone can enter God's kingdom is to experience a spiritual rebirth, and this is precisely what Jesus is emphasizing to Nicodemus.

The problem is, Nicodemus did not initially comprehend Jesus' meaning. Nicodemus wrongly concluded that Jesus was speaking of something related to physical birth, but could not understand how a person could go through physical birth a second time (John 3:4). Jesus picked up on Nicodemus' line of thought and sought to move the argument from physical birth to spiritual birth.

Notice how Jesus went about His explanation to Nicodemus. He first speaks about being "born of water and the Spirit" in John 3:5, and then explains what He means by this in verse 6. It would seem that "born of water" in verse 5 is parallel to "born of the flesh" in verse 6, just as "born of...the Spirit" in verse 5 is parallel to "born of the Spirit" in verse 6. Jesus' message, then, is that just as each person has had a *physical* birth to live on earth, so he or she must also have a *spiritual* birth in order to enter the spiritual kingdom of God. A person must be "born from above." Seen in this light, *this verse has nothing whatsoever to do with water baptism.*

I should note that the fact that some of the early church fathers believed this verse referred to baptism is not decisive for us. Indeed, the fathers were finite and fallible human beings. Only the Bible is infallible. Further, the fathers often offered mistaken and conflicting interpretations of the same verse. Hence, there is no consensus among the fathers on many issues. This being the case, the fathers cannot be cited as some infallible indicator of what the correct interpretation must be.

Ask...

- Would you please read aloud from John 3:5? What two kinds of birth does Jesus mention?

- Would you please read aloud from John 3:6? What two kinds of birth does Jesus mention?

- In context, is it not clear that Jesus defines what He means in verse 5 by the more precise statement in verse 6?

- Is it not clear that "born of water" (verse 5) and "born of the flesh" (verse 6) are referring to the same thing—that is, physical birth?

- That being the case, isn't Jesus saying that just as a person has had a physical birth ("born of the flesh"), so also must a person have a spiritual birth if he wants to enter the spiritual kingdom of God?

- If this is correct, the phrase "born of water" cannot be interpreted to mean baptism, can it?

Mark 16:16—Is Baptism Necessary for Salvation?

The Roman Catholic Teaching: In Mark 16:16 we read, "He who has believed and has been baptized shall be saved; but he who has disbelieved shall be condemned." Roman Catholics teach that in this verse Jesus is saying that baptism is necessary for salvation. We are told that "through Baptism as through a door men enter the Church."[29]

Response: Notice the latter part of the verse: "He who has believed and has been baptized shall be saved; but *he who has disbelieved shall be condemned*" (Mark 16:16, emphasis added). It is *unbelief* that brings damnation, not a lack of being baptized. When someone rejects the gospel, refusing to believe it, that person is damned.

In regard to the question of whether baptism is necessary for salvation, consider the words of the apostle Paul: "For Christ did not send me to baptize, but to preach the gospel—not with words of human wisdom, lest the cross of Christ be emptied of its power" (1 Corinthians 1:17 NIV). Paul here draws a clear distinction between baptism and the gospel. And since it is the gospel that saves (1 Corinthians 15:1,2), baptism is clearly not necessary to attain salvation.

That is not to say that baptism is unimportant. Baptism should be the first act of obedience to God following a person's conversion to Christ. But even though we should obey God and get baptized, we must not forget that our faith in Christ is what saves us (Acts 16:31; John 3:16), not baptism. Baptism is basically a public profession of faith. It says to the whole world, "I'm a believer in Christ and have identified my life with Him."

Ask...

- Would you read aloud from Mark 16:16? According to the last half of the verse, what is the basis of damnation?

- According to 1 Corinthians 15:1,2, does baptism save or the gospel?

- Would you read aloud from 1 Corinthians 1:17? If the gospel saves, and if Paul draws a clear distinction between the gospel and baptism, doesn't that mean that baptism has no part in salvation?

(Next you might read aloud from 1 Corinthians 15:1-4, where the apostle Paul clearly defines what he means by "the gospel.")

Titus 3:5—Is Baptism Necessary for Salvation?

The Roman Catholic Teaching: In Titus 3:5 we read, "He saved us, not on the basis of deeds which we have done in righteousness, but according to His mercy, by the washing of regeneration and renewing by the Holy Spirit." This verse is interpreted as meaning that baptism leads to regeneration. "It is through baptism that this regeneration takes place; hence Paul calls this Sacrament 'the bath of regeneration' (Tit. 3:5)."[30]

Response: The Greek word for baptism (*baptizo*) is *not* used in this verse. Paul did not use this word because he was not referring to baptism. Paul refers to "washing of regeneration" (Greek: *loutrou*) to describe how believers are cleansed of guilt at the moment of salvation.

The fact that this is a "washing of regeneration" indicates that a *spiritual* washing is in view, not a literal water-baptism kind of washing. Besides, the very words used in this verse point out beyond any doubt that our salvation is not a result of doing things (like getting baptized) but is based entirely on God's mercy.

Ask... _____

- If baptism is so necessary for salvation, as Roman Catholicism teaches, why didn't Jesus baptize anyone (John 4:2)?

- If baptism is so necessary for salvation, how did the thief on the cross get saved (Luke 23:43)? (*Jesus told him, "Truly I say to you, today you shall be with Me in Paradise."*)

- If baptism is so necessary for salvation, why did the apostle Paul say, "Christ did not send me to baptize, but to preach the gospel" (1 Corinthians 1:17)?

- If baptism is so necessary for salvation, how do you explain the fact that Cornelius was a recipient of the Holy Spirit (thereby indicating his salvation) prior to his baptism (Acts 10:44-48)?

- If baptism is so necessary for salvation, why is it that close to 200 times in the New Testament salvation is said to be solely by faith in Christ, with no mention of baptism? Wouldn't Scripture be deceptive in these 200 verses if baptism were a requirement for salvation?

10

Sacramentalism—Part 1

"Religion that is merely ritual and ceremonial can
never satisfy.... Man's craving is for the spiritual."[1]
Samuel Shoemaker (1893–1963)

In Roman Catholic theology there are seven sacraments:
baptism, penance, the Eucharist, confirmation, matrimony, holy orders, and the anointing of the sick. The word
sacrament communicates the idea of conveying grace.
Sacraments in Roman Catholic theology are not just viewed
as metaphors pointing to the reality of grace, but rather these
sacraments are actually said to be *containers* of grace, and
this grace gets infused into the believer when participating in
the sacraments. The Council of Trent said, "A sacrament is
something presented to the senses, which has the power, by
divine institution, not only of signifying, but also of effi-
ciently conveying grace."[2]

This grace, which is said to be available to people only
because of the merits of Jesus Christ, is viewed as necessary for salvation. The Roman Catholic Church has traditionally taught that without this infusion of grace through

the sacraments, salvation is impossible. The *Catechism of the Catholic Church* tells us, "The Church affirms that for believers the sacraments of the New Covenant are necessary for salvation."[3] The Council of Trent said: "If anyone says that the sacraments...are not necessary for salvation...and that without the desire of them men obtain from God through faith alone the grace of justification...let him be anathema."[4] The sacrament of baptism, for example, is thought to bestow initial sanctifying grace. When someone sins and loses that grace, the sacrament of penance becomes necessary in order to restore lost grace.

Roman Catholics teach that the sacraments convey two kinds of grace: sanctifying grace and actual grace. Sanctifying grace is at the very heart of the Roman Catholic view of salvation. Indeed, when a person is infused with sanctifying grace through the sacraments, he or she is thereby made holy and acceptable to God. This kind of grace is a "created sharing or participation in the life of God himself."[5] It is first infused into the person at the sacrament of baptism, and each respective sacrament continues the process of infusing grace. Catholic theologian Ludwig Ott tells us that "supernatural life is generated by Baptism; brought to growth by Confirmation; nourished by the Eucharist; cured from the disease of sins and from the weakness arising from these by Penance and Extreme Unction."[6] Sanctifying grace is maintained within the person so long as he or she does not commit a mortal sin (at which point sanctifying grace is virtually erased from the person's soul). So long as the person does not commit a mortal sin, he or she is in a "state of grace."

Actual grace, by contrast, "is a transient help of God which enlightens the mind and strengthens the will to do good and avoid evil."[7] As a person lives from day to day by grace, seeking to do good and avoid evil, this kind of grace becomes depleted and hence must be replenished through regular participation in the sacraments. This grace involves a temporary strengthening, and passes as it is utilized. It must continually be replenished, like a car needing to be refueled. This spiritual "refueling" is done through the sacraments.

According to Roman Catholic theology, the graces mentioned above are communicated to people *by the ritual being conducted*—that is, the grace is dispensed by the actual conducting of the ritual itself, regardless of the spiritual state of the priest. It is feasible that the priest himself could be in a state of sin when he performs the rite, and yet God's grace is nevertheless communicated to participants by the ritual being conducted.[8] What this means is that the effectiveness of the rite is independent of the spiritual condition of the priest.

The reason the attitude or merits (or lack thereof) of the priest are not important in the sacraments is that the sacramental act is viewed as an act of Christ Himself, operating *through* His servant, the priest (called "another Christ"). As one Catholic document put it:

> A sacramental celebration does not depend for its validity on the disposition of the minister; its action has its effect from the power of Christ as the due sacramental action is performed (*ex opere operato*). It is not in itself affected by lack of faith, state of grace, or holiness on the part of the minister but only on the fact that the minister is divinely empowered according to the institution of Christ.[9]

Catholics are careful to point out, however, that the *participant* must be spiritually prepared in order for the sacrament to yield a transferal of grace to his or her soul. To receive this sacramental grace, there must already be sanctifying grace in the person's soul (which first comes at baptism), and the person must have faith. When a person meets these and other requirements, he or she is prepared for a valid reception of grace through the performing of the sacrament. A lesser-prepared person might receive proportionally less grace from God than a person who is optimally prepared.

Understanding the Roman Catholic view on the sacraments helps us to comprehend why the Church has traditionally viewed salvation outside the Church as being impossible. If it is true that sacraments performed by the priest are necessary for the reception of the grace that is essential for salvation, then obviously, if someone places himself or herself outside the Church, that person is cut off from this necessary grace. The Roman Catholic Church has historically viewed itself as the "true" and "only instrument" of salvation.

Since Vatican II, the Church has changed its tone a bit, now claiming that other Christian denominations and religions have remnants of truth, and people can be saved in these non-Catholic groups. But anyone who wants to have the full truth and who desires to join the true church on earth must leave their group and join the Roman Catholic Church. These "separated brethren" are urged to return to the "Mother Church."

The Eucharist—the "Most Blessed Sacrament"

The Eucharist* (or Mass)—the single most important of the Roman Catholic sacraments—involves a resacrificing of Jesus (or, more accurately, a "re-presenting" or "renewing" of the sacrifice of Jesus) over and over again. We are told that the Mass constitutes a "true and proper sacrifice."[10] Karl Keating writes, "The Church insists that the Mass is the continuation and re-presentation of the sacrifice of Calvary."[11] The *Catholic Encyclopedia* asserts, "We may establish that the Eucharist is a true sacrifice."[12] Whether you call it "resacrifice" or "re-presenting" the sacrifice, Roman Catholics say that in every single Mass, *God is appeased.*

As defined by the Council of Trent, the same Christ who offered himself in a bloody manner on the cross is during the

---

* The Eucharist is often popularly called "Mass" because "the liturgy in which the mystery of salvation is accomplished concludes with the sending forth (*missio*) of the faithful, so that they may fulfill God's will in their daily lives" (*Catechism of the Catholic Church*, p. 370).

Mass (or Eucharist) present and offered in an unbloody manner. Consequently, the Mass is viewed as a truly propitiatory sacrifice by which the Lord is appeased.[13]

Pivotal to a proper understanding of the Mass is the Catholic teaching that the bread and wine miraculously turn into the actual body and blood of Jesus Christ. This happens at the prayer of consecration said by the priest. Even though the bread and wine still look and feel and taste like bread and wine, in fact, there is a change such that it turns into Jesus Christ in His full deity and humanity. As the *Catechism of the Catholic Church* puts it, "In the most blessed sacrament of the Eucharist 'the body and blood, together with the soul and divinity, of our Lord Jesus Christ and, therefore, the whole Christ is truly, really, and substantially contained.'"[14] Vatican II proclaimed that "in the sacrament of the Eucharist Christ is present, in a manner altogether unique, God and man, whole and entire, substantially and continuously."[15]

The theological term used to describe this is *transubstantiation*—from the Latin term *transubstaniato*, meaning "change of substance." This term was incorporated into the creed of the Fourth Lateran Council in A.D. 1215.[16]

Consider the implications of this viewpoint. The Roman view is that every single crumb of bread and every drop of wine contains Christ's entire body and blood. If a crumb of bread should fall to the floor, that means the body of Christ is on the floor. If someone spills a drop of wine, that means a drop of Christ's blood is on the floor.

In any event, once the bread and wine are transformed into the body and blood of Jesus at the prayer of consecration, *He is upon the altar as a sacrificial victim.* He is then offered up as a living sacrifice. After consecrating the bread and wine, the priest prays: "We offer to you, God of glory and majesty, this holy and perfect sacrifice, the bread of life and the cup of eternal salvation."[17] This sacrifice is said to soothe God's wrath and cover people's sins.

Catholics believe that the sacrifice of Christ at the cross and the sacrifice of the Mass are one and the same sacrifice. At the cross, Jesus offered Himself as a sacrifice to the Father directly. At the Mass, Jesus is said to offer Himself to the Father through the agency of the priest. Yet even here Christ is nevertheless viewed as the main offerer.

Catholics teach that it was Christ Himself who instituted the Mass (or Eucharist). He did this in order that "the church might have a perpetual Sacrifice, by which our sins might be expiated, and our heavenly father, oftentimes grievously offended by our crimes, might be turned away from wrath to mercy, from the severity of just chastisement to clemency."[18] Indeed, every time the Mass is performed by a priest, God's wrath is said to be appeased.

Roman Catholics claim that the doctrine of the Mass does not detract from the atonement that Christ wrought on the cross, but is the primary means of applying the benefits of Christ's death to the faithful. We are told that the Mass is "the source and summit of the Christian life." It is "the sum and summary of our faith."[19]

The Eucharist is also a source of grace, as one of the seven sacraments of the Roman Catholic Church. In fact, it is known as the primary and most sacred channel of grace to Catholics. Through this sacrament, Roman Catholics receive both kinds of grace: *sanctifying grace*, which helps them on their road to heaven, and *actual grace*, which helps them to do good and avoid evil.

You can see, then, how important the Mass (or Eucharist) is to Roman Catholicism. It is only through this sacrament, we are told, that people can receive the grace necessary for eternal salvation. Only through this sacrament can satisfaction be made for sins.

After parishioners partake of the bread and wine, the priest takes what is left of the bread and wine and puts it in a small safe called a "tabernacle"—a gold-plated structure on one of the church altars. The reason why such care is given these "leftovers" is that Christ is said to "continuously" be in the bread and wine so long as they remain incorrupted.

Related to this is the Roman Catholic teaching regarding the *Exposition of the Blessed Sacrament*—a time (at annual feasts) involving adoration of the bread. The priest places the bread in a glass receptacle and then mounts it on a gold stand upon an altar. Catholics then worship the bread, believing that it is actually Christ. There are even religious orders authorized by the Roman Catholic Church whose members dedicate their lives to the perpetual adoration of the "Blessed Sacrament." The Council of Trent pronounced that "there is, therefore, no room left for doubt that all the faithful of Christ...offer in veneration the worship of *latria* [adoration] which is due to the true God, to this most Holy Sacrament."[20]

The *Catechism of the Catholic Church* likewise tells us:

> In the liturgy of the Mass we express our faith in the real presence of Christ under the species of bread and wine by, among other ways, genuflecting or bowing deeply as a sign of adoration of the Lord. The Catholic Church has always offered and still offers to the sacrament of the Eucharist the cult of adoration, not only during Mass, but also outside of it, reserving the consecrated hosts with the utmost care, exposing them to the solemn veneration of the faithful, and carrying them in procession.[21]

Catholics are instructed that refusing to attend Mass is a mortal sin. Certainly there are some recognized reasons for not meeting this obligation. If a person is sick, or is caring for ill family members, for example, he or she can legitimately miss attending Mass. But to deliberately choose not to attend Mass when able to is a mortal sin. If someone commits this sin, the person must go to a priest and make confession.

Other Roman Catholic Sacraments

The Sacrament of Baptism

I have already discussed the sacrament of baptism in the chapters dealing with justification. I covered baptism in that part of the book because, in Roman Catholic theology, baptism is closely related to initial justification. But inasmuch as baptism is one of Catholicism's seven sacraments, I mention it here briefly for the sake of continuity.

In a capsule, baptism is thought to confer initial justification and the new birth (regeneration). It allegedly purifies a person from sins, makes him or her a new creature, renders the individual an adopted son of God, and infuses sanctifying grace into his or her soul.[22]

Of course, the grace someone receives at baptism is erased if he or she commits a mortal sin. Should someone get baptized and then commit a mortal sin—and then die *before participating in the sacrament of penance*—that person goes straight to hell. (I will discuss mortal sin in detail in chapter 12.)

The Sacrament of Penance

I will address the issue of penance in detail in chapter 12—"Sin and the Sacrament of Penance." At the present juncture, allow me simply to emphasize that in Roman Catholic theology, should someone commit a mortal sin following baptism, that person *must* participate in the sacrament of penance or be assured of going to hell upon death. *The Catholic Encyclopedia* affirms: "The result of mortal sin is the loss of sanctifying grace, the loss of the gifts of the Holy Spirit, remorse, and the punitive effect of eternal separation from God."[23] The only thing that can reverse this damnable destiny is penance.

What is involved in penance? Briefly, there must be *contrition* (sorrow for sins), *confession* to a priest, and then *satisfaction* (acts of penance as prescribed by the priest). The

Council of Florence (A.D. 1439) summarized the three aspects of penance this way:

> The first of these is contrition of heart, which consists of sorrow for sin committed and the intention not to sin in the future. The second is oral confession, whereby the sinner confesses to the priest all the sins he remembers in their entirety. The third is satisfaction for sins according to the judgment of the priest, which is mainly achieved by prayer, fasting and almsdeeds. The form of this sacrament is the words of absolution spoken by the priest when he says: *I absolve thee* etc....The effect of this sacrament is absolution from sins.[24]

The Sacrament of Confirmation

In Roman Catholic theology, confirmation is said to complete the sacrament of baptism. Indeed, "if baptism is the sacrament of re-birth to a new and supernatural life, confirmation is the sacrament of maturity and coming of age."[25] Confirmation is not strictly necessary for salvation, "but it is eminently important in contributing to Christian perfection and there is a grave obligation to receive it in due time."[26]

The bishop administers confirmation by laying his hands on the head of the parishioner, by which act the person is said to receive the Holy Spirit, strengthening him to live up to his profession of faith. *The Essential Catholic Handbook* tells us:

> Along with baptism and the Eucharist, confirmation is a sacrament of initiation—in this case, initiation into the life of adult Christian witness. The deepened presence of the Spirit, who comes to us in this sacrament, is meant to sustain us in a lifetime of witness to Christ and service to others.[27]

The Sacrament of Holy Orders

In this sacrament, "spiritual power is transferred to one of the faithful by the imposition of hands and prayer of the priest, together with grace to exercise this power in a manner pleasing to God."[28] This sacrament involves ordination to the offices of bishop, priest, or deacon, conferring "on a man the spiritual power and grace to sanctify others."[29] We are told that the Sacrament of Holy Orders confers upon the soul of the man ordained a special indelible mark or character of Jesus Christ which will remain for all eternity.[30] Such individuals are consecrated to shepherd God's people, each in accord with his own grade of orders.[31]

The Sacrament of Matrimony

In this sacrament two marriageable people of different sexes "receive grace for the fulfillment of the special duties of their state."[32] The Council of Florence (A.D. 1439) declared that a triple good attaches to the sacrament of matrimony: "The first is the begetting of children and their education to the worship of God. The second is the faithfulness which each spouse owes to the other. The third is the indissolubility of marriage because it represents the indissoluble union of Christ and the Church."[33]

The Sacrament of Anointing of the Sick

The sacrament of anointing of the sick is for those who are sick or who are near the point of death. It is said to take away the infirmity left by sin. It removes that which might be an obstacle to the clothing with glory of the resurrection.[34] The sacrament of anointing of the sick is done with a view to commending to the Lord "the faithful" who are "dangerously sick" so that He can relieve and save them. This sacrament is conferred by anointing the sick person with oil and reciting the following words: "Through this holy anointing and His most loving mercy, may the Lord assist you by the grace of the Holy Spirit, so that, freed from your sins, He may save you and in His goodness raise you up."[35]

Answering Roman Catholics

Sacraments and Grace

The key emphasis in Scripture is a personal relationship with Christ, not an endless series of rituals to appease God. External rites ultimately mean very little; rather, one's inner spiritual heart attitude toward God is all-important. God calls us to worship Him "in spirit and in truth" (John 4:24).

Evangelical Protestants challenge the very idea that rites and sacraments infuse grace into participants at all. As noted in previous chapters, the biblical view of salvation involves faith in Christ (John 3:16; Acts 16:31), not a continual infusion of grace. Such an idea is entirely foreign to the pages of Scripture.

We will look in vain for references to seven sacraments that are needed for a regular supply of grace. Indeed, God's grace is given to us not through ritualistic ceremonies, but comes straight from God to all who believe in the Person of Jesus Christ: "Therefore having been justified by faith, we have peace with God through our Lord Jesus Christ, through whom also we have obtained our introduction by faith *into this grace in which we stand*; and we exult in hope of the glory of God" (Romans 5:1,2, emphasis added).

Eternal life, according to Scripture, cannot be earned. Verse after verse in Scripture indicates that eternal life is a free gift that comes as a result of believing in the Savior, Jesus Christ. Jesus said: "Truly, truly, I say to you, he who believes *has* eternal life" (John 6:47; emphasis added). "The *free gift of God* is eternal life in Christ Jesus our Lord" (Romans 6:23, emphasis added). "I will give to the one who thirsts from the spring of the water of life *without cost*" (Revelation 21:6, emphasis added).

Not through rites, but *through Christ alone* we have peace with God (Romans 5:1,2). Our salvation is available as a once-for-all free gift resulting from faith in Christ (Ephesians 2:8,9). As Ephesians 2:18 puts it, through Jesus we have our "access in one Spirit to the Father." Indeed, "there is one God, and one mediator also between God and men, the man Christ Jesus" (1 Timothy 2:5). We need no priests to mediate between us and God.

There is another issue that bears mentioning. History reveals that the sevenfold sacramental system of Roman Catholicism was not initiated until the twelfth century A.D. and was not a permanent part of Catholicism until the fifteenth century. While baptism and the Lord's Supper were universally celebrated by Christians from the first century, the sevenfold sacramental system of Roman Catholicism was not officially acknowledged until the Council of Florence in A.D. 1439. What are we to conclude from this? Were Roman Catholics for over 1000 years missing out on some of the critically important grace-infusing sacraments now said to be so important for salvation?

Ask...

• If the sevenfold sacramental system of Roman Catholicism was not officially acknowledged until the Council of Florence in A.D. 1439, does that mean that Catholics for over 1000 years were missing out on some of the grace-infusing sacraments now said to be so important for salvation?

The Problem with Transubstantiation

There are many problems with the doctrine of transubstantiation. First, note that Jesus Christ was physically present with the disciples when He said the bread and wine were His body and blood (Luke 22:17-19). Obviously He intended that His words be taken figuratively.

Further, we must keep in mind the scriptural teaching that drinking blood is forbidden to anyone (Genesis 9:4; Leviticus 3:17). The disciples, schooled in the commandments of God, would never have understood Jesus to be instructing them to go directly against the commandments of God.

Related to this, keep in mind that some months later Peter said, "I have never eaten anything unholy and unclean" (Acts 10:14). Peter could not have said this if he thought he had actually ingested the body and blood of Jesus Christ, for the law defines such an act as unholy and unclean (Leviticus 3:17). Further, the Jerusalem Council repeated an injunction contained in the Old Testament law to the effect that Christians are to abstain from blood (see Acts 15:29). This would not make much sense if those at the council thought they had actually drunk the real blood of Jesus.

Ask... _____

- In view of the scriptural teaching that drinking blood is forbidden, do you think the disciples, schooled in the commandments of God, would have understood Jesus to be instructing them to go directly against these commandments?

- Do you think Peter could have later said, "I have never eaten anything unholy and unclean" (Acts 10:14), if he knew he had violated God's commandment against drinking blood (Leviticus 3:17)?

Jesus conceded that He often used figurative language. In fact, at the end of His Upper Room Discourse recorded for us in John 14–16, Jesus acknowledged: "These things I have spoken to you in figurative language" (John 16:25). Jesus also often used figurative language in His teachings through the use of parables (Matthew 13ff.). His consistent use of figurative language certainly fits in with His instruction regarding the intended meaning of the Lord's Supper: "Do this in remembrance of Me" (Luke 22:19). The literal Roman Catholic viewpoint would have required Jesus to say,

"Do this to ingest Me." The word *remembrance* literally means "bring to mind," not "ingest into the stomach."

It is worth noting that elsewhere in Scripture we are exhorted to pay attention to empirical evidence based on our five senses. For example, Jesus told doubting Thomas to stick his fingers into His crucifixion wounds as a way of proving to Thomas that indeed He had risen from the dead (John 20:27). In Luke 24:39 the resurrected Jesus told His followers, "See My hands and My feet, that it is I Myself; touch Me and see, for a spirit does not have flesh and bones as you see that I have." We read in 1 John 1:1 that John and the apostles spoke of "what we have heard, what we have seen with our eyes, what we beheld and our hands handled, concerning the Word of Life." Yet in regard to the bread and wine, we are exhorted to ignore what our senses plainly tell us—that is, that it is still bread and wine—and instead believe that even though it looks and feels and tastes like bread and wine, it has really been changed into the body and blood of Jesus Christ! This just does not make sense.

Ask... _____

- Would you please read John 20:27 aloud?

- Would you please read Luke 24:39 aloud?

- Would you please read 1 John 1:1 aloud?

- Can you see from these verses that we are often exhorted to pay attention to empirical evidence based on our five senses?

- In view of this, is it reasonable to ignore what our senses plainly tell us—that is, that the bread and wine *are still* bread and wine—and instead believe that even though these look and feel and taste like bread and wine, they have really been changed into the body and blood of Jesus Christ?

Yet another problem arises when we consider that Roman Catholic churches all over the world have Masses on a regular basis. This fact would require that Christ's human body be omnipresent (everywhere-present). In the book *Heresies: The Image of Christ*, Harold O. J. Brown tells us that "in order to be bodily present at thousands of altars, the body of Christ must possess one of the so-called attributes of the majesty of God, namely, omnipresence or ubiquity."[36] Moreover, as Millard Erickson notes, "To believe that Jesus was in two places at once is something of a denial of the incarnation, which limited his physical human nature to one location."[37] The Scriptures clearly indicate that Christ's human body is localized in heaven (see Revelation 1:13-16). When Stephen was being stoned, he said, "Behold, I see the heavens opened up and the Son of Man standing at the right hand of God" (Acts 7:56). Scripturally speaking, only Christ's divine nature is omnipresent (Matthew 18:20; 28:20; John 1:47-49).

Ask...

- Is it possible for a human body to be in more than one place at a time?

- If Roman Catholic churches all over the world hold Mass every Sunday, wouldn't Jesus' human body have to be omnipresent (everywhere-present)?

- Did you know that Scripture teaches that *only* Christ's divine nature—not His human nature (and body)—is omnipresent?

- Did you know that Scripture consistently portrays Christ's human body as now being localized in heaven (Revelation 1:13-16)?

- Transubstantiation seems to contradict Scripture, doesn't it?

The memorial view of the Lord's Supper makes much more sense. In this view there is no change in the elements, and the ordinance is not intended as a means of communicating grace to the participant. The bread and wine are merely symbols and reminders of Jesus in His death and resurrection (1 Corinthians 11:24,25). It also reminds us of the basic facts of the gospel (11:26), our anticipation of the second coming (11:26), and our oneness as the body of Christ (10:17). This viewpoint, I believe, best fits the context of 1 Corinthians 11:24-26.*

The Unbiblical Nature of the Mass

Roman Catholics believe that the Mass really does not detract from the atonement wrought by Christ at the cross. Protestants respond by reminding Catholics of what the Council of Trent said: "This sacrifice [of the Mass] is truly propitiatory....For by this oblation the Lord is appeased...and he pardons wrongdoing and sins, even grave ones."[38] Because the Mass is said to bring about the forgiveness of sins, *it is a necessity* in the Catholic system of salvation. This very much detracts from the final salvation that Christ accomplished at the cross (see John 19:30).

For Protestants the idea that the Mass is in any sense a repetition of the death of Christ seems reminiscent of the repeated sacrifices of the old covenant, which were "a reminder of sins year by year" (Hebrews 10:3). As opposed to believers having the full assurance of complete forgiveness

---

* There are two other views held by Protestants. The Lutheran view is known as consubstantiation. This view says that Christ is present *in, with,* and *under* the bread and wine. There is a real presence of Christ, but no change in the elements. The mere partaking of the elements after the prayer of consecration communicates Christ to the participant along with the elements. The Reformed view is that Christ is spiritually present at the Lord's Supper, and it is a means of grace. There is said to be a dynamic presence of Jesus in the elements made effective in the believer as he partakes. The partaking of His presence is not a physical eating and drinking, but an inner communion with His Person.

of sins through the *once-for-all* sacrifice of Christ (Hebrews 10:12), the Mass gives a constant reminder of sins and remaining guilt to be atoned for week after week.[39]

Ask...

- Did you know that Scripture says that one of the detracting things about the Old Testament sacrificial system is that people were reminded year after year of their sins (Hebrews 10:3)?

- Did you know that Scripture says one of the great things about the *once-for-all* sacrifice of Christ is that people have full assurance of complete forgiveness of sins (Hebrews 10:12)?

- Doesn't the Roman Catholic Mass resemble the Old Testament system in that it constantly serves to remind us of our sin instead of the fact that our sin has once for all been taken care of by Christ?

Protestants are resolute in their conviction that Scripture strongly argues against the doctrine of the Mass. Recall what Jesus said upon the cross in regard to His sacrificial death: "It is finished" (John 19:30). This proclamation from the Savior's lips is fraught with meaning. The Lord was doing more than announcing the termination of His physical life. That fact was self-evident. What was not known by those who were carrying out the brutal business at Calvary was that somehow, despite the sin they were committing, *God through Christ had completed the final sacrifice for sin.* The work long contemplated, long promised, long expected by prophets and saints, is done.

It is highly significant that the phrase "it is finished" can also be translated "paid in full." The backdrop to this is that in ancient days, whenever someone was found guilty of a crime, the offender was put in jail and a "certificate of debt" was posted on the jail door (Colossians 2:14). This certificate listed all the crimes the offender was found guilty of. Upon release, after serving the prescribed time in jail, the offender was given the certificate of debt, and on it was stamped "paid in full." Christ took the certificate of debt of all our lives (including all our sins) and nailed it on the cross. And Jesus said, "paid in full" upon the cross (John 19:30).

Hence, Jesus' words do not constitute a moan of defeat nor a sigh of patient resignation. Rather, His words were a triumphant recognition that He had now fully accomplished what He came into the world to do. The work of redemption was completed at the cross. Nothing further needed to be done. He had paid in full the price of our redemption (2 Corinthians 5:21). And "when He had made purification of sins, He sat down at the right hand of the Majesty on high" (Hebrews 1:3), where He remains to this day.

Ask...

• How do you reconcile Jesus' statement, "It is finished" (John 19:30), with the continual re-presenting of Christ's sacrifice in the Mass?

(Share the above insights on the phrase "it is finished.")

Jesus completed the work of redemption at the cross with a single *once-for-all* sacrifice. No more sacrifices (or "re-presentings") would occur. It was a "done deal"—*a finished transaction*—at that point. Consider the Book of Hebrews. God assures believers that "their sins and their lawless deeds I will remember no more" (Hebrews 10:17). And "where there is forgiveness of these things, there is no longer any offering for sin" (10:18). Christ made a sacrificial offering "once for all when He offered up Himself" (7:27). He did so "not through the blood of goats and calves, but through His own blood, He entered the holy place once for all, having obtained eternal redemption" (9:12). By the death of Christ "we have been sanctified through the offering of the body of Jesus Christ once for all" (10:10).

Ask... _____

- Would you please read aloud from Hebrews 10:18?

- How do you reconcile this with the continual "re-presentings" of Christ's sacrifice in the Mass?

_____

Yet another evidence that points against this idea of Christ being "re-presented" over and over again in sacrifice is Romans 6:9, which notes that "Christ, having been raised from the dead, is never to die again; death no longer is master over Him." Christ today is portrayed as "the living One... alive forevermore" (Revelation 1:18).

Ask... _____

- Would you please read aloud from Romans 6:9?

- Does this verse seem compatible with the Catholic doctrine of the Mass?

_____

The Priesthood of Every Believer

Christians have no need of intermediating priests because there are no further sacrifices being made to God today. *Jesus has done it all.* Furthermore, it is critical to understand that every Christian is a member of the priesthood of believers. Consider:

— Revelation 1:6 tells us: "He has made us to be a kingdom, priests to His God and Father; to Him be the glory and the dominion forever and ever. Amen."

— In Revelation 5:10 we read: "Thou hast made them to be a kingdom and priests to our God; and they will reign upon the earth."

— Revelation 20:6 tells us: "Blessed and holy is the one who has a part in the first resurrection; over these the second death has no power, but they will be priests of God and of Christ and will reign with Him for a thousand years."

— First Peter 2:5 tells us: "You also, as living stones, are being built up as a spiritual house for a holy priesthood, to offer up spiritual sacrifices acceptable to God through Jesus Christ."

As "priests," we do offer sacrifices, but not the kind the Roman Catholic Church speaks about. We are to offer up our own bodies in sacrifice to God (Romans 12:1). We are to engage in a sacrifice of praise to God, for this is well-pleasing to Him (Hebrews 13:15). *But the Eucharist?* No!

In fairness, the Roman Catholic Church does recognize a general priesthood of believers, and a person becomes a member of this priesthood through baptism. But the emphasis is on the *ministerial* priesthood, which is open only to unmarried, celibate men. After ordination they are said to have the authority to consecrate and offer the body and blood of the Lord at the Eucharist.

The Bible knows nothing of such a distinction in priesthoods. The Bible simply says that every believer in Christ is part of the priesthood (Revelation 1:5,6; 5:10; 20:6). And for that reason, Protestants reject the Catholic view as unbiblical.

Sometimes Roman Catholics will try to argue that references in the New Testament to "elders" point to the office of priest. Some Catholic translations even translate *elder* as *priest* in an effort to build support for their case. For example, the (non-Catholic) New American Standard Version says at Titus 1:5: "For this reason I left you in Crete, that you might set in order what remains, and *appoint elders* in every city as I directed you" (emphasis added). The Douay Rheims (Catholic) version, by contrast, translates this same verse: "For this cause I left thee in Crete, that thou shouldest...

ordain priests in every city, as I also appointed thee" (emphasis added).

This is not honest scholarship. The Greek word for "elder" is *presbuteros*, whereas the Greek word for "priest" is *hiereus*. The word *presbuteros* is used in Titus 1:5. Any honest look at the lexical use of these words in the Bible shows that two entirely different offices are in view with these words.

Ask...

- Did you know that the Greek word for "elder" is *presbuteros* whereas the Greek word for "priest" is *hiereus*?

- In view of the fact that the word *presbuteros* is used in the Greek version of Titus 1:5, do you think it is honest to use the word *priest* in the English translation of this verse? Shouldn't it be translated as *elder*?

11

Sacramentalism—Part 2

Reasoning from the Scriptures

"That doctrine which maintains a change of the substance of
bread and wine, into the substance of Christ's body and blood
(commonly called transubstantiation) by consecration of a priest,
or by any other way, is repugnant, not to Scripture alone,
but even to common sense, and reason."[1]
Westminster Confession of Faith

In the previous chapter we examined and answered a number of issues related to Roman Catholic sacramentalism.
In the present chapter our attention will focus on some specific verses that typically come up in discussions with
Roman Catholics on transubstantiation and the Mass. We
begin with John 6:52,53, a verse often cited in support of
transubstantiation.

John 6:52,53—Biblical Support for Transubstantiation?

The Roman Catholic Teaching: In John 6:51-55 we read
the words of Jesus:

> "I am the living bread that came down out of heaven; if
> anyone eats of this bread, he shall live forever; and the
> bread also which I shall give for the life of the world is
> My flesh." The Jews therefore began to argue with one

another, saying, "How can this man give us His flesh to eat?" Jesus therefore said to them, "Truly, truly, I say to you, unless you eat the flesh of the Son of Man and drink His blood, you have no life in yourselves. He who eats My flesh and drinks My blood has eternal life, and I will raise him up on the last day. For My flesh is true food, and My blood is true drink."

Roman Catholics have often cited this verse in support of their view of transubstantiation. Ludwig Ott, a respected Roman Catholic authority, says there are a number of factors pointing to a literal interpretation of the passage. For example, someone could argue from the nature of the words used in this passage: "true food" and "true drink."[2] One could also argue, Ott says, from the difficulties created by a figurative interpretation. He suggests that "in the language of the Bible to eat a person's flesh and drink his blood in the metaphorical sense means to persecute him in a bloody fashion, to destroy him."[3] Hence, if Jesus' words about eating and drinking Him are to be taken metaphorically, then we must surmise that Jesus was asking His followers to persecute Him. One can further argue, Ott says, from the reaction of Jesus' listeners: "This is a difficult statement; who can listen to it?" (John 6:60). Apparently, His listeners understood Jesus to be speaking literally.[4]

Response: In the broader context of John 6, Jesus had just performed a tremendous miracle in feeding 5000 people with five barley loaves and two fishes. Then, in verse 27, Jesus builds into His main message: "Do not work for the food which perishes, but for the food which endures to eternal life, which the Son of Man shall give to you, for on Him the Father, even God, has set His seal" (John 6:27). The crowd had eaten a meal that satisfied their *physical* hunger, but Christ wanted to give them something to satisfy their *spiritual* hunger and give them eternal life. It comes by partaking of the bread of life, Jesus Himself.

In context, John 6:53 is saying that just as we must consume or partake of physical food to sustain physical life, so we must spiritually appropriate Christ to have spiritual life. Just as the ancient Jews were dependent on manna (bread) to sustain physical life, so we are dependent on Jesus (the bread of life) for our spiritual life. Food that is eaten and then digested is assimilated so that it becomes a part of the body. Likewise, people must spiritually appropriate Christ and become one with Him *by faith* to receive the gift of eternal life.

The references to *flesh* and *blood* in this verse point us to the work of Christ on the cross. It was there that His flesh was nailed to the cross and His blood was shed to make man's salvation possible. By placing faith in the crucified Christ, we appropriate Him and His work of salvation.

Regarding how this verse relates to the death of Christ, expositors Robert Jamieson, A. R. Fausset, and David Brown make a keen observation:

> [Jesus] says they must not only "eat His flesh" but "drink His blood," which could not but suggest the idea of His death—*implied in the separation of one's flesh from his blood.* And as He had already hinted that it was to be something very different from a natural death, saying, "My flesh I will give for the life of the world" (John 6:51), it must have been pretty plain to candid hearers that He meant something above the gross idea which the bare terms expressed....The truth really conveyed here is no other than that expressed in John 6:51, though in more emphatic terms—that He Himself, in the virtue of His sacrificial death, is the spiritual and eternal life of men.[5]

Ask...

- If, hypothetically, a person were to eat someone's flesh and drink his blood, would that not presuppose the fact that the blood had been separated from the flesh?

- • Wouldn't that separation of the blood from the body entail physical death?

- • Can you see the possibility that Jesus' words in John 6 were intended as a graphic metaphor representing His death on the cross, where He would indeed shed His blood after His flesh was nailed to the cross?

There are other evidences that stand against the Roman Catholic interpretation of this passage. Consider:

— As noted in the previous chapter, Scripture teaches that drinking blood is forbidden to anyone (Genesis 9:4; Leviticus 3:17). The disciples, schooled in the commandments of God, would never have understood Jesus to be instructing them to go directly against the commandments of God.

— Peter said, "I have never eaten anything unholy and unclean" (Acts 10:14). Peter could not have said this if he thought he had actually ingested the body and blood of Christ (Leviticus 3:17).

— There is no mention of wine in John 6:52,53. If this passage were referring to the Eucharist, wine would be mentioned along with the bread.

Ask... _____

- • If John 6:52,53 is referring to the Eucharist, why isn't wine mentioned in this passage?

— The context for understanding Jesus' statement in John 6:54 ("He who eats My flesh and drinks My blood has eternal life") is set for us 15 verses earlier, in John 6:40: "For this is the will of My Father, that everyone who beholds the Son and *believes in Him*, may have eternal life; and I Myself will raise him up on the last day" (emphasis added). Contextually, the discussion centers on salvation by believing in Jesus, not on the Lord's Supper.

What about the Roman Catholic argument that some of Jesus' listeners understood Him to be speaking literally when He announced that people were to eat of His flesh (John 6:52)? The fact that some of Jesus' Jewish listeners understood Him this way does not prove that the Roman Catholic position is correct, for indeed, the Jews often misunderstood what Jesus taught. For example, when Jesus spoke of destroying "this temple," after which Jesus would raise it again in three days, the Jews misunderstood and thought Jesus was referring to the literal temple made of stones (John 2:19-21; other Jewish misunderstandings are found in John 3:4; 4:15; and 6:32-34). My point is that just because the Jews may have understood Jesus to be referring to literal flesh in John 6 does not mean that that interpretation is correct. As we have seen, the context indicates that Jesus was speaking figuratively of believing in Him for salvation (see verse 40).

Theologians Norman Geisler and Ralph MacKenzie note that the Bible often uses ingestive language to speak of our relationship with God.[6] We read, "O taste and see that the LORD is good; how blessed is the man who takes refuge in Him!" (Psalm 34:8). David, while in the wilderness of Judah, prayed, "My soul thirsts for Thee" (Psalm 63:1). He later affirmed, "My soul is satisfied as with marrow and fatness, and my mouth offers praises with joyful lips" (Psalm 63:5). The psalmist also said, "How sweet are Thy words to my taste! Yes, sweeter than honey to my mouth" (Psalm 119:103). In 1 Peter 2:2,3 we read of longing "for the pure milk of the word, that by it you may grow in respect to salvation, if you have tasted the kindness of the Lord." In Hebrews 5:14 we read, "But solid food is for the mature, who because of practice have their senses trained to discern good and evil." These are all simple metaphors pointing to spiritual realities. The same is true of John 6:52,53.

Ask... _____

- Would you please read aloud from Psalm 34:8?

- Is the tasting of the Lord in this verse literal or figurative?

- Did you know that ingestive language is often used in Scripture as a figurative way of speaking about our relationship with God? (*Share some examples.*)

- Do you think the same is possible in John 6, where Jesus says, "I am the living bread that came down out of heaven" (verse 51)?

What about Ludwig Ott's objection that "in the language of the Bible to eat a person's flesh and drink his blood in the metaphorical sense means to persecute him in a bloody fashion, to destroy him"? This is a weak objection, for Ott assumes that if Jesus' words are used metaphorically, the metaphor *can only have one meaning* (that is, the meaning Ott attaches to it). In context, however, Jesus Himself indicated the meaning of the metaphor by what He said in John 6:40: "For this is the will of My Father, that everyone who beholds the Son and believes in Him, may have eternal life." *The metaphor refers not to persecuting Jesus, but rather refers to placing faith in Jesus.*

There is one more point that bears mentioning. If the bread Jesus held in His hands were actually His body, then He would have been incarnated into two places at the same time—an unreasonable view that contradicts other verses on the nature of the Incarnation (for example, Hebrews 2:14; 10:5). Taken in its immediate context and in the broader context of all of Scripture, it seems best to hold that in John 6:52,53 Jesus was using a vivid metaphor for placing faith in Him who would soon have His flesh nailed to the cross and His blood shed for the sins of humankind.

Matthew 26:20-30; Mark 14:17-26; Luke 22:14-38—Biblical Support for Transubstantiation and the Mass?

The Roman Catholic Teaching: In Matthew 26:20-30 we read:

> Now when evening had come, He was reclining at the table with the twelve disciples. And as they were eating, He said, "Truly I say to you that one of you will betray Me." And being deeply grieved, they each one began to say to Him, "Surely not I, Lord?" And He answered and said, "He who dipped his hand with Me in the bowl is the one who will betray Me. The Son of Man is to go, just as it is written of Him; but woe to that man by whom the Son of Man is betrayed! It would have been good for that man if he had not been born." And Judas, who was betraying Him, answered and said, "Surely it is not I, Rabbi?" He said to him, "You have said it yourself." And while they were eating, Jesus took some bread, and after a blessing, He broke it and gave it to the disciples, and said, "Take, eat; this is My body." And when He had taken a cup and given thanks, He gave it to them, saying, "Drink from it, all of you; for this is My blood of the covenant, which is poured out for many for forgiveness of sins. But I say to you, I will not drink of this fruit of the vine from now on until that day when I drink it new with you in My Father's kingdom." And after singing a hymn, they went out to the Mount of Olives.

Roman Catholic scholars often say this passage, along with the parallel passages in Mark 14:17-26 and Luke 22:14-38, provides biblical support for transubstantiation. They assume Jesus was teaching that the bread and wine were miraculously transformed into His actual body and blood. Hence, Christ gave His real flesh and blood to the disciples to eat and drink in the elements of the bread and wine.

Ludwig Ott says that the principal biblical proof for the "Eucharistic Real Presence" lies in the words of Matthew, Mark, and Luke.[7] He notes that the words found in the Gospels should be taken literally, especially in view of the wording: "There is nothing in the text to support a figurative interpretation; for bread and wine are neither of their nature nor, by current speech-usage, symbols of body and blood."[8]

Roman Catholics also argue that a present tense is used in the original Greek throughout this passage ("This *is* my body," "this *is* My blood of the covenant...").[9] Since Christ's sacrifice is spoken of in present-tense terms, this must mean it was happening *at that very instant*. That would mean that as they partook of the Lord's Supper, a sacrifice was *then* taking place. The Masses today are just like that first "Mass" at the Lord's Supper.

Response: The Roman Catholic viewpoint is reading something into the text that is not there. The fact that Jesus was present with the disciples when He said of the bread, "Take, eat; this is My body," is more than enough clue to indicate that Jesus was speaking metaphorically. If the Roman Catholic interpretation is correct, that would mean that Jesus was incarnated in two places at once: in His own body and in the bread. Scripture always presents Jesus as being incarnated only in a human body (Hebrews 2:14; 10:5).

Ask...

• Doesn't the fact that Jesus was physically present with His disciples when He said to them of the bread, "Take, eat; this is My body," indicate that He was speaking figuratively of the bread?

Jesus never said that the elements of bread and wine are actually transformed into His body and blood. He did not say, "This *becomes* My body and blood." He said, "This *is* My body and blood." The present tense does not mean a sacrifice was then taking place, but simply indicates that the bread and wine were at that present moment metaphorical symbols of His impending death for the sins of man. The verb is carries the idea of "represents": "The bread and wine *represent* My body and blood."

Jesus often spoke figuratively of Himself in Scripture. Consider a few of Jesus' other metaphors:

— "I am the light of the world" (John 8:12).
— "I am the door" (John 10:9).
— "I am the true vine" (John 15:1).

These statements, like Jesus' statement "I am the bread of life" (John 6:48), are figures of speech. They are not to be taken literally, but rather in each case they indicate something about Jesus. "I am the door," for example, indicates that Jesus is the way of salvation for His people. The bread and wine likewise are not to be taken literally, but rather are symbolic of the sacrifice Jesus made upon the cross.

Ask...

• Did you know that Jesus often spoke figuratively of Himself in Scripture?

• When Jesus said "I am the door" (John 10:9) and "I am the true vine" (John 15:1), He was not speaking literally, was He?

• In this same Gospel, when Jesus calls Himself the "bread of life" (John 6:48), do you think it is possible that He is also speaking figuratively here?

Further, as I noted in the previous chapter, if the elements of the bread and wine become the actual body and blood of Christ in Roman Catholic churches throughout the world every Sunday, this means that the body of Christ is spread all over the planet (and hence would require omnipresence). But nowhere in Scripture is Christ's human body portrayed as being omnipresent. Only Christ *in His divine nature* (as spirit—John 4:24) is omnipresent.

Revelation 1 makes it quite clear that Christ is now bodily in heaven, where He ascended from earth in Acts 1:9-11. And one day from heaven Christ will bodily come again at the second coming, where every eye will see this one (nonfragmented) body of Jesus (Revelation 1:7). So the idea that Christ's body is somehow omnipresent in Roman Catholic church services all over the world contradicts the biblical facts.

All things considered, Matthew 26:20-30 does not provide biblical proof for either the doctrine of transubstantiation or the Mass. In fact, both doctrines are directly refuted by Scripture.

John 4:19-21—Does Jesus' Prophecy Support the Doctrine of the Mass?

The Roman Catholic Teaching: In John 4:19-21 we read of an encounter Jesus had with a Samaritan woman, to whom Jesus spoke about her many husbands:

> The woman said to Him, "Sir, I perceive that You are a prophet. Our fathers worshiped in this mountain, and you people say that in Jerusalem is the place where men ought to worship." Jesus said to her, "Woman, believe Me, an hour is coming when neither in this mountain, nor in Jerusalem, shall you worship the Father."

Some Roman Catholics conclude that since worship would not be "in this mountain" or "in Jerusalem," it would indeed be all over the world—and hence this must refer to the Mass being performed in Roman Catholic churches all over the world.[10]

Response: Notice that Jesus said only that "worship" would not be limited to the "mountain" or to "Jerusalem." He made virtually no reference or allusion to any kind of sacrifice or to the Mass. Roman Catholics are practicing eisegesis (reading a meaning into the text) when they say this verse supports their view of the Eucharist.

Eisegesis can make a verse say virtually anything. For example, in reading John 4:21—"Jesus said to her, 'Woman, believe Me, an hour is coming when neither in this mountain, nor in Jerusalem, shall you worship the Father'"—an atheist might read into this passage the idea that Jesus was teaching the growth of atheism. An apocalyptic radical might read this verse as meaning that the mountain and Jerusalem will be nuked. A biohazard specialist might suggest that these areas might one day become infested and uninhabitable (and hence, no worship will take place there). Eisegesis is never an appropriate way to read the Bible. The important question is, *What does the context of John 4:19-21 reveal about its meaning?*

As a contextual backdrop, the Jews considered the Samaritans an "unclean" mixed breed—with Israelite and Assyrian ancestry. Because of this, the Jews were harshly prejudiced against the Samaritans and discriminated against them. This cultural hostility led the Samaritan woman to ask Jesus; "'You are a Jew and I am a Samaritan woman. How can you ask me for a drink?' (For Jews do not associate with Samaritans)" (John 4:9 NIV).

During the ensuing discussion, the woman asked Jesus which cultural place of worship was valid: Mount Gerizim where the Samaritans built their temple, or Jerusalem where the Jews built theirs. Theologian Anthony Evans alerts us to the significance of Jesus' response:

> Jesus does not hesitate to let her know that once you bring God into the picture, the issue is no longer culture, but truth. He informs her that the question is not Mt. Gerizim or Jerusalem, that it is not according to Samaritan tradition or Jewish tradition (v. 21). In fact, He denounces her cultural heritage in relation to worship, for He told her, "Ye worship ye know not what" (v. 22). When she began

to impose her culture on sacred things, Christ invaded her cultural world to tell her she was spiritually ignorant.[11]

Jesus transcended the whole issue of culture in discussing spiritual issues with the woman. When it came to her relationship with God, the issue moved from her cultural heritage to her heart, and the criterion for that relationship was truth. Jesus acknowledged cultural distinctions, but disallowed them when they interfered in any way with truth about God. A principle we can derive from this is, Culture must always take a backseat to the truth of God as revealed in Scripture.

As for localizing God in either Jerusalem or Samaria, it is the clear teaching of Scripture that God is spirit (John 4:24) and cannot be localized by human beings. God is everywhere. And He seeks a relationship with all people all over the world, regardless of their cultural heritage.

Seen in this light, there is not even the slightest hint of the Mass in John 4:19-21.

Ask... _____

(First share the above contextual setting of John 4:19-21.)

- In view of this context, do you think it is legitimate to cite this verse in support of the doctrine of the Mass?

Hebrews 9:12—Biblical Support for the Mass?

The Roman Catholic Teaching: In Hebrews 9:12 we read, "Not through the blood of goats and calves, but through His own blood, He entered the holy place once for all, having obtained eternal redemption." Roman Catholics sometimes argue that this verse supports the doctrine of the Mass. In fact, in the book *Crossing the Threshold of Hope*, Pope John Paul II writes:

> The Church is the instrument of man's salvation. It both contains and continually draws upon the mystery of

Christ's redemptive sacrifice. Through the shedding of His own blood, Jesus Christ constantly "enters into God's sanctuary thus obtaining eternal redemption" (cf. Hebrews 9:12).[12]

Response: James McCarthy[13] has made some keen observations for us in regard to this quote from the pope's book:

— The original biblical text renders Hebrews 9:12, "...through His own blood, He entered the holy place once for all, having obtained eternal redemption." *Entered* is an aorist tense in the Greek, indicating a one-time past event. Yet the pope renders it in the present tense, *enters.*

— Though the wording of Hebrews 9:12 is changed from what is recorded in Scripture, the pope puts it in quotation marks, implying that the source of his words is in fact Hebrews 9:12.

— The pope adds *constantly* ("constantly 'enters into God's sanctuary'") and leaves out *once for all.*

— The pope changes the once for all "*having obtained* eternal redemption" so that it reads, "*thus obtaining* eternal redemption."

All this completely changes the meaning of the biblical text. The way the pope renders the verse, it comes out sounding like it supports the Mass. But in reality the pope has changed what Scripture says. Not even an apostle or prophet of God would ever dare change what God said (see Galatians 1:8; John 10:35)!

Ask... _____

• Would you please read aloud from Hebrews 9:12?

• Whereas this verse indicates that Jesus "entered the holy place *once for all,*" why does the pope translate it, "*enters* into God's sanctuary" (present tense), as if it is still an ongoing process?

• Why does the pope change "*having obtained* eternal redemption" (a past event) so that it reads, "*thus obtaining* eternal redemption" (present tense)?

• Isn't the pope changing what Scripture says here?

• Did you know that not even a prophet or apostle—*and not even Jesus Himself*—ever dared change Scripture (Matthew 5:18; John 10:35; Galatians 1:8; Revelation 22:18,19)?

First Corinthians 10:21—Biblical Support for the Mass?

The Roman Catholic Teaching: In 1 Corinthians 10:21 we read, "You cannot drink the cup of the Lord and the cup of demons; you cannot partake of the table of the Lord and the table of demons." The Council of Trent substitutes *altar* for *table* here, and then argues that the Lord's Supper is a sacrifice. (After all, altars are used for sacrifices.)[14]

Response: The apostle Paul did not use the word *altar* (Greek: *thusiasterion*); he used the word *table* (Greek: *trapeza*). As Robert Jamieson, A. R. Fausset, and David Brown put it, "The Lord's Supper is a feast on a table, not a sacrifice on an altar. Our only altar is the cross, our only sacrifice that of Christ once for all."[15]

In Bible times, tables were places of fellowship (people would eat "fellowship meals"). In the city of Corinth, there were cultic meals as well. Some who were involved in pagan religion would sit down at a table, believing they were dining and fellowshiping with pagan gods. Paul thus said you cannot eat at *that* kind of table and at the table of the Lord. It is one or the other—Christians must "choose whom ye shall follow." But there is no indication of any kind of sacrifice in this verse. Hence, it cannot be applied in support of the Mass.

Psalm 110:4—Biblical Support for the Mass?

The Roman Catholic Teaching: In Psalm 110:4 we read, "The LORD has sworn and will not change His mind, 'Thou art a priest forever according to the order of Melchizedek.'" Roman Catholics say this verse supports their view of the Eucharist.

The backdrop to understanding this is in Genesis 14:18 where we read: "And Melchizedek king of Salem brought out bread and wine; now he was a priest of God Most High." This is said to support the doctrine of the Mass, prefiguring the offering of Christ's body and blood, since Jesus Himself is called a priest *forever* according to the order of Melchizedek (Psalm 110:4). "The Church sees in the gesture of the king-priest Melchizedek, who 'brought out bread and wine,' a prefiguring of her own offering."[16]

Response: The Roman Catholic interpretation is a huge stretch. A plain reading of the text in Genesis 14 indicates that as Abraham arrived with his troops and came before Melchizedek, Melchizedek brought out some food (bread and wine) to feed all these hungry guys. The verse makes no reference, or even the slightest allusion, to Melchizedek making any kind of sacrificial offering to God akin to the Mass.

Ask...

- Doesn't a plain reading of the text of Genesis 14:17-20 point to the fact that Melchizedek was simply providing food for a bunch of hungry warriors?

Protestants concede that Melchizedek is a "type" of Christ, prefiguring Christ in His work and ministry. They note that Melchizedek's name is made up of two words meaning "king" and "righteous." Melchizedek was also a priest. Thus, Melchizedek foreshadows Christ as a righteous king/priest. Melchizedek was also the king of "Salem" (which means "peace"). This points forward to Christ as the King of peace.

Yet, despite this typological parallel, the bread and wine in Genesis 14 have no typological significance, but simply portray Melchizedek being hospitable in providing something to eat for some hungry warriors. Nothing more, nothing less. There is no mention or allusion to any kind of sacrifice akin to the Mass.

Malachi 1:11—Malachi's Prophecy a Support for the Mass?

The Roman Catholic Teaching: In Malachi 1:11 we read, "'For from the rising of the sun, even to its setting, My name will be great among the nations, and *in every place incense is going to be offered to My name*, and a grain offering that is pure; for My name will be great among the nations,' says the LORD of hosts" (emphasis added). The Roman Catholic New American Bible (NAB) renders the above italicized portion of the verse, "and everywhere they bring sacrifice to my name." Roman Catholics believe that the Mass or Eucharist is a fulfillment of Malachi 1:11, inasmuch as sacrifices are offered everywhere (in Roman Catholic churches all over the planet). Also, the term translated "grain offering" in the New American Standard Bible (NASB) is translated "pure offering" in the Catholic NAB, and is also believed to support the doctrine of the Mass.

Catholic theologian Ludwig Ott writes:

> The Sacrifice of the Cross cannot be meant, as this was offered in one place only. The prophecy is fulfilled in the Holy Sacrifice of the Mass, which is offered "in all parts"...and which, in view of the sacrificial gift and of the primary sacrificing priest, is a clean oblation [pure offering].[17]

Response: Contextually this verse has nothing to do with the Eucharist. For one thing, most translators today believe the word translated *sacrifice* in the NAB carries the meaning "to cause to rise up in smoke," which is why the NASB translates it, "in every place incense is going to be offered to My name." It is noteworthy that the ancient Septuagint (a Greek translation of the Hebrew Old Testament that predates the time of Christ) renders the word as *incense*. This Hebrew word is certainly not the normal word used for sacrifice in the Old Testament, and its unique use in Malachi 1:11 bears no resemblance to what takes place at the Eucharist.[18]

Further, many scholars believe the "pure offering" of the NAB is probably a grain offering (see Leviticus 6:14-23), as the NASB renders it. If this is correct, it would not make sense for Roman Catholics to apply this to the Eucharist, since the Eucharist does not involve grain offerings.

It seems likely that this verse is pointing prophetically to the time following Christ's second coming. The verse does not seem to apply to the present day because God's name is ridiculed and scorned by so many people. God is not presently universally accepted. Following the second coming of Christ, however, Christ will set up His kingdom, and indeed His name will be great among the nations.[19]

12

Sin and the Sacrament of Penance

"No sin is small. No grain of sand is small
in the mechanism of a watch."[1]
Jeremy Taylor (1613–1667)

I noted earlier in the book that Roman Catholics believe that when Adam and Eve fell into sin, they lost the divine life God had bestowed upon them through sanctifying grace. Since then, every human being born into the world has been born without this divine life or sanctifying grace.[2] This is the Roman Catholic understanding of original sin.

To remedy original sin, there must be a restoration of sanctifying grace to the soul. Catholics believe that at the moment of baptism, this grace is restored. Indeed, sanctifying grace is bestowed and infused into the person and the spiritually dead person becomes spiritually alive. The spiritual transformation that takes place at baptism is referred to as initial justification.

Following this initial justification, the second aspect of justification occurs throughout life as the person progresses in good works and merits the further grace necessary for him to enter eternal life. This means that the person must sustain his new relationship with God and cooperate with the continuing grace of Christ in order to gain full and final justification, being cautious along the way not to commit a mortal sin (conscious, deliberate, serious sin), which erases grace from the soul.

But how does someone know when he or she has committed a mortal sin? How does it differ from a venial sin? And if someone does commit a mortal sin, what does that person do about it? It is to these important issues that we now shift our attention. In what follows, I will set forth the Roman Catholic view on these issues, and then will offer a biblical evaluation.

Venial Sins

Venial sins, in Roman Catholic theology, are lesser sins that can be pardoned. Indeed, the word *venial* comes from the Latin term *venia*, which means "pardon" or "easily forgiven."[3] Such sins do involve a violation of God's holy law, but they do not have any bearing as to whether a person goes to heaven or not. Venial sins can weaken someone's spiritual vitality—thus making him or her more vulnerable to falling into deeper sin—but venial sins cannot keep a person out of heaven. Someone might have to suffer some temporal punishment for these sins, but they are not serious enough to put a person outside the family of God. Unlike mortal sins, venial sins do not kill the soul. They just make you spiritually sick, so to speak.

In *Dogmatic Theology for the Laity* we read:

> We commit a *venial sin* (one which can be forgiven outside confession) whenever we transgress a commandment of God either in a matter which is not so serious, or without full knowledge, or without full consent of the will... for example, deliberate distraction at prayer, petty thievery, idleness, white lies, lack of love and generosity in small things, etc.[4]

What this means is that a person can commit a venial sin not only by engaging in a lesser form of sin, but also if that individual engages in a more serious sin but is not sufficiently aware of the evil involved or does not fully consent to the sin.[5] God forgives the sinner for such venial sins if he or she confesses them to God in prayer and sincerely repents.

Mortal Sins

Unlike venial sins, mortal sins are deadly or mortal in the sense that they virtually deplete the soul of God's sanctifying grace. We read in *Dogmatic Theology for the Laity*: "We commit *mortal sin* when we transgress a commandment of God in a serious matter, with full knowledge, and free consent of the will. Serious matter is, for example, unbelief, hatred of our neighbor, adultery, serious theft, murder, etc."[6]

Every bit as much as a "clear" button removes all the numbers on a calculator, so mortal sins—grave sins in which one is fully aware of violating God's holy law—"clear" the soul of God's sanctifying or justifying grace that comes at the moment of baptism.[7] These kinds of serious sins deplete the life of God within a person. *The Catholic Concise Encyclopedia* affirms: "The result of mortal sin is the loss of sanctifying grace, the loss of the gifts of the Holy Spirit, remorse, and the punitive effect of eternal separation from God."[8] Mortal sins are thus *deadly* sins. Should a Roman Catholic die in a state of having committed (and not dealt with) a mortal sin, that person will end up in hell.

For a person who commits such a sin, there is only one way to escape the damnable destiny of hell and find redemption, and that is found in confession of sin in the sacrament of penance. By confession of such sins to a priest, a person can do penance as instructed by the priest and can be absolved of his sins. At that point, grace is restored to the soul and the person essentially becomes "re-justified."

The *Catechism of the Catholic Church* puts it this way:

Christ instituted the sacrament of Penance for all sinful members of his Church: above all for those who, since Baptism, have fallen into grave sin, and have thus lost their baptismal grace and wounded ecclesial communion. It is to them that the sacrament of Penance offers a new possibility to convert and to recover the grace of justification. The Fathers of the Church present this sacrament as "the second plank [of salvation] after the shipwreck which is the loss of grace."[9]

What Is Involved in the Sacrament of Penance?

According to Roman Catholic theology, there are three primary aspects of penance: there must be *contrition*, *confession* to a priest, and then *satisfaction*. Contrition of heart consists of sorrow for the sins one has committed and the intention not to commit such sins in the future. In confession the sinner confesses to the priest all the sins he remembers in their entirety. Satisfaction for sins is then made according to the judgment of the priest, which is mainly achieved by the confessing sinner's prayers, fasting, and good deeds.[10]

In the sacrament of penance, the priest and confessing parishioner go through a programmed ritual in which each verbalizes responses and prayers. Though the ritual is programmed, I have spoken to Catholics who say the procedure is dreadfully embarrassing. In the course of the ritual, the parishioner verbally confesses his sins, admits how often they occurred, and acknowledges sorrow for such moral failure. Following this, the parishioner is assigned some acts of penance and is instructed to say an "Act of Contrition"—a penitential prayer that indicates personal sorrow for the sins committed. A typical "Act of Contrition" goes like this:

O my God, I am heartily sorry for having offended You. And I detest all my sins because of Your just punishment, but most of all because they offend You, my God, who are all good and deserving of all my love. I firmly resolve with the help of Your grace to confess my sins, to do penance, and to amend my life. Amen.[11]

At this point, the priest typically extends his right hand toward the parishioner and absolves him of his sins. To absolve means "to release from the consequences of guilt." The priest's prayer goes like this:

God, the Father of mercies, through the death and resurrection of His Son has reconciled the world to himself and sent the Holy Spirit among us for the forgiveness of sins; through the ministry of the Church may God give you pardon and peace, and I absolve you from your sins in the name of the Father, and of the Son, and of the Holy Spirit.[12]

The person then engages in the "acts of penance" assigned by the priest, typically involving praying ten "Our Fathers" and ten "Hail Marys." He sits in the pew until this assigned task is completed. Following this, he goes home thinking that all is well with his soul. He goes home with the conviction that sanctifying/justifying grace has been restored to his soul and that he has been reconciled to God. His slate has been wiped clean—for the time being.

Some persons not familiar with Roman Catholicism may wonder what the reasoning is behind the "acts of penance" mentioned above. Parishioners are instructed by the priest to engage in acts of penance as a way of making satisfaction for the *temporal punishment* of whatever sin or sins they committed. You see, the priest has the power to absolve a penitent sinner of the *guilt* and the *eternal punishment* of the sin, but he does not necessarily remove the *temporal punishment* for that sin. So the priest assigns an act of penance by which the sinner provides "satisfaction" for his sins, thereby removing the temporal punishment.

The priest assigns such acts of penance according to the seriousness of the sins committed. A lesser sin will require a lesser act of penance than a more serious sin. Such acts of penance might include fasting for a time, giving a financial gift or material goods to the poor, rendering a service to a neighbor, or, as is most often the case, recite "Hail Mary." By fulfilling such acts of penance as instructed by the priest, the temporal punishment for the sin is allegedly removed. (Any temporal punishment not removed in this life will allegedly be purged in purgatory following death.)

Answering Roman Catholics

A *Minimizing of Sin*

Many Protestants believe that the Roman Catholic view of salvation minimizes sin. According to Catholic theology, at the moment of baptism a person is cleansed of original sin and infused with sanctifying grace. This allegedly renders the person acceptable to God. At this moment the person is considered "born again."

Even infants who get baptized, though completely unaware of what is going on around them, are viewed as born again and a part of God's forever family. These infants then grow up thinking that they have already been made right with God by virtue of their baptism. Their sin problem has already been taken care of, in their thinking (except in the event they commit a mortal sin).

The scriptural viewpoint is that baptism does not save anyone, but rather takes place *after* one has become a Christian (Acts 2:41; 8:13; 18:8). Biblically, one is "born again" the moment he or she places personal faith in Jesus Christ (John 3:1-5; Titus 3:5). A parent cannot make that decision on his or her child's behalf. It is something that each person must do for himself or herself, realizing that he or she is a sinner in need of redemption. It is those who personally trust in Christ that become a part of God's forever family (Acts 16:31).

As we read in John 1:12,13, "*As many as received Him, to them He gave the right to become children of God, even to those who believe in His name, who were born not of* blood, nor of the will of the flesh, nor of the will of man, but of God." This wonderful privilege of gaining entrance into God's forever family depends upon personally "receiving" Him in faith. These are the ones who have had their sin problem taken care of.

There is also a problem in the Roman Catholic distinction between mortal sins and venial sins. If a person grows up thinking that most of his sins have been venial sins, then he may view himself as basically a good person. He may not see himself as being in dire need of a Savior. Even if the person does commit a mortal sin, the solution involves just going to a priest and participating in the sacrament of penance. Easy enough. The slate is wiped clean all over again.

I do not mean to imply that *all* Catholics view sin in this way. I am quite sure that many Catholics feel genuine remorse for sins. My point is that a lax attitude toward sin can easily result from the Catholic distinction between mortal sins and venial sins.

The Bible makes no such distinction between mortal sins and venial sins. It is true that some sins are worse than others (Proverbs 6:16-19). But never does Scripture say that only certain kinds of sin lead to spiritual death.* *All* sin leads to spiritual death, not just one category of sin (Romans 3:23).

There are two points I want to make in this regard. First, the biblical reality is that every single sin a person commits is a

---

* The Greek word for death *(thanatos)* literally means "separation." Physical death involves the separation of the spirit from the body. But spiritual death involves the separation of the sinner from God. *All* sin spiritually separates us from God (Romans 6:23). *All* sin leads to spiritual death.

In view of this, some readers may wonder how 1 John 5:16 relates to this. In this verse John makes reference to "a sin not leading to death." Most interpreters believe this is referring to the issue of premature death as a result of heinous sin. Christians can commit such horrendous sins that God judges them with premature death (see 1 Corinthians 11:30 for an example). But the great majority of sins a Christian commits do not fall into this severe category. So while *all* sins lead to spiritual death (that is, "spiritual separation from God"—Romans 6:23), *not all* sins lead to premature physical death (1 John 5:16). The key word here, of course, is *premature.* Ultimately all sin leads to both spiritual and physical death.[13]

mortal sin in the sense that it brings about spiritual death and separates us from God. Even the smallest sin makes us legally guilty before God and is worthy of eternal punishment. As the apostle Paul put it in Romans 6:23, "The wages of sin is death."

Second, and most important, even the most serious sins (so-called "mortal sins") are fully forgiven for the person who comes to Christ for salvation. Someone does not have to go to a priest a thousand times throughout life to obtain absolution, but rather the person who has trusted in Christ is simply in a state of forgiveness. Christ has done it all.

An example would be the believers in the city of Corinth. Consider the apostle Paul's words from 1 Corinthians 6:9-11:

> Do you not know that the unrighteous shall not inherit the kingdom of God? Do not be deceived; neither fornicators, nor idolaters, nor adulterers, nor effeminate, nor homosexuals, nor thieves, nor the covetous, nor drunkards, nor revilers, nor swindlers, shall inherit the kingdom of God. And such were some of you; but you were washed, but you were sanctified, but you were justified in the name of the Lord Jesus Christ, and in the Spirit of our God.

These Corinthians had been guilty of committing all kinds of "mortal sins" for years and years, and yet their slate had been wiped clean as a result of their faith in the Savior, who attained eternal redemption for them at the cross. They were "washed," "sanctified," and "justified" in the name of the Lord Jesus Christ.

Ask...

- Did you know there is not a single reference in the Bible to "mortal sins" and "venial sins"? Don't take my word for it. Check it out for yourself. *(If your Roman Catholic acquaintance appeals to tradition for support for the distinction between mortal sins and venial sins, consult chapters 3 and 4, which deal with "sola scriptura versus tradition.")*

- Did you know that from a scriptural perspective, all sins cause spiritual death? (*Read Romans 6:23. Explain that "spiritual death" involves spiritual separation from God as a result of sin.*)

- Would you please read aloud from 1 Corinthians 6:9-11?

- These Corinthians were guilty of plenty of mortal sins, weren't they?

- Yet what words are used to describe their present spiritual standing as a result of believing in Christ? (*"Washed," "sanctified," "justified."*)

- Did you know that Scripture says we are justified and made right with God not by works but solely by faith in Christ? (*Read Romans 3:26,28; 4:3; 5:1.*)

A Biblical View of Sin

As noted above, from a biblical perspective *all sin is deadly*. Indeed, the penalty for "sin" (not just "mortal sin," but *all* sin) includes both spiritual and physical death (Romans 6:23; 7:13). Death means "separation." Spiritual death, then, is spiritual separation from God. Physical death results from spiritual death, and involves separation of the soul from the body. After Adam and Eve sinned, both they and their descendants experienced spiritual separation from God, and they eventually died physically (Romans 5:12).

The apostle Paul stressed that all human beings fall short of God's glory (Romans 3:23). *Fall short* is a single word in the Greek and is in the present tense. This indicates continuing action. Human beings perpetually fall short of God's glory. The word *glory* here refers not just to God's splendor, but also to the outward manifestation of His attributes— including His righteousness, justice, and holiness. Human beings fall short of God in these and other areas.

The seriousness of man's sin problem comes into clearest focus in the teachings of Jesus Christ. Jesus taught that as a result of the fall, human beings are evil (Matthew 12:34) and that man is capable of great wickedness (Mark 7:20-23). Moreover, He said that man is utterly lost (Luke 19:10), that he is a sinner (Luke 15:10), and that he is in need of repentance before a holy God (Mark 1:15).

Jesus often spoke of sin in metaphors that illustrate the havoc sin can wreak in someone's life. He described sin as blindness (Matthew 23:16-26), sickness (Matthew 9:12), being enslaved in bondage (John 8:34), and living in darkness (John 8:12; 12:35-46). Moreover, Jesus taught that this is a universal condition and that all people are guilty before God (Luke 7:37-48).

Jesus also taught that both inner thoughts and external acts render a person guilty (Matthew 5:28). He taught that from within the human heart come evil thoughts, sexual immorality, theft, murder, adultery, greed, malice, deceit, envy, slander, arrogance, and folly (Mark 7:21-23). Moreover, He affirmed that God is fully aware of every person's sins, both external acts and inner thoughts; nothing escapes His notice (Matthew 22:18; Luke 6:8; John 4:17-19).

So, sin—any sin, all sin, sins *of the heart*, not just "mortal" sin—causes death and separates us from God. And it is in view of the horrific nature of sin that the wonder of the salvation provided in Jesus Christ comes into clear focus. For Scripture indicates that those sinners who come to Christ and place their faith in Him and *Him alone* are recipients of the most wonderful gift in the world: the gift of eternal salvation (Ephesians 2:8,9). And once someone receives this gift, it is a permanent transaction. A person does not lose this gift and regain it by continual visits to a priest. *It is a gift forever.* This is the glorious good news of the gospel (Luke 7:47-50; 18:9-14; Acts 10:43; Romans 3:25,28,30; 8:33,34; Galatians 4:21–5:12; 1 John 1:7–2:2).

A Biblical View of Confession

When we as Christians sin, the Holy Spirit convicts us and we experience a genuine sense of conviction that Scripture calls a "godly sorrow" (2 Corinthians 7:8-11). This leads to a sense of guilt, a sense of estrangement from God. So, what do we do when the Holy Spirit convicts us of a sin?

Scripture says we need to confess that sin not to a priest but to *God* (1 John 1:9). The Greek word for *confess* literally means "to say the same thing." When I confess my sin to God, that means I am saying the same thing about my sin that God says about it. I am agreeing with God that I did wrong. *No excuses!* And following my confession, I can thank God that I am forgiven, because Jesus paid for my sin on the cross (2 Corinthians 5:21; Colossians 2:14). Instantly my fellowship with the Father is restored. My goal from that point forward is to walk in the power of the Holy Spirit so I will have the power to resist such sins in the future (Galatians 5:22,23).

What happens if the Christian refuses to respond to the Holy Spirit's conviction and chooses to continue sinning? That is not a wise thing to do. God loves us too much to let us perpetually remain in sin. Scripture reveals that if a child of God sins and refuses to turn from it and confess it, God—with a motive of love—brings discipline into that child's life to bring him or her to a point of confession (Hebrews 12:4-11; see also Psalm 51). God's desire is to restore fellowship with His child.

It is much the same in a human family. If my son or daughter does something wrong and refuses to turn from it, I may find it necessary to discipline that child. That child is still in my family. Nothing will change that. But because I love my child, I cannot let him or her persist in doing wrong without taking action. In the same way, because God loves us, He takes disciplinary action when we refuse to turn from sin and confess it.

I want to reiterate that our confession is to be to God and Him alone. We are not required to make confession to a human mediator like a priest.* Recall that after committing adultery with Bathsheba, David made confession directly to God: "I acknowledged my sin to Thee, and my iniquity I did not hide; I said, 'I will confess my transgressions to the LORD'; and Thou didst forgive the guilt of my sin" (Psalm 32:5; see also Nehemiah 1:4-11; Daniel 9:3-19; Ezra 9:5-10). This same pattern of confession to God is seen in the New Testament. In fact, in Hebrews 4:16 we are exhorted, "Let us therefore draw near with confidence to the throne of grace, that we may receive mercy and may find grace to help in time of need." *We do not need a priest as an intermediary.*

Ask...

- Would you please read aloud from Psalm 32:5?

- To whom did David confess his sins?

- Would you please read aloud from Hebrews 4:16?

- Would you say this verse indicates you and I can approach the very throne of God without having to go through a priest?

Reasoning from the Scriptures
John 20:23—Biblical Support for Confession to a Priest?

The Roman Catholic Teaching: In John 20:23 we read the words of Jesus, "If you forgive the sins of any, their sins have been forgiven them; if you retain the sins of any, they have

---

* Of course, Scripture does admonish us to confess our sins to *one another* (James 5:16), not because such confession has anything to do with our forgiveness before God (it does not), but because it brings reconciliation among Christians. Confessing our sins to other people also makes it possible for Christians to pray more intelligently for one another. This verse, however, offers no support for the idea of making confession to a priest.

been retained." Roman Catholics often teach that in this verse Jesus was giving priests the power to forgive Christians who had succumbed to sin: "This power to forgive sins Christ delegated to His Apostles (John 20:23), thereby, according to the solemn teaching of the Council of Trent, instituting the Sacrament of Penance, in which this same power to forgive sins continues to be exercised by the priests of the Church."[14]

Response: Only God can judicially forgive sins committed against Him (Mark 2:7). All John 20:23 is saying is that when people respond positively to the gospel and accept it, we have the right to declare to them, "Your sins are forgiven," based on the promise of Jesus. Likewise, when people respond negatively to the gospel and reject it, we have the right to declare to them, "Your sins are not forgiven," based on the promise of Jesus. We are simply declaring or announcing heaven's verdict regarding what will happen if people respond one way or the other in regard to Christ. Further, the context of the verse indicates that this declarative power is not limited to some select group (like priests), but every Christian has this right. After all, every single believer is a priest before God (1 Peter 2:5,9).

Of course, if it is true that we are all priests unto God, then this has implications regarding whether it is necessary for believers to go to a priest for confession. After all, *priests confess directly to God* (see Hebrews 4:16). If we are priests, as Scripture indicates, then we confess directly to God, not to another priest.

The scriptural reality is that there is not a single verse in the New Testament (including John 20:23) that instructs us to confess our sins to some priest. Nor do we see a single example in the Book of Acts or any other biblical book of anyone making confession to a priest (or disciple). Confession is to be made to God alone (Psalm 32:5; Nehemiah 1:4-11; Daniel 9:3-19; Ezra 9:5-15).

Ask...

- • Can you think of a single example in the Book of Acts or any other biblical book of a believer having to go to a priest to confess his sins? *(There is none.)*

- • Since the Bible indicates that all of us are priests (1 Peter 2:5,9), and since all priests confess directly to God (Hebrews 4:16), what does this tell you about the privilege of every single believer? (*We can confess directly to God instead of having to go through another priest.*)

Matthew 16:24—Biblical Support for the Need for Penitential Works?

The Roman Catholic Teaching: In Matthew 16:24 we read, "Then Jesus said to His disciples, 'If anyone wishes to come after Me, let him deny himself, and take up his cross, and follow Me.'" Some Roman Catholics say that Jesus' instruction here refers to the necessity of doing penitential works.[15]

Response: This verse refers not to doing penitential works (which Roman Catholics typically say are necessary for salvation), but rather refers to the life of commitment of one who has already become saved. Christ is calling on those who have already trusted in Him for salvation to totally commit themselves to living for Him on a daily basis.

These words of Jesus would certainly have made sense to His first-century hearers, since the cross as a tool of execution was quite common. When a man had been condemned to die, and the time of execution had arrived, the man would be required by the Roman executioners to carry his own cross to the place of execution. This is much as it was with Jesus when the time of His execution came: "Carrying his own cross, he went out to the place of the Skull (which in Aramaic is called Golgotha)" (John 19:17 NIV).

As we "take up" our "cross" and follow Jesus, we are willingly submitting ourselves to suffering and even dying for His sake. Jesus is quite obviously calling for a total commitment. The idea is this: "If you really want to follow Me, do not do so in word only, but put your life on the line and follow Me on the path of the cross—a path that will involve sacrifice, suffering, and possibly even death."

It is important to keep in mind that there is a distinction between becoming saved and following Christ as a disciple. Scripture is clear that we become saved by placing faith in Jesus Christ. Close to 200 times in the New Testament, salvation is said to be by faith alone. Here are a few representative verses:

— In John 5:24 (NIV) Jesus said, "I tell you the truth, whoever hears my word and believes him who sent me has eternal life and will not be condemned; he has crossed over from death to life."

— In John 11:25 (NIV) Jesus said, "I am the resurrection and the life. He who believes in me will live, even though he dies."

— In John 12:46 (NIV) Jesus said, "I have come into the world as a light, so that no one who believes in me should stay in darkness."

Clearly, salvation is by faith in Christ!

A life of discipleship, however, goes beyond the initial conversion experience and calls for a life of sacrifice and commitment. The disciple is to "deny" himself. He must turn his back on selfish interests. He is no longer to live his life with self on the throne of his heart, but Christ must reign supreme. As Bible scholar William Lane put it,

> Jesus stipulated that those who wish to follow him must be prepared to shift the center of gravity in their lives from a concern for self to reckless abandon to the will of

God. The central thought in self-denial is a disowning of any claim that may be urged by the self, a sustained willingness to say "No" to oneself in order to be able to say "Yes" to God. This involves a radical denunciation of all self-idolatry and of every attempt to establish one's own life in accordance with the dictates of the self.[16]

Ask...

- Did you know the Bible draws a distinction between becoming saved and following Christ as a disciple?

- We become saved by faith in Christ. *(Read aloud from John 3:16; 5:24; 11:25; 12:46.)*

- We become disciples by "taking up our crosses" (denying ourselves) and following Jesus on a day-to-day basis.

Some scholars have noted that in ancient times the very act of having to bear one's cross en route to the place of execution showed one's submission to the authority against which the person had previously rebelled. There is a lesson we learn here. Formerly we ourselves were of the world, and we certainly were not in submission to Jesus Christ (Ephesians 2:1-3). But the act of taking up our crosses and following Him involves openly showing our submission to the One against whom we formerly rebelled.

It is also interesting to note that, among the ancients, when a person had been sentenced to die and was carrying his cross to the place of execution, he would often pass by crowds of people who would mock and scorn him. The condemned person was made to feel condemned on his way to the place of execution. There is a parallel in the life of the Christian. As we take up our crosses to follow Jesus on a day-to-day basis, there very well may be times when we are scorned for following Him (see Matthew 5:11; John 15:18-21). We must be prepared for this. It will likely happen. This is a part of following Christ on the path of the cross.

There is one further observation that bears mentioning. When Jesus instructed those listening to take up their crosses and "follow" Him, the word *follow* in the Greek is what is called a "present imperative." This is highly significant. The present tense indicates continuous action. We are to perpetually and unceasingly follow Jesus, day in and day out. (It is not just a Sunday thing.) The imperative indicates it is a command. It is not a mere option for the Christian. We are commanded to follow Jesus on a daily basis.

2 Corinthians 2:10—Biblical Support for Performing Absolution?

The Roman Catholic Teaching: In 2 Corinthians 2:10 we read the apostle Paul's words: "But whom you forgive anything, I forgive also; for indeed what I have forgiven, if I have forgiven anything, I did it for your sakes in the presence of Christ." Roman Catholic theologians often say that in this verse we find the apostle Paul exercising the power of absolution given to him by Christ. Christ likewise "promised to His Church and transmitted to His Church the power to forgive sins without limitation."[17]

Response: This verse has nothing to do with exercising the power of absolution. In context the verse deals with an incident of church discipline in the church at Corinth. The person of whom Paul was speaking had committed a serious offense and, as a result, severe church discipline was imposed upon him. Paul now urged the Corinthian believers to lovingly restore this person to fellowship in view of the remorse the person had shown. The person had repented, and hence forgiveness was in order. After all, the purpose of church discipline is to restore a person to fellowship, not to permanently injure him.

It was in this context that the apostle Paul said, "But whom you forgive anything, I forgive also; for indeed what I have forgiven, if I have forgiven anything, I did it for your sakes in the presence of Christ." Paul then indicated that it was important for the offender to be restored so that the incident would not become an occasion for Satan to drive a wedge between the church and Paul (verse 11).

Many Bible scholars believe that in this verse Paul was personally forgiving an offense directed at him, and then urged the Corinthian believers to forgive the person and restore him to fellowship. Bible Scholar Colin Kruse notes that Paul had "found himself the object of a hurtful attack (2:5; 7:12) made by a certain individual,"[18] and this situation caused disruption not just for Paul but for the church as well.

Expositor Murray H. Harris agrees, adding:

> The man referred to in these verses is almost certainly not the man guilty of incest (1 Corinthians 5). Rather, after Paul's painful visit some powerful insult had been directed against him or one of his representatives by a visitor to Corinth or by a Corinthian, who perhaps headed the opposition against Paul at Corinth.[19]*

This individual ended up repenting of his attack against Paul after being disciplined by the church. Bible scholar David Clines notes: "The leader of the opposition to Paul has been punished by the church, and has repented of his rebellion. Paul therefore forgives him, and asks the church also to forgive him."[21]

If this view is correct, as the evidence seems to indicate, then in verse 10 Paul is simply saying that he has already forgiven the man in question, if, in fact, there was anything to

---

* The person in question here has been traditionally identified with the incestuous man of 1 Corinthians 5. This view is unacceptable for several reasons: (1) The Corinthians' attitude to this offender is portrayed as a matter of obedience to Paul (2 Corinthians 2:9), whereas in the case of the incestuous man it was a matter of ethics. (2) Here, the church discipline has been sufficient punishment, and the offender is to be restored (verses 6,7), whereas in 1 Corinthians 5:5 the wrongdoer has been delivered to Satan for the destruction of the flesh. (3) It would be putting things too mildly to say that the incestuous man caused pain to the church only "in some degree"[20] (2 Corinthians 2:5).

forgive in the first place. Paul was taking the initiative in the matter of forgiveness, making sure the Corinthians followed suit. Seen in this light, the verse cannot be used to support the Roman Catholic view of a priest absolving people from their sins. *Paul himself was expressing personal forgiveness.*

Ask... _____

(First explain the contextual setting of 2 Corinthians 2:10.)

- Since the context indicates that an individual who had personally attacked Paul had repented after being disciplined by the Corinthian church, does it make sense to you that Paul would want to verbalize his personal forgiveness of the offender to the Corinthians?

- Since Paul was just expressing personal forgiveness in this verse, can you see that he was not exercising some alleged power of absolution given to him by Christ?

Luke 13:3—Biblical Support for Penance?

The Roman Catholic Teaching: A Roman Catholic translation of Luke 13:3 reads, "The Lord also said: 'Except you do penance, you shall all likewise perish.'" Roman Catholics say this verse supports the sacrament of penance.[22]

Response: The Roman Catholic translation of this verse is incorrect. A better translation is the New American Standard Version: "I tell you, no, but unless you repent, you will all likewise perish." The Greek word in question, *metanoe*, means "to change one's mind," "to repent."[23] Indeed, *Friberg's Greek Lexicon* tells us the word is used "predominately of a religious and ethical change in the way one thinks about acts—[meaning] repent, change one's mind, be converted."[24] The *Louw-Nida Greek Lexicon* says the word means, "to change one's way of life as the result of a complete change of thought and attitude with regard to sin and righteousness—'to repent, to change one's way, repentance.'"[25]

Clearly, then, the phrase in question in Luke 13:3 should be translated, "Unless you *repent*, you will all likewise perish" (New American Standard Version), not "Except you do *penance*, you shall all likewise perish" (Roman Catholic translation). Obviously there is a big difference between the sacrament of penance and a call to repentance.

As for what is going on in the context of Luke 13:1-3, in verse 1 we find record of some Galileans who had been slain by Pilate's soldiers while offering sacrifices at the temple so that their blood and that of the sacrifices were mixed. Christ's subsequent point in verses 2 and 3 is that this horrible thing did not happen to them because they were worse sinners than all other Galileans, but that *all* people needed to repent. Death is a common denominator for the whole human race. Only repentance can bring life as people prepare to enter into God's holy kingdom. "Unless you repent, you will all likewise perish." *Penance is nowhere in view here.*

Acts 2:38—Biblical Support for Penance?

The Roman Catholic Teaching: A Roman Catholic translation of Acts 2:38 reads, "Do penance and be baptized every one of you." Roman Catholics say this supports the sacrament of penance. We are told that Peter recommended "penance to sinners about to receive baptism."[26]

Response: The Roman Catholic translation is a mistranslation. A better translation is the New American Standard Version: "Repent, and let each of you be baptized in the name of Jesus Christ for the forgiveness of your sins; and you shall receive the gift of the Holy Spirit." The same Greek word used for *repent* in Luke 13:3, *metanoe*, is used in this verse. It means, "to change one's mind," "to repent."[27] There is a big difference between the sacrament of penance and a call to repentance.

What is it the people in Acts 2 were called to "change their minds" about? In context, Peter was speaking to the Jews ("men of Judea" [verse 14], "men of Israel" [verse 22]) who had rejected Jesus Christ as being the Messiah. It is logical that Peter would call on them to repent (or change their mind) regarding their rejection of Jesus as the Messiah. In other verses, repentance has to do with sin in general, but in the present context it would seem that the Jews are being called to repent regarding the one primary sin of rejecting Jesus.

13

Purgatory and Indulgences

"There is therefore now no condemnation
for those who are in Christ Jesus."[1]
The Apostle Paul

The Doctrine of Purgatory

Purgatory may be defined as "a place or state in which are detained the souls of those who die in grace, in friendship with God, but with the blemish of venial sin or with temporal debt for sin unpaid. Here the soul is purged, cleansed, readied for eternal union with God in Heaven."[2] The *Catechism of the Catholic Church* tells us that "all who die in God's grace and friendship, but still imperfectly purified, are indeed assured of their eternal salvation; but after death they undergo purification, so as to achieve the holiness necessary to enter the joy of heaven."[3]

The Roman Catholic teaching on purgatory was pronounced as Church dogma in A.D. 1438. The best way to describe it is that it is a temporary hell with the sole purpose of working off the temporal punishment for a person's sins.

Here is the backdrop: The Council of Trent taught that the temporal punishments of sins committed prior to the sacrament of baptism are remitted by that baptism. If someone sins after baptism, however, even when these sins are forgiven through the sacrament of penance, the temporal punishments remain. These punishments can be expiated by works in this life or in the future (following death) in purgatory.

Consider the following scenario by way of illustration. A Roman Catholic parishioner dies, having persevered to the end in a state of sanctifying grace. This is a "saved" person. He is headed for heaven. Yet, despite this, the person still needs to "pay off" the remaining temporal punishment for his sins that he was unable to pay for while he was alive on earth. (Remember—the temporal punishment for sins must be paid even if the actual guilt of sins has been forgiven by participation in the sacrament of penance.) To make satisfaction for this outstanding debt, the person must suffer for a time in purgatory before going to his ultimate destiny in heaven. Matthew 5:26 indicates that every last ounce ("up to the last cent") of temporal punishment must be paid for.

To most Roman Catholics, the doctrine of purgatory makes good sense—especially in the context of a works-oriented system of salvation. After all, most people know they are not good enough for heaven. Most people seem to have an intuitive awareness that they have done enough bad things in life that they do not deserve to spend eternity in heaven. Seen in this way, a little punishment for the wrongs committed in this life is not viewed as unreasonable for those on the road to heaven. Purgatory meets this need.

As the *Pocket Catholic Dictionary* puts it:

> The souls of those who have died in the state of grace suffer for a time a purging that prepares them to enter heaven. The purpose of purgatory is to cleanse one of imperfections, venial sins, and faults, and to remit or do away with the temporal punishment due to mortal sins that have been forgiven in the Sacrament of Penance. It is an intermediate

state in which the departed souls can atone for unforgiven sins before receiving their final reward.[4]

Of course, because people have varying levels of sin in their lives, they spend varying amounts of time in purgatory depending on the level of temporal punishment that must be paid off before going to heaven. This is much as it is with the justice system on earth. People who commit more serious crimes spend more time in jail than minor offenders. The way some Roman Catholics put it, some sins "stick to the soul" with more vigor than others, and hence more "purging" is necessary in purgatory.

Once someone passes through purgatory and is purified, he or she is henceforth allegedly unselfish and is capable of perfect love. A person's selfish ego, along with its yearning for perpetual self-satisfaction, is purged away forever, never again to resurface. The individual is transformed into a "new you," ready for the joys of heaven.[5]

Roman Catholics have differing opinions regarding the nature of suffering in purgatory. Most believe that suffering the physical pain of burning in fire is required. Others believe that a sense of separation from God is all that is involved. Either way, by spending time in purgatory a person is purged of all remaining temporal punishment for sins that he or she was unable to pay for while on earth.

Catholics believe that if you have a loved one in purgatory, there are things you can do to shorten the person's stay there. For example, you can say prayers, give alms, and perform a variety of good works. All of these are viewed as meritorious and can aid a soul in purgatory. But if you really want to help your loved one, ask the priest to say a Mass on his or her behalf. That yields big results.

The Doctrine of Indulgences

The Roman Catholic Church teaches that the Church is the steward of a vast reservoir of merit called the "treasury of the Church" or "treasury of merit." This treasury was allegedly earned by the works and prayers of Jesus Christ, His mother Mary, and the saints of all ages. This treasury of merit is so vast that it can never be exhausted or depleted.

According to Roman Catholic theology, the Church has the power to dispense from this reservoir "indulgences," which are said to cancel the debt of temporal punishment.* Because Christ, Mary, and various Catholic saints have provided "super-abundant satisfactions" to God through their many merits, the Catholic Church believes it can offer these same merits to Catholic believers in exchange for remission of punishment.

Catholics speak of both a "partial indulgence" and a "plenary indulgence." A partial indulgence is one that takes away just a portion of a person's temporal punishment. A plenary indulgence cancels *all* the temporal punishment a person has accumulated. The more temporal punishment remitted through indulgences in this life, the less time someone will have to spend in purgatory. Understandably, the partial indulgence requires fewer acts of piety than a plenary indulgence.

Once a person has earned an indulgence, he or she can apply it either personally (thereby reducing his or her own temporal punishment for sins committed), or can by prayer apply it to the account of a dead loved one believed to be in purgatory. So indulgences can benefit both oneself and one's dead loved ones.[6]

What kinds of things must a person do for an indulgence? One of the most common is merely doing the sign of the cross (which grants an indulgence of three years less time in purgatory). Reciting the rosary in a family group can grant a partial indulgence of ten years.[7] Visiting a Catholic shrine can also grant an indulgence.

---

* Some Roman Catholics may try to minimize or play down the use of indulgences in the modern Roman Catholic Church. However, the modern Roman Catholic teaching on indulgences has been stated and clarified in three documents, dating from 1967 (*Indulgentiarum doctrina*, of Paul VI), 1968 (The new *Enchiridion of Indulgences*, issued by the Sacred Apostolic Penitentiary), and 1983 (the new Code of Canon Law of the Roman Catholic Church).

To gain a plenary indulgence, there are three conditions that must be met in addition to performing the specific requirements of that particular indulgence: sacramental confession, Eucharistic communion, and prayer for the pope (as well as, of course, abstaining from willful sin). When a person performs the specific requirements for an indulgence, the Roman Catholic Church then has the power to grant that indulgence based on the merits of Christ and the earned merits of Mary and Catholic saints.

Answering Roman Catholics

The Doctrine of Purgatory

Consider what Roman Catholics are saying in regard to the doctrine of purgatory. Let's say you are a good-hearted Catholic, and you do all the things required of your Church throughout life. You regularly attend Mass, you work hard to maintain sanctifying grace in your soul by being faithful, and you confess your sins to a priest when you do wrong. You are always careful to participate in the sacrament of penance after committing what you think may be a mortal sin. (The line of demarcation between mortal sins and venial sins is not always a clear one in Catholic theology.) You do all this and more, in keeping with what your Church tells you. When you die, *you will likely still have to go to purgatory before being granted entrance into heaven.* Throughout someone's lifetime he or she could attend over a thousand Masses *and still die not fully purified from sin.* Protestants respond that this hardly seems like the "good news" of the gospel (Ephesians 2:8,9).

Ask... _____

• Did you know that the word *gospel* means "good news"?

• Does it sound like "good news" to you that you can attend over a thousand Masses throughout your life *and still die not fully purified from sin?*

- By contrast, does the following statement by the apostle Paul sound like "good news": "For by grace you have been saved through faith; and that not of yourselves, it is the gift of God; not as a result of works, that no one should boast" (Ephesians 2:8,9)?

The doctrine of purgatory is an outgrowth of the insufficient Roman Catholic view of justification (see chapters 7, 8, and 9). Since only perfectly righteous people get into heaven, and since in the Roman Catholic view of justification someone is not absolutely and once for all declared righteous by God, then somehow a person must become perfectly righteous before entrance into heaven is granted. This happens via purgatory (among other things). Contrary to the Catholic view, the biblical view of justification involves a singular and instantaneous event in which God declares the believing sinner to be righteous.

From a scriptural perspective, when Jesus died on the cross He said, "It is finished" (John 19:30). Jesus completed the work of redemption *at the cross*. No purgatory is needed for those who trust in Christ. In His high priestly prayer to the Father, Jesus said, "I have brought you glory on earth by *completing* the work you gave me to do" (John 17:4 NIV, emphasis added). First John 1:7 (NIV) says, "The blood of Jesus, his Son, purifies us from *all* sin" (emphasis added). Romans 8:1 (NIV) says, "Therefore, there is *now* no condemnation for those who are in Christ Jesus" (emphasis added).

We are cleansed not by some alleged fire of purgatory but by the blood of Jesus Christ (Hebrews 9:14). Jesus "Himself is the propitiation for our sins" (1 John 2:2). It is through Jesus' work on the cross that we are made righteous (2 Corinthians 5:21). The apostle Paul spoke of his life as "not having a righteousness of my own derived from the Law, but that which is through faith in Christ, the righteousness which comes from God on the basis of faith" (Philippians 3:7-9). It is through this wonderful work of Christ on the cross that believers are "blameless," and hence are in no need of some alleged purgatory (Jude 1:24; see also Ephesians 1:4).

A key verse you will want to share with the Roman Catholic is Hebrews 10:14: "For by one offering He has *perfected for all time* those who are sanctified" (emphasis added). In other words, no further purging is necessary because Christ has perfected "for all time" those who have believed in Him. *That which is already perfect "for all time" needs no further purging.* There is no need for purgatory for those who have truly trusted in Christ as Savior.

Ask... ———————————————————————————————

- Would you please read aloud from Hebrews 10:14?

- How do you think this verse relates to the Catholic doctrine of purgatory?

- More specifically, how do you think the phrase "perfected for all time" relates to the Catholic doctrine of purgatory?

- Would you please read aloud from Romans 8:1, placing special emphasis on the word *now?*

- How do you think this verse relates to the Catholic doctrine of purgatory?

———————————————————————————————

It is the clear teaching of Scripture that, at the moment of death, believers go directly into the presence of God. The apostle Paul said, "I am hard-pressed from both directions, having the desire to depart and be with Christ, for that is very much better" (Philippians 1:23). Paul is saying that the very moment after physical death occurs, he will be with Christ. How do we know this? It is clear from the Greek text. Without going into too much detail, suffice it to say that an aorist infinitive ("to depart") is linked by a single article with a present infinitive ("to be with Christ"). The infinitives thus belong together: "The single article ties the two infinitives together, so that the actions depicted by the two infinitives are to be considered two aspects of the same thing, or two sides of the same coin."[8] So Paul is saying that the very moment after he departs the body or dies, he will be with Christ in heaven.

Moreover, for believers "to be absent from the body" is to be "at home with the Lord." We read in 2 Corinthians 5:6-8:

> Therefore, being always of good courage, and knowing that while we are at home in the body we are absent from the Lord—for we walk by faith, not by sight—we are of good courage, I say, and prefer rather to be absent from the body and to be at home with the Lord.

The Greek of this passage is highly revealing. The phrases "at home in the body" and "absent from the Lord" in the first part of the passage are present tenses (which indicate continuing action). Hence, we might paraphrase it: "Therefore, being always of good courage, and knowing that while we are *continuing to be at home in the body* we are *continuing to be absent from the Lord*."[9]

By contrast, the latter part of the passage contains two aorist infinitives: "absent from the body" and "at home with the Lord." Such aorists indicate a sense of "once for all." Hence, we might paraphrase it: "We are of good courage, I say, and prefer rather to be *absent from the [mortal, perishable] body* and to be *once for all at home with the Lord*."[10]

Regarding all this, Bible scholar Anthony Hoekema comments:

> Whereas the present tenses in verse 6 picture a continuing at-homeness in the body and a continuing away-from-homeness as to the Lord, the aorist infinitives of verse 8 point to a once-for-all momentary happening. What can this be? There is only one answer: *death*, which is an immediate transition from being at home in the body to being away from home as to the body.[11]

The moment a Christian dies, he or she is immediately in the presence of Christ.

It is also noteworthy that the Greek word *pros* is used for *with* in the phrase "be at home *with* the Lord." This word suggests very close (face-to-face, as it were) fellowship. It is a word used of intimate relationships. Paul thereby indicates that the fellowship he expects to have with Christ immediately following his physical death will be one of great intimacy.

In view of such verses, there is clearly no stopover at purgatory for believers who die. Rather, the instant they die, all believers are ushered directly into the presence of Christ.

Ask...

(First go over Philippians 1:23 and 2 Corinthians 5:8.)

• Since Philippians 1:23 and 2 Corinthians 5:8 clearly teach that *all* believers in Christ go straight to heaven at the moment of death, how do you reconcile this with the Catholic doctrine of purgatory?

John Ankerberg and John Weldon have noticed an occult connection to the doctrine of purgatory. They note that throughout the history of the Roman Catholic Church there have been widespread apparitions from the alleged dead:

> As an example we could cite *The Dogma of Purgatory*, containing both Catholic seals of approval (the *nihil obstat* and *imprimatur*), signifying a book is "free of doctrinal or moral error." This book is full of stories of the alleged spirits of deceased Catholics appearing to the faithful and warning them of the torments of purgatory. The result? Inevitably it is a greater bonding to Roman Catholic beliefs and practice.[12]

This is nothing more than spiritism. And all forms of spiritism are condemned by God as a heinous sin. Deuteronomy 18:10,11 (NIV) is clear: "Let no one be found among you who...consults the dead. Anyone who does these things is detestable to the Lord."

The Doctrine of Indulgences

As is true with the doctrine of purgatory, the Roman Catholic use of indulgences is an outgrowth of the insufficient Roman Catholic view of justification. Because the Church has offered an insufficient view of justification, it presents many little Band-Aid fixes—including indulgences—to help the believer on his or her road to salvation.

Consider the logical implications of this doctrine. A person must not only do meritorious works throughout life to help earn salvation, but must then suffer for a time in purgatory after death. His surviving loved ones can then do good works and gain indulgences to help shorten his time in purgatory. How can it be argued that this is not a works-oriented view of salvation?

Protestants believe the doctrine of indulgences compromises the atonement wrought by Christ on the cross. If the doctrine of indulgences is true, this means that Christ did not accomplish *full* redemption on the cross. Christ got only part of the job done. Biblically, though, Christ *did* get the job done (2 Corinthians 5:19-21), and the Bible tells us that for those who trust in Christ, their sins are *fully* forgiven: "And when you were dead in your transgressions and the uncircumcision of your flesh, He made you alive together with Him, *having forgiven us all our transgressions*" (Colossians 2:13, emphasis added).

As noted earlier in the book, Protestants view justification as a singular and instantaneous event in which God declares the believing sinner to be righteous. Justification viewed in this way is a judicial term in which God makes a legal declaration. It is not based on performance or good works. It involves God's pardoning of sinners and restoring them to a state of righteousness. This declaration of righteousness takes place the moment a person trusts in Christ for salvation (Romans 3:25,28,30; 8:33,34; Galatians 4:21–5:12; 1 John 1:7–2:2).

Romans 3:24 (NIV) tells us that God's declaration of righteousness is given to believers "freely by his grace." The word *grace* literally means "unmerited favor." It is because of God's unmerited favor that believers can freely be declared righteous before God. Indulgences play no role! Indeed, we will look in vain in Scripture for a single explicit reference to indulgences.

Reasoning from the Scriptures— The Doctrine of Purgatory

First Corinthians 3:10-15—Biblical Support for Purgatory?

The Roman Catholic Teaching: In 1 Corinthians 3:10-15 we read:

> According to the grace of God which was given to me, as a wise master builder I laid a foundation, and another is building upon it. But let each man be careful how he builds upon it. For no man can lay a foundation other than the one which is laid, which is Jesus Christ. Now if any man builds upon the foundation with gold, silver, precious stones, wood, hay, straw, each man's work will become evident; for the day will show it, because it is to be revealed with fire; and the fire itself will test the quality of each man's work. If any man's work which he has built upon it remains, he shall receive a reward. If any man's work is burned up, he shall suffer loss; but he himself shall be saved, yet so as through fire.

Roman Catholics often interpret this passage as referring to purgatory. Indeed, Catholic authority Ludwig Ott tells us that the Latin fathers took 1 Corinthians 3:15 "to mean a transient purification punishment in the other world."[13] Vatican II described purgatory as a place where the souls of the dead make expiation "in the next life through fire and torments or purifying punishments."[14] The *Catechism of the Catholic Church* describes purgatory as a place of "cleansing fire."[15]

Response: This passage says nothing about purgatory. It indicates that the believer's *works* will be tested by fire at the judgment seat of Christ, not that *the believer himself* will be purged by fire. That is an entirely different thing. The verse has nothing to do with purging sin from a person, but rather has to do with reception or loss of rewards based on works done on earth *after one has trusted in Christ and has been saved.* (The Greek word for *reward* used here, *misthos,* refers to a reward or "recompense given for the moral quality of an action."[16]) If the saved person's works withstand the fire, he or she will receive an eternal reward. If the saved person's works do not withstand the fire, he or she will not receive a reward. Either way, the person is still saved, even if his works should be burned up (verse 15).

Ask ...

(Read through 1 Corinthians 3:10-15 aloud.)

- According to this passage, what is subject to the fire—the *believer*, or the *works* of the believer?

- Can you see that there is a big difference between purging a person of sin *(the Catholic view)*, and testing a person's works to determine if they are worthy of reward *(Paul's statement in 1 Corinthians 3:10-15)*?

- Since this passage is talking about rewards (for faithfulness) and loss of rewards (for a lack of faithfulness), this passage is not dealing with purgatory at all, is it?

It is critical to understand that the Book of 1 Corinthians was written "to those who have been sanctified in Christ Jesus" (1 Corinthians 1:2). These individuals were already in full possession of salvation. No further purging was necessary for them, for all their sins had already been purged by

Christ at the cross. They were secure in their salvation (compare with Ephesians 4:30 and Romans 8:29,30). Paul's comments in 1 Corinthians 3, as noted above, have to do *not* with purgatory but with receiving or losing rewards based on a person's level of faithfulness.

The broader backdrop to this is that all believers (not just some) will one day stand before the judgment seat of Christ (Romans 14:8-10). At that time each believer's life will be examined in regard to deeds done while in the body. Personal motives and intents of the heart will be weighed.

The idea of a judgment seat relates to the athletic games of Paul's day. After the athletic races and games concluded, a dignitary, or perhaps even the emperor himself, took his seat on an elevated throne in the arena. One by one the winning athletes would come up to the throne to receive a reward—usually a wreath of leaves, a victor's crown.[17] In the case of Christians, each of us will stand before Christ the Judge and receive (or suffer the loss of) rewards.

Christ's judgment of us will not be in a corporate setting—like a big class being praised or scolded by a teacher. Rather it will be *individual* and *personal*. "We will all stand before God's judgment seat" (Romans 14:10 NIV). Each of us will be judged on an individual basis.

It seems to be the testimony of Scripture that some believers at the judgment may have a sense of deprivation and suffer some degree of forfeiture and shame. Indeed, certain rewards may be forfeited that otherwise might have been received, and this will involve a sense of loss. The fact is, Christians differ radically in holiness of conduct and faithfulness in service. God in His justice and holiness takes all this into account. Some believers will be without shame and others *with* shame at the judgment seat of Christ.

Second John 8 (NIV) warns us, "Watch out that you do not lose what you have worked for, but that you may be rewarded fully." In 1 John 2:28, John wrote about the possibility of a believer actually being ashamed at Christ's coming.

In terms of the judgment mentioned in 1 Corinthians 3:10-15, notice that the materials Paul mentions in this passage are combustible in increasing degrees. Obviously, the hay and straw are the most combustible. Then comes wood. Precious metals and stones are not combustible.

It also seems clear that some of these materials are useful for building, while others are not. If you construct a house made of hay or straw, it surely will not stand long. (And it can burn to the ground very easily.) But a house constructed with solid materials such as stones and metals will stand and last a long time.

What do these building materials represent? Pastor Douglas Connelly insightfully suggests that "gold, silver, and costly stones refer to the fruit of the Spirit in our lives; they refer to Christ-honoring motives and godly obedience and transparent integrity. Wood, hay, and straw are perishable things—carnal attitudes, sinful motives, pride-filled actions, selfish ambition."[18]

I think it is interesting that fire in Scripture often symbolizes the holiness of God (Hebrews 12:29). And there are clear cases in the Bible in which fire portrays God's judgment upon that which His holiness has condemned (Genesis 19:24; Mark 9:43-48). God, then, will examine our works, and they will be tested against the fire of His holiness.

Perhaps the passage is intended to communicate that those works performed with a view to glorifying God are the works that will stand. Those works performed with a view to glorifying self, performed in the flesh, are those that will be burned up.

It is sobering to read in Scripture that some believers will suffer such loss at the judgment seat of Christ that practically all—*if not all*—of their works will go up in flames. Paul describes this person as being saved, "but only as one escaping through the flames" (1 Corinthians 3:15 NIV). Theologian Merrill F. Unger explains it this way:

Imagine yourself waking out of sleep to find your house ablaze. You have no time to save a thing. You flee with only the nightclothes on your back. Even these are singed away by the flames that engulf you. You escape with literally nothing but your life....In this fashion believers who have lived carnally and carelessly or who have worked for self and self-interest instead of for the Lord will find that all their works have been burned up. They shall have no reward. No trophies to lay at Jesus' feet! No crowns to rejoice in [on] that Day of Judgment![19]

Yet, despite the fact that our *works* will be tested by fire, 1 Corinthians 3:10-15 makes no mention of—not even a slight allusion to—believers being purged of sin by fire. The passage has only to do with rewards or losing rewards at the future judgment seat of Christ. *Make this distinction clear!*

Two passages you will want to continually come back to in refuting the doctrine of purgatory are Hebrews 10:14 and Romans 8:1. Keep coming back to the finished work of Christ.

Matthew 12:32—Biblical Support for Purgatory?

The Roman Catholic Teaching: In Matthew 12:32 we read, "And whoever shall speak a word against the Son of Man, it shall be forgiven him; but whoever shall speak against the Holy Spirit, it shall not be forgiven him, either in this age, *or in the age to come*" (emphasis added). Roman Catholics sometimes reason that if certain sins like blasphemy against the Holy Spirit cannot be forgiven in the "age to come," then other sins *may* be forgiven in the "age to come."[20] The *Catechism of the Catholic Church* tells us:

As for certain lesser faults, we must believe that, before the Final Judgment, there is a purifying fire. He who is truth says that whoever utters blasphemy against the Holy Spirit will be pardoned neither in this age nor in the age to come. From this sentence we understand that certain offenses can be forgiven in this age, but certain others in the age to come.[21]

Response: When this text says that the sin against the Holy Spirit will not be forgiven in this age or the age to come, this is simply a Jewish idiomatic way of saying that the sin will *never* be forgiven. This becomes clear in the parallel account in Mark 3:29: "But whoever blasphemes against the Holy Spirit *never has forgiveness, but is guilty of an eternal sin*" (emphasis added). Hence, there is no support for the Roman Catholic doctrine of purgatory to be found in these verses.

Ask...

- Would you please read aloud from Matthew 12:32?

- Now, please read aloud from the parallel account in Mark 3:29.

- Can you see that the phrase "it shall not be forgiven him, either in this age, or in the age to come" is simply another way of saying that this sin will *never* be forgiven?

- Seen in this light, can you see that there is no support here for a future purgatory?

The broader backdrop to understanding Matthew 12:32 is that the Jews who had just witnessed a mighty miracle of Christ should have recognized that Jesus performed this miracle in the power of the Holy Spirit. After all, the Hebrew Scriptures, with which the Jews were well familiar, prophesied that when the Messiah came He would perform specific mighty miracles in the power of the Spirit—like giving sight to the blind, opening deaf ears, and enabling the lame to walk (see Isaiah 35:5,6). Instead, these Jewish leaders claimed that Christ did these miracles in the power of the devil, the unholy spirit. This was a sin against the Holy Spirit. This shows that these Jewish leaders had completely hardened themselves against the things of God.

I believe that Matthew 12 describes a unique situation among the Jews, and that the actual committing of this sin requires the presence of the Messiah on earth doing His messianic miracles. In view of this, I do not think this sin can be duplicated today exactly as described in Matthew 12.

Bible expositors point out that "blaspheming the Spirit" involves opposing Jesus' messiahship so firmly and definitively that a person resorts to accusations of sorcery to avoid the impact of the Holy Spirit's miraculous signs that confirm Christ's messianic identity. This is truly a damning sin, for there is no other provision for man's sin than the work of the one true Messiah, as attested by the Holy Spirit.

Moreover, inasmuch as it is the particular function of the Holy Spirit to bring conviction upon people and lead their hearts to repentance—making people open and receptive to salvation in Jesus Christ—the person who blasphemes the Holy Spirit effectively separates himself from the only One who can lead him or her on the path to salvation in Jesus Christ. This is precisely what happened to the Jewish leaders.

Matthew 5:26—Biblical Support for Purgatory?

The Roman Catholic Teaching: In Matthew 5:26 we read the words of Jesus: "Truly I say to you, you shall not come out of there, until you have paid up the last cent." Some Roman Catholic theologians such as Ludwig Ott believe this parable lends support to the doctrine of purgatory, teaching a "time-limited condition of punishment in the other world."[22]

Response: The Roman Catholic interpretation is completely foreign to the context. That Jesus is referring to a *physical prison* during earthly life and not a *spiritual prison* in the afterlife is clear from the previous verse: "Make friends quickly with your opponent at law while you are with him on the way, in order that your opponent may not deliver you to the judge, and the judge to the officer, and you be thrown into prison" (Matthew 5:25). Jesus is simply giving a practical teaching about reconciliation of human conflicts and the avoidance of situations that naturally lead to anger and personal injury (see Matthew 5:21-26).

Ask...

- Would you please read aloud from Matthew 5:25,26?

- In context, this is referring to a *physical* prison and not a future *spiritual* prison, right?

- So can you see that this has nothing to do with purgatory?

I know I mentioned this earlier in the book, but it bears repeating: The very idea of a prison-like purgatory contradicts the clear teaching of Scripture that Christ on the cross paid for all the consequences of our sins. In Colossians 2:14 we read that Jesus "canceled out the certificate of debt consisting of decrees against us and which was hostile to us; and He has taken it out of the way, having nailed it to the cross." In ancient days, whenever someone was found guilty of a crime, the offender was put in jail and a "certificate of debt" was posted on the jail door. This certificate listed all the crimes the offender was found guilty of. Upon release, after serving the prescribed time in jail, the offender was given the certificate of debt, and on it was stamped *Paid in Full*. Christ took the certificate of debt of all our lives (including all our sins) and nailed it on the cross. And Jesus said, "Paid in full" upon the cross (John 19:30). ("Paid in full" is another way of translating the Greek words for "It is finished," which Jesus uttered upon the cross in John 19:30.)

Second Timothy 1:18—Biblical Support for Purgatory?

The Roman Catholic Teaching: In 2 Timothy 1:18 we read Paul's words concerning Onesiphorus: "The Lord grant to him to find mercy from the Lord on that day—and you know very well what services he rendered at Ephesus." Roman

Catholics believe this verse supports the doctrine of purgatory. "Paul also shows his belief in purgatory when, in his second letter to Timothy, he prays for the deceased Onesiphorus. 'May the Lord grant him to find mercy from the Lord on that day' (2 Timothy 1:18)."[23]

Response: Roman Catholics are reading something into this verse that simply is not there. Onesiphorus was likely still alive and well when Paul prayed that God would have mercy on him on the future "day" of his reward at the judgment seat of Christ (which, as noted earlier, is entirely different from purgatory). Hence, any suggestion that this verse supports purgatory is unwarranted.

Some Catholics may object and point to 2 Timothy 1:16 where Paul says, "The Lord grant mercy to the house of Onesiphorus for he often refreshed me, and was not ashamed of my chains." They may reason that since Paul mentions Onesiphorus's *house,* Onesiphorus must have died. Such a conclusion is unwarranted. Paul's statement proves only that he wished blessings not only on Onesiphorus, but on his family as well. *Vine's Expository Dictionary of New Testament Words* tells us that the Greek word for "house" here, *oikos,* can be used by metonymy to refer to "members of a household or family" (Luke 10:5; Acts 7:10; 11:14; 1 Timothy 3:4,5).[24] In the present case, Paul expressed well wishes for Onesiphorus's entire family because Onesiphorus had faithfully served in Ephesus where Paul had worked for three years (2 Timothy 1:18; see also 4:19).

It was not uncommon for Paul to express well wishes for his acquaintances in regard to the afterlife and end times. Paul wrote to the Thessalonians, "Now may the God of peace Himself sanctify you entirely; and may your spirit and soul and body be preserved complete, without blame at the coming of our Lord Jesus Christ" (1 Thessalonians 5:23). It was in this same spirit that Paul wrote about his good wishes for Onesiphorus and his household. Purgatory is nowhere in view.

Revelation 21:27—Biblical Support for Purgatory?

The Roman Catholic Teaching: In Revelation 21:27 we read that "nothing unclean and no one who practices abomination and lying, shall ever come into [God's heavenly kingdom]." Roman Catholics interpret this as supporting the doctrine of purgatory, for "only completely pure souls [can] be assumed into Heaven (Apoc. 21:27)."[25]

Response: Roman Catholics are reading something into this verse that is not there. It is true that "nothing unclean and no one who practices abomination and lying, shall ever come into" God's kingdom, but that does not thereby mean that purgatory is the instrument through which people become purged of uncleanness. As I have stated numerous times in this book, our cleansing and purging from sin is based entirely on the finished work of Christ. First John 1:7 (NIV) says, "The blood of Jesus, his Son, purifies us from all sin." Romans 8:1 (NIV) says, "Therefore, there is now no condemnation for those who are in Christ Jesus" (see also Hebrews 10:14).

Ask...

* Would you please read aloud from 1 John 1:7?

* According to this verse, how do we get purged of uncleanness?

Reasoning from the Scriptures— The Doctrine of Indulgences

Job 1:5—Biblical Support for Indulgences?

The Roman Catholic Teaching: Job 1:5 declares that Job offered sacrifices for his children for, he said, "Perhaps my sons have sinned and cursed God in their hearts." Some Catholics cite this verse in support of their view of the so-called "treasury of merit" by teaching that one person can make up for the temporal consequences of another person's sins.[26]

Response: There is virtually no mention in this verse of a treasury of merit. Nor does the verse say that God accepted what Job did on behalf of his children. Bible expositors are careful to note that this verse is *descriptive*, not *prescriptive*. In other words, the verse only describes what Job did; it does not instruct us (or prescribe) what ought to be done. Moreover, Scripture is clear that one person's virtue is not transferable to another: "The righteousness of the righteous *will be upon himself*, and the wickedness of the wicked *will be upon himself*" (Ezekiel 18:20, emphasis added).

Ask...

- Does it make sense to you that simply because Scripture records what someone did in Old Testament times does not mean that that person's action is correct, or that it is regulative upon Christians for all time?

- Do you think it is possible that Job 1:5 is *descriptive*, and not *prescriptive*, like many scholars believe?

- Would you please read aloud from Ezekiel 18:20?

- Do you think this verse contradicts the Catholic concept of a treasury of merit?

2 Corinthians 12:15—Biblical Support for Indulgences?

The Roman Catholic Teaching: In 2 Corinthians 12:15 we read the apostle Paul's words to the Corinthian believers: "And I will most gladly spend and be expended for your souls." Some Roman Catholic theologians say this verse lends support to the doctrine of indulgences by which the merits of one person can be transferred to another.[27]

Response: Neither purgatory nor indulgences are mentioned or alluded to in the verse. Paul's desire to "spend and be expended" for the Corinthians is for *living* believers (verse 14), not dead believers in a place of suffering (purgatory). Further, Paul's suffering has nothing to do with the temporal consequences of the Corinthians' sins, but rather relates to Paul's burden to minister the grace of Christ to them (see verses 11-18). He is willing not only to spend his money but also to expend *himself* on behalf of these (living) Corinthian believers whom he loved. Contextually, then, this verse cannot be cited to support the doctrine of indulgences.

Ask...

(*Read 2 Corinthians 12:14,15.*)

- According to verse 14, was Paul desiring to "spend and be expended" for *living* believers or for *dead* believers? (*Living believers.*)

- Did Paul say he was doing this because of the Corinthians' sins? (*No.*)

- Contextually, is it not clear that Paul was desiring simply to minister the grace of Christ to the Corinthians?

- This passage really has nothing to do with indulgences, does it?

Galatians 6:2—Biblical Support for a "Treasury of Merit" and Indulgences?

The Roman Catholic Teaching: The apostle Paul in Galatians 6:2 exhorts, "Bear one another's burdens, and thus fulfill the law of Christ." Some Roman Catholic authorities say this verse lends credence to the belief in indulgences based on the merit of other saints and those of Christ and Mary that are stored in a treasury of merit.[28]

Response: A look at the context clearly shows that Paul is not saying we can bear the *punishment* for someone else's sin. After all, just two verses later Paul reminds us that "whatever a man sows, this he will also reap" (verse 7). The "burdens" Paul refers to are not *sins,* but rather the *problems* that all of us face from time to time. The spirit of the verse is this: "When life throws your brother or sister a punch, help them in any way you can."

The Greek word for *burdens* here carries the idea of "weights." Often weights can exceed the strength of the person trying to do the lifting, and can overwhelm the person to the point of giving up. And so it is with life's problems. Sometimes they get too heavy to bear. That is why Paul says we should help other people carry their load in life. By doing this, we fulfill the law of Christ—namely, "love" (see Galatians 5:14).

Ask...

- According to the context, this verse is not talking about bearing the punishment for someone else's sin, is it?

- Doesn't this verse rather speak of helping our brothers and sisters in Christ when life throws them a punch?

14

The Exaltation of Mary—Part 1
The Roman Catholic View

"I am the way, and the truth, and the life;
no one comes to the Father, but through Me."[1]
Jesus Christ

The Mary of Roman Catholicism is far different than the one portrayed in the pages of Scripture. In a number of ways, the Mary of Roman Catholicism is a powerful, almost godlike being. She is viewed as being beyond sin altogether—spotless, undefiled, holy, innocent in every way, pure in soul and body, stainless. She is said to have been immaculately conceived, according to Pope Pius IX, thus being preserved from the stain of inherited sin from Adam.

Mary is also said to have been *perpetually* a virgin—meaning that she retained her virginal state both *during* the birth of Jesus and *afterward*, even though married to Joseph. At the end of her earthly life, since she was "sinless," she was allegedly taken up bodily into heaven. Catholics tell us that she has appeared to people throughout history, including in Guadalupe (Mexico), 1531; Rue de Bac (France), 1830; Salette (France), 1846; Lourdes (France), 1858; Fatima

(Portugal), 1917; Beauraing (Belgium), 1933; Banneau (Belgium), 1933; and Medjugorje (Bosnia-Herzegovina) 1980s.

To date, over ten million Catholics have traveled to Medjugorje to witness the appearances of Mary since they began. In these appearances, Mary speaks of distinctly Catholic doctrines—calling people to perform acts of penance and to pray the Rosary. She also asks that people express greater devotion to her. These appearances are referred to as "apparitions of Mary." The word "apparition" comes from the Late Latin word *apparitio*, which means "appearance" or "presence." While the Church community has officially approved a number of apparitions and shrines, the Church does not view the messages communicated to persons in supernatural appearances as part of official Catholic doctrine.

The Mary of Roman Catholicism has many honorific titles, including "Mother of God," "Mother of the Church," and "Co-redeemer of Mankind." She is presently said to be in heaven in the role of "Queen of Heaven and Earth." She is also called the "Mother of Grace," and is the one through whom Christ bestows all graces to those on earth.

Many Catholics today wear medals that bear an image of Mary. Mary allegedly promised Pope John that any Catholics who wore the scapular medal (which bears an image of Mary) would be delivered from purgatory the first Saturday following their death.[2] That is quite a deal (if you are a believer in purgatory)!

Pope John Paul II is quite devoted to Mary. In fact, he believes Mary saved him from an assassin's bullet early in his pontificate. The motto inscribed on his coat of arms— *Totus Tuus sum Maria*—means, "Mary, I am totally yours."[3]

To get a better grasp on this important Roman Catholic doctrine, let us consider some of these points in greater detail.

The Immaculate Conception of Mary

Roman Catholics believe that in order for Mary to be an appropriate habitation for Christ, God had to preserve her from the corruption of original sin (Adam's sin). This doctrine, called the "Immaculate Conception," was officially defined in A.D. 1854. Pope Pius IX in the *Ineffabilis Deus* declared that "the most Blessed virgin Mary, in the first instant of her conception, by a singular grace and privilege granted by Almighty God, in view of the merits of Jesus Christ, the Savior of the human race, was reserved free from all stain of original sin, is a doctrine revealed by God and therefore to be believed firmly and constantly by all the faithful."[4]

In Roman Catholic theology, then, Mary had no sin nature and was absolutely free of all blemish of sin. As well, she was free from every personal sin for the duration of her life. Mary was never subject to the curse, being "immune from all sin, personal or inherited."[5]

Now, I must be careful in how this is communicated, for Roman Catholics *do not* say that Mary needed no Savior. Indeed, Catholics suggest that the merits of Christ were applied to Mary in an anticipatory way prior to her birth. It was allegedly in this way that she was born without sin. God preemptively saved Mary, as it were, while all other human beings are saved after the fact of needing salvation. James White summarizes how some Roman Catholic apologists explain it:

> If you keep someone from falling into a mudhole, you can be said to have "saved" that person. In the same way, if they fall in, and you pull them out and clean them off, you also can be said to have "saved" them. In the one case you saved them preemptively from getting dirty, and in the other, you saved them *after* they became dirty. Hence, the argument is that God saved Mary from *contracting* the stain of original sin (and thus, in life, all personal sin) through the *preemptive* application of the merits of Christ to her.[6]

The Perpetual Virginity of Mary

Jesus' birth from the womb of Mary was unique in a number of ways. For one thing, Roman Catholics tell us that

Mary, unlike all other human women, suffered virtually no pain during the birth. She was apparently exempt from the curse God spoke to Eve as a result of the fall: "I will greatly multiply your pain in childbirth, in pain you shall bring forth children" (Genesis 3:16). Catholic theologian Ludwig Ott says that "Mary gave birth in miraculous fashion without opening of the womb and injury to the hymen, and consequently also without pains."[7] Christ's birth "did not diminish his mother's virginal integrity but sanctified it."[8] Ancient writers such as Ambrose, Augustine, and Jerome employed a variety of analogies to illustrate how this could be so: the emergence of Christ from the sealed tomb, His going through closed doors, penetration of light through glass, and the going out of human thought from the mind.[9]

Further, following the birth of Jesus, Mary perpetually remained a virgin. She never engaged in any sexual relations with her husband, Joseph. Catholics offer a number of reasons why the perpetual virginity of Mary makes good sense. Thomas Aquinas is sometimes cited in his argument that it was "becoming" for Jesus to be the only-begotten son of His mother in-as-much as He was the only-begotten Son of the Father. He also argued that Mary's womb—a "shrine" of the Holy Spirit—would have been defiled had she engaged in sexual relations with Joseph. Still further, it was argued, sexual relations would have been beneath Mary's dignity and would have implied that she was not satisfied with merely being the mother of Jesus.[10]

As for those verses in the New Testament that make reference to Jesus' brothers (for example, Matthew 13:55,56), Catholics often argue that in reality they were Jesus' cousins. Karl Keating argues that the Hebrew and Aramaic (which Jesus and His disciples spoke) did not have a word for "cousin." Even though the Greek language (in which the New Testament was written) does have a word for "cousin," it was common for the Jews to continue the Hebrew practice of referring to relatives as "brothers." He cites evidence for this in the Septuagint (the Greek translation of the Old Testament that predates the time of Christ). So, Jesus' "brothers" can be interpreted to be His cousins. Seen in this light, the fact that Jesus is said to have "brothers" in the New Testament does not argue against the perpetual virginity of Mary.

Mary as Mother of God

As the mother of the Lord Jesus, Mary is considered by Catholics to be the mother of God. The term "mother of God" is a "title of the blessed Virgin Mary as the physical parent of Jesus, who is God."[11] Jesus was true God, and Mary was truly the mother of Jesus. As Ignatius of Antioch put it, "Our God Jesus Christ was carried in Mary's womb, according to God's plan of salvation."[12]

"As the mother of God," Ludwig Ott comments, "Mary transcends in dignity all created persons, angels and men, because the dignity of a creature is the greater the nearer it is to God.... As a true mother she is related by blood to the Son of God according to His human nature."[13]

The *Catechism of the Catholic Church* tells us that "Mary is truly 'Mother of God' since she is the mother of the eternal Son of God made man, who is God himself."[14] Indeed, "the One whom she conceived as man by the Holy Spirit, who truly became her Son according to the flesh, was none other than the Father's eternal Son, the second person of the Holy Trinity."[15]

The Veneration of Mary

In view of Mary's unique role in giving birth to the divine Messiah—as well as the many other roles the Roman Catholic Church attributes to her, along with her many alleged virtues—Mary is venerated by Catholics worldwide. Catholics are quick to point out that the veneration they give Mary (called *hyperdulia*) is less than the adoration they give God (called *latria*), but is nevertheless higher than that rendered to angels and other saints (called *dulia*).[16]

What evidence is there that Mary should be venerated? While there is no explicit scriptural support, Catholic apologist Scott Hahn, speaking to a Protestant friend, offered an argument for Marian devotion that goes like this:

1. Christ obeyed the law perfectly, right?
   (Friend answers, "Right.")

2. The Ten Commandments sum up that law, right?
   (Friend answers, "Right.")

3. One commandment reads, "Honor your father and mother," right?
   (Friend answers, "Right.")

4. When Christ fulfills the law He fulfills that commandment, right?
   (Friend answers, "Right.")

5. So Christ bestows honor and glory upon His mother, right?
   (Friend answers, "Right.")

Hahn then says that we are called to imitate Christ. There you have it. Marian devotion.[17]

The most common way Catholics venerate Mary today is by saying the rosary. This is considered an "epitome of the whole gospel." It is a series of prayers counted on a string of beads. These beads are arranged in groups of ten small beads separated by one large bead. There are five sets of these so-called "decades." On the large bead, the "Our Father" or "Lord's Prayer" is said. On each of the ten small beads, Catholics pray, "Hail Mary, full of grace, the Lord is with thee. Blessed art thou among women and blessed is the fruit of thy womb, Jesus. Holy Mary, Mother of God, pray for us sinners now and at the hour of our death. Amen."

Mary as Co-redeemer and Mediatrix

Many Catholics speak of Mary as the co-redeemer of humanity. They offer a number of arguments in support of this idea. For example, Mary's very agreement to bear in her womb the human-divine Messiah shows a cooperation on her part with (and a taking part in) the divine plan of humankind's redemption.

For this reason, the Second Vatican Council tells us, a number of the early church fathers asserted that "the knot of Eve's disobedience was untied by Mary's obedience: what the virgin Eve bound through her disbelief, Mary loosened by her faith." Comparing Mary with Eve, they claim: "death through Eve, life through Mary."[18]

Moreover, Mary is often portrayed as offering her son to the Father on Golgotha. Hence, it is argued, Mary played a pivotal role in the redemption of humankind. She is thus referred to as "co-redemptor."

> She so grievously suffered and almost died with her suffering and dying Son, she so wholeheartedly renounced her maternal rights over her Son for the salvation of men and immolated her Son, as far as was in her power, to placate God's justice, that she may deservedly be said to have redeemed the human race along with Christ.[19]

Roman Catholic apologists are careful to clarify what is meant when Mary is called "co-redeemer." Mark Miravalle argues that the prefix "co" does not mean "equal," but means "with." When Mary is called co-redemptrix, this is not to imply that she is on a level of equality with Jesus. Rather, she shared with her son in the saving work of redemption for humankind. She participated in the redemptive work of her Savior-son. "Mary, who is completely subordinate and dependent to her redeeming Son even for her own human redemption, participates in the redemptive act of her Son as his exalted human mother."[20]

There are other titles given to Mary in Roman Catholicism. For example, she is presently in heaven in the role of "Queen of Heaven and Earth." This title is due in no small part to her alleged role in man's redemption. And as Queen of Heaven and Earth, she can answer our prayers. We read in *Ineffabilis Deus*:

> Since she has been appointed by God to be the Queen of heaven and earth, and is exalted above all the choirs of angels and saints, and even stands at the right hand of her only-begotten Son, Jesus Christ our Lord, she presents our petitions in a most efficacious manner. What she asks, she obtains. Her pleas can never be unheard.[21]

Mary is also sometimes called "Mediatrix of Grace." Catholics typically argue that while Jesus is Mediator between man and God; nevertheless, Mary holds a secondary mediatorship that is subordinate to that of Christ. Mary's role as "mediatrix" is said to carry two important connotations, according to Catholic theologian Ludwig Ott: "1. Mary is the Mediatrix of all graces by her cooperation in the Incarnation. And 2. Mary is the Mediatrix of all graces by her intercession in Heaven."[22] Ott tells us that "according to God's positive ordinance, the redemptive grace of Christ is conferred on nobody without the actual intercessory co-operation of Mary."[23]

St. Alphonsus Ligouri, a Roman Catholic canonized saint, tells us that it is God's will that all graces come to humankind by the hands of Mary. Indeed, we are told that "the plenitude of grace was in Christ, as the *Head* from which it flows, as from its source; and in Mary, as in the *neck* through which it flows."[24] We must not forget that "all graces are dispensed by Mary, and all who are saved are saved only by the means of this divine Mother."[25]

Roman Catholic literature sometimes portrays a disjunction between Jesus and Mary in terms of justice and mercy. Mary is portrayed as a Queen of Mercy, whereas Jesus is portrayed as the King of Justice. The idea is that we need another mediator (Mary) to go between us and the stern Judge Jesus.

The 1891 Encyclical *Octobri Mense* written by Pope Leo XIII declared that because people are fearful of the justice of

God, an advocate is needed where none will be refused: "Mary is such a one, Mary worthy of all praise; she is powerful, mother of the all-powerful God.... So God gave her to us.... We should place ourselves under her protection and loyalty, together with our plans and our deeds, our purity and our penance, our sorrows and joys and pleas and wishes. All that is ours we should entrust to her."[26]

It is no wonder that with such titles and virtues ascribed to Mary, she is venerated by so many people within the Roman Catholic Church. We look in vain, however, for such titles in the pages of Scripture.

The Assumption of Mary

Roman Catholics teach that when Mary's life on earth was over, she was bodily assumed into heaven. Indeed, Pope Pius XII on November 1, 1950, proclaimed this as Church dogma: "The Immaculate Mother of God, Mary ever Virgin Mary, when the course of her earthly life was finished, was taken up body and soul into the glory of heaven."[27] It is argued that because Mary was full of grace (Luke 1:28) and because she was preserved from original sin, she was also kept free from the consequences of sin—namely, corruption of the body after death.[28]

Pope Pius XII said that "her body was preserved unimpaired in virginal integrity, and therefore it was fitting that it should not be subject to destruction after death, and that since Mary so closely shared in Christ's redemptive mission on earth, she deserved to join him also in bodily glorification."[29]

In view of all the above, it is understandable why the issue of Mariology has become a dividing point between Catholics and Protestants. Indeed, the Mary of Catholicism and the Mary of Protestantism seem like two different individuals.

15

The Exaltation of Mary—Part 2
Answering Roman Catholics

"For there is one God, and *one mediator* also
between God and men, the man Christ Jesus."[1]
The Apostle Paul

In many ways the Roman Catholic Mary ends up being a
female counterpart to Jesus. Jesus was born without sin—
Mary was conceived without original sin; Jesus was sinless—Mary lived a sinless life; Jesus ascended to heaven
following His resurrection—Mary was bodily assumed into
heaven at the end of her earthly life; Jesus is a Mediator—
Mary is a mediatrix; Jesus is a Redeemer—Mary is a co-
redemptrix; Jesus is the King—Mary is the Queen of
Heaven.[2] Yet none of these ideas about Mary are found anywhere within the pages of Scripture.

The Mary of the Bible is far different from the picture
portrayed above. Indeed, the biblical Mary is a "bondslave
of the Lord" (Luke 1:38)—a humble servant of God. The
Greek word for "bondslave" *(doulos)* here "speaks of one
whose will is swallowed up in the will of another," "one who
serves another to the disregard of [her] own interests."[3] Mary

was not one who sought others to express "greater devotion" to her, as the Mary of the apparitions does. The humble attitude of the biblical Mary is far removed from the *hyperdulia* (veneration) paid to her by Romanism.

The reality is that the peculiar doctrines about Mary held by Roman Catholics are nowhere to be found in the pages of Scripture. There is nothing in the Bible about the perpetual virginity of Mary. There is nothing in the Bible regarding Mary as co-redeemer or mediatrix. There is nothing in the Bible about venerating Mary. There is nothing in the Bible about the "assumption" of Mary. Certainly there are some verses which Roman Catholics *claim* refer to some of these things, but as we will see in the next two chapters, Roman Catholics have consistently misinterpreted the words of Scripture.

In view of the tremendous attention paid to Mary in Roman Catholic churches, it might be instructive to ask Catholic acquaintances to read straight through the New Testament over a few months and keep track of how much attention is paid to Mary there. They may be very, very surprised.

Ask...

- Here is a challenge: Would you read through the New Testament over the next few months, and pay special attention to what you read about Mary? *(Encourage them to keep a record.)*

- Let's talk again when you are finished!

From the pages of the Bible, we know that Mary was a godly woman, and was well-versed in the Old Testament Scriptures. Her scriptural literacy is more than evident in the Magnificat (Luke 1:46-55). But she certainly was not gifted with any kind of supernatural insight into God's doings, as evidenced in Jesus' response to her when she and Joseph found Him in the temple as a child (Luke 2:38-50).[4]

We are told in Luke 1:48 that Mary is "blessed" among women. But is this blessedness based on something intrinsic to Mary's own being that separates her from all other women and makes her worthy of such blessedness? Or is it simply based on the fact that God chose her to give birth to the Messiah? The context of Scripture clearly indicates that the latter is the case. Mary's blessedness was due not to something within her, but was rather related entirely to what God Himself chose to do by allowing her to give birth to the Messiah.

Protestant apologists Elliot Miller and Ken Samples make this keen observation about Mary, the mother of Jesus:

> Without wishing to detract from her rightful honor, it must be stated that Mary's part in the incarnation was merely as the vehicle chosen by the Triune God for the Logos's entry into this world. After this she was also called to provide maternal care for the divine child. In Scripture, after these functions are accomplished she recedes into the background and we read little of her. (In this sense she has rightly been compared with John the Baptist, who, after he accomplished his preparatory purpose, said: "He must increase while I must decrease" [John 3:30].)[5]

It is highly revealing that Jesus never exalted His mother Mary like Roman Catholics have done. Indeed, He is often seen downplaying His relationship with her. Miller and Samples suggest this is illustrated in the several occasions where He calls His mother "woman" instead of "mother" (John 2:1-4; 19:26)—something that was not customary for a Jewish son to do.[6]

The Alleged Immaculate Conception and Sinlessness of Mary

Certainly I have no interest in being offensive to Roman Catholics, and I most certainly have no interest in saying anything negative about Mary. Truly she is blessed among

women—*but not venerated above women and all humanity.*
The biblical fact of the matter is that Mary had a sin nature
just as all other human beings do. That is not to say that
Mary was a bad person, or that she was as bad a sinner as
every other sinner. But she definitely had a sin nature and
was in need of a Savior. She knew this to be true of herself
(Luke 1:47).

It is the consistent testimony of Scripture that every single
human being—with the one exception of Jesus Christ,
whose conception was by the Holy Spirit (Luke 1:35)—has
been born into the world with a sin nature. Romans 5:12 tells
us that "through one man sin entered into the world, and
death through sin, and so death spread to *all* men, because
all sinned" (emphasis added). We are assured that "*all* have
sinned and fall short of the glory of God" (Romans 3:23,
emphasis added). "There is *none* righteous, *not even one*;
there is *none* who understands, there is *none* who seeks for
God; *all* have turned aside...there is *none* who does good,
there is *not even one*" (Romans 3:10-12, emphasis added).
"There is not a righteous man on earth who continually does
good and who never sins" (Ecclesiastes 7:20). Jesus Himself
asserted, "*No one* is good except God alone" (Luke 18:19,
emphasis added).

Scripture indicates that Mary was in need of redemption,
as are all other people (Luke 1:47). She even presented an
offering to the Jewish priest as prescribed arising out of her
state of sin (Luke 2:22-24; Leviticus 12).

Moreover, in a heavenly scene we read the following
words ascribed to God by those present in heaven: "*Thou
alone* art holy" (Revelation 15:4, emphasis added). You must
keep in mind that Mary herself is in heaven too as this future
scene is unfolding. And yet only God is recognized as holy
by nature. The implication is clear: Mary is not holy by
nature. My words here should not be taken as an attack
against Mary. They should be taken as a simple affirmation

that Mary is just like the rest of us when it comes to being a sinner in need of a Savior.

Ask... _____

(First read aloud from Revelation 15:4.)

• Since only God in this heavenly scene is recognized as being holy, and since Mary herself is in heaven at this time, what does this tell you about Mary?

(Spend some time discussing Romans 3:10-12,23; 5:12; and Luke 18:19.)

_____

On a historical note, it is highly revealing that it was not until the Council of Trent in A.D. 1547 that the Roman Catholic Church proclaimed the sinlessness of Mary as dogma. Further, most of the significant doctrines concerning Mary have been promulgated in little more than the past 100 years.[7] If these doctrines were really true, then they would be reflected in the pages of Scripture, as opposed to emerging over 1500 years after the fact.

Ask... _____

• Did you know that Mary's alleged sinlessness was not proclaimed as dogma by the Roman Catholic Church until A.D. 1547?

• If this doctrine were really true, don't you think it would be reflected in the pages of Scripture, as opposed to emerging over 1500 years after the fact?

_____

The Alleged Perpetual Virginity of Mary

The idea that Mary was a perpetual virgin—that is, that she remained a virgin following the birth of Jesus—is directly contradicted by the biblical account. Indeed, in Matthew 1:25

we read that Joseph "kept her a virgin *until* she gave birth to a Son; and he called His name Jesus" (Matthew 1:25, emphasis added). The word *until* implies that normal sexual relations between Joseph and Mary took place following the birth of Jesus.

Further, when Jesus spoke in His hometown, some of the people there inquired, "Is not this the carpenter's son? Is not His mother called Mary, and His brothers, James and Joseph and Simon and Judas? And His sisters, are they not all with us?" (Matthew 13:55,56).

We also read that Jesus "went down to Capernaum, He and His mother, and His brothers, and His disciples; and there they stayed a few days" (John 2:12). The fact that Jesus had brothers clearly shows that Mary gave birth to other children following the birth of Jesus.

Not too long prior to the crucifixion, we find some of Jesus' brothers taunting Him, not having yet placed faith in Him: "Not even His brothers were believing in Him" (John 7:5). Again, the fact that He had brothers shows that Mary and Joseph gave birth to other children following His own birth.

In later books in the New Testament, we discover that Jesus' brothers indeed did end up coming to faith. We read that on one occasion the apostles gathered for prayer "along with the women, and Mary the mother of Jesus, and with His brothers" (Acts 1:14). James, "the Lord's brother" (Galatians 1:19), became a leader in the church at Jerusalem (Galatians 2:9-12).

The Roman Catholic claim that references to Jesus' "brothers" actually refer to cousins is not convincing. It is true that the Greek term for *brother* (*adelphos*) can be used in a sense not referring to a literal brother (for example, it can refer to Jewish brothers, just like we today refer to our Christian brothers). Yet, unless the context indicates otherwise, Greek scholars agree that the term should be taken in its normal sense of a literal brother.

Further, there was a perfectly appropriate word in the Greek language that could have been used in the biblical text for "cousin" (*anepsios*), but this word is not used in the verses cited above. And since these "brothers" are always mentioned as being *with* Mary, the context is clear that *literal* brothers are in view.

Furthermore, in a messianic prophecy in the Old Testament that was literally fulfilled in the life of Jesus, we read: "I have become estranged from my brothers, and an alien to my mother's sons" (Psalm 69:8). That this psalm is messianic in nature[8] is clear at numerous points of comparison:

— compare verse 8 with John 7:3-5;
— compare verse 9 with John 2:17 and Romans 15:3;
— compare verse 21 with Matthew 27:34;
— compare verse 25 with Matthew 23:38.

Clearly, then, since verse 8 is a messianic reference to Christ's alienation "to my mother's sons," Mary most definitely had other children besides Jesus.

Ask...

• Would you please read aloud from Psalm 69:8?

• Since this is a messianic prophecy, referring to Jesus the Messiah, is it not clear that the reference to "my mother's sons" proves that Jesus had brothers?

I should also note that while Catholic apologists point to examples of the term *brother* being used of cousins in the Septuagint (the Greek translation of the Hebrew Old Testament that predates Christ), there is not a single example of this usage to be found in the pages of the New Testament. We also note that Colossians 4:10 (NIV) gives us an example of the apostle Paul making reference to "Mark, the cousin of Barnabas," showing us that in the New Testament a distinction between brothers and cousins was made.

Ask...

- Since there was a Greek word for *cousins*, don't you think the biblical writers would have used this word instead of the Greek word for *brothers* when referring to James, Joseph, Simon, and Judas (Matthew 13:55-57)?

- Since these "brothers" are specifically mentioned in contexts *with Mary*, is it not clear that the literal brothers of Jesus are meant?

As for the Roman Catholic claim that "Mary gave birth in miraculous fashion without opening of the womb and injury to the hymen, and consequently also without pains,"[9] there is virtually no biblical support for such a view. In fact, every verse in Scripture that addresses the birth of Jesus speaks of that birth as being quite normal, with no miracle having taken place. Jesus was "born of a woman" (Galatians 4:4), "brought forth" (Luke 2:7), delivered (Luke 2:6), and "born" (Matthew 2:2). Roman Catholics are reading something into the text of Scripture that simply is not there.

Sexual Relations Between Mary and Joseph Would Have Been Appropriate

Sexual relations within the marriage relationship bring no defilement, but are rather good and proper (see Genesis 2:24; Matthew 19:5; 1 Corinthians 6:16; Ephesians 5:31). It is only sexual relations outside of marriage that Scripture condemns.

Sex was a part of God's "good" creation. Indeed, God created sex, and "everything created by God is good" (1 Timothy 4:4). But again, it is good only within the confines of the marriage relationship, which God Himself ordained (see Hebrews 13:4). So there would have been no defilement for Mary if she and her husband, Joseph, engaged in sexual relations following the birth of Jesus. As noted above, the biblical text clearly indicates that Joseph and Mary bore other children (Matthew 1:25; 13:55,56).

To say that Joseph would have violated Mary if he had sex with her—knowing that the Holy Spirit had caused a divine conception in her womb—has no biblical warrant. There is no evidence in Scripture that Mary's womb was any kind of "shrine" for the Holy Spirit. The miraculous point in the Gospel account is the *conception* of Jesus, which was brought about in Mary's womb by the Holy Spirit. Following that divine conception, we can surmise that there was a controlling, sanctifying ministry of the Holy Spirit in the fetal state. But the birth itself was normal in every way. And following that birth, Scripture indicates that normal sexual relations between Joseph and Mary took place (see Matthew 1:25).

Was Mary the Mother of God?

The exalted position Mary occupies in the Roman Catholic Church today is actually the result of many centuries of development. Mary was first recognized as the "Mother of God" at the Council of Ephesus in A.D. 431. That council carefully qualified the expression by declaring that Mary was the "mother of God according to the manhood" of Jesus. Mary was truly a mother of Christ's human nature and was the "mother of God" in the limited sense that she conceived and bore the second Person of the Godhead, not according to His divine nature but only according to His assumed human nature.

Hence, the phrase "Mother of God" was meant to uphold the fact that the man born of Mary was, in His divine nature, *truly God*, and, at the same time, that this second Person of the eternal Godhead was truly *man*, by virtue of His taking upon Himself the full nature of man as born from the womb of Mary. He was not just a human baby with deity dwelling in Him, but was 100 percent God and 100 percent human. Jesus did not have some kind of third compound nature, partially human and partially divine. The child born from Mary's womb was fully God and fully man.

In view of the fact that Mary did not give rise to the divinity of Jesus but was only the human instrument through whom the Incarnation took place, *there is nothing in this doctrine that exalts Mary at all*. Because this is so critically important, I want to provide a brief biblical backdrop to the Incarnation.

In the first chapter of Luke's Gospel we read: "In the sixth month, God sent the angel Gabriel to Nazareth, a town in Galilee, to a virgin pledged to be married to a man named Joseph, a descendant of David. The virgin's name was Mary. The angel went to her and said, 'Greetings, you who are highly favored! The Lord is with you'" (Luke 1:26-28 NIV).

Earlier in man's history, the angel Gabriel had given special revelations from God regarding the coming Messiah to the prophet Daniel (Daniel 8:16; 9:21). Now, over 500 years later, this same angel appeared to Mary with the news that the prophesied Messiah would be given birth by her, a virgin. This is in fulfillment of Isaiah 7:14, which prophesied that the Messiah would be born of a virgin.

Mary's humble status is evident in that she was a resident of Nazareth in Galilee. Galileans in general were looked down on by the Jews in Jerusalem as an inferior people. They were considered second-class citizens. Nazareth was especially a place of vice in biblical times. "Nazareth had become a military camp town with which all manner of sin and corruption were associated. The Nazarenes were particularly despised by the rest of the Jews."[10]

Mary was a simple countrywoman in this less-than-desirable city, and she was betrothed to Joseph, a humble carpenter. Betrothal in ancient times, which usually lasted one year, was much stronger than marital engagements are today. In fact, a betrothed couple was considered husband and wife except that they did not live together until after the wedding.[11] So strong was the betrothal relationship that the betrothed woman was considered a widow if her fiancé died.[12]

This serves as a very important backdrop for our study of the virgin birth, for it was in the context of a betrothed relationship that Mary would soon be found pregnant due to the supernatural work of the Holy Spirit. She no doubt mused over what her fiancé, Joseph, would think when she was found to be pregnant.

Following Gabriel's greeting to Mary, she was "greatly troubled at his words and wondered what kind of greeting this might be" (Luke 1:29 NIV). Apparently, in her modesty and humility, Mary did not understand why a heavenly angel greeted her in such terms and told her that the Lord was with her.

Gabriel then said,

> Do not be afraid, Mary, you have found favor with God. You will be with child and give birth to a son, and you are to give him the name Jesus. He will be great and will be called the Son of the Most High. The Lord God will give him the throne of his father David, and he will reign over the house of Jacob forever; his kingdom will never end (Luke 1:30-33 NIV).

The angel's pronouncement that the child would be called *Jesus* is full of meaning. The name *Jesus* means "*Yahweh* saves" or "*Yahweh* is salvation." This name is the counterpart of the Old Testament name *Joshua*. Just as Joshua in the Old Testament led Israel out of the wilderness experience into a new land and a new life, so Jesus would lead people out of a spiritual wilderness experience into a new sphere of existence and a new life.

Theologian Robert Reymond has suggested that the meaning of Jesus' name, "*Yahweh* saves," is an evidence for His deity. He qualifies what he means by noting that the name meaning "*Yahweh* saves" in itself

> does not *need* to mean that the one who bears this name is identical with *Yahweh*; others bore the name under the Old Testament economy to symbolize the fact that *Yahweh*

was at work in the salvation of his people. But I suggest that in Jesus' case we should understand that it connotes more than a mere symbol, inasmuch as some intimation of the identity between Jehovah [*Yahweh*] and the Messiah seems to be contained in the words of the angel (Matthew 1:21).[13]

Moreover, Reymond suggests,

When one adds to this compelling data first the fact that *Yahweh* again and again in the Old Testament declares that He alone is Israel's "Savior" (Isaiah 43:3,11; 45:21; 49:26; 60:16; Hosea 13:4; cf. 1 Samuel 10:19; 14:39; 2 Samuel 22:3; Psalm 7:10; 17:7; 106:21; Isaiah 45:15; 63:8; Jeremiah 14:8) and then the fact that Jesus is often declared (along with God the Father) to be "the Savior" in the New Testament (Luke 2:11; John 4:42; Acts 5:31; 13:23; Ephesians 5:23; Philippians 3:20; 1 Timothy 4:10; 2 Timothy 1:10; Titus 1:4; 2:13; 3:6; 2 Peter 1:1,11; 2:20; 3:2, 18; 1 John 4:14), it is difficult to avoid the conclusion that when Jesus was named "*Yahweh* saves," the name connoted more than merely that He stood as one more in the long line of "saviors" (cf. Judges 3:9,15; 6:36; 2 Kings 13:5; Nehemiah 9:27). Rather His name meant that in Him, as Himself *Yahweh* incarnate, the line of "saviors" had now been consummated in a transcendent manner.[14]

In any event, besides informing Mary of the Savior's name, Gabriel also informed her that Jesus would be called "Great"; he would be called the "Son of the Most High"; and He would reign on "the throne of his father David." Each of these three descriptions is highly revealing of Jesus' true identity. The term *great* is a title which, when unqualified, is usually reserved for God alone.[15] Being called "the Son of the Most High" is significant, for *Most High* is a title often used of God in the Old Testament (see, for example, Genesis 14:19; 2 Samuel 22:14; Psalm 7:17).

Bible expositor John A. Martin suggests that

> Mary could not have missed the significance of that terminology. The fact that her Baby was to be called the "Son of the Most High" pointed to His equality with *Yahweh*. In Semitic thought a son was a "carbon copy" of his father, and the phrase "son of" was often used to refer to one who possessed his "father's" qualities.[16]

This "great" one—*eternal God in human flesh*—would rule, according to Gabriel, on the throne of David. Jesus, who in His humanity was a direct descendant of David (Matthew 1:1), will rule from David's throne during the future millennial kingdom in which there will be perfect righteousness and justice (2 Samuel 7:16; Psalm 89:3,4,28-39). This kingdom will be inaugurated immediately following the second coming of Christ (Revelation 19).

To describe this future rule of Christ, three significant words are used in Luke 1:32,33 (NIV): *throne, house,* and *kingdom* ("The Lord God will give him the *throne* of his father David, and he will reign over the *house* of Jacob forever; his *kingdom* will never end"). It is significant that each of these words is found in the covenant God made with David in which God promised that someone from David's line would rule forever (2 Samuel 7:16). Gabriel's words must have immediately brought these Old Testament promises to mind for Mary, a devout young Jew. Indeed, Gabriel's words constituted "an announcement as clear as it was possible to make it that Mary's Son would come into this world to fulfill the promise given to David that one of David's sons would sit on David's throne and rule over David's kingdom."[17] Jesus would come not only to be the *Savior,* but also to be the *Sovereign.*

Mary then responded to Gabriel's announcement by inquiring, "How will this be..., since I am a virgin?" (Luke 1:34 NIV). The angel answered,

> The Holy Spirit will come upon you, and the power of the Most High will overshadow you. So the holy one to be

born will be called the Son of God. Even Elizabeth your relative is going to have a child in her old age, and she who was said to be barren is in her sixth month. For nothing is impossible with God (verses 35-37 NIV).

It is important that you not miss this point: *The Holy Spirit's ministry in this miraculous conception was necessary because of Christ's preexistence as eternal deity* (see Isaiah 7:14; 9:6; Galatians 4:4). The Holy Spirit's supernatural work in Mary's body enabled Christ—*eternal God*—to take on a human nature. "From the production of the egg out of Mary's ovary to the actual birth, the fetal state in Mary's womb was entirely under the controlling, sanctifying ministry of the Holy Spirit."[18] And through this incarnation a key aspect of the eternal plan of salvation came to fruition. Our eternal Savior became flesh with the specific purpose of dying on our behalf so that those who trusted in Him would be saved and dwell with God forever.

Through the miracle of the virgin birth, the eternal Son reached out and took to Himself a true and complete humanity without diminishing His essential deity. He united deity and humanity inseparably and eternally in one Person.

A fact that is often overlooked in theological discussions is that all three Persons of the Trinity were involved in this Incarnation. Though the Holy Spirit played the central role and was the Agent through whom the Incarnation was brought about (Luke 1:35), we are told in Hebrews 10:5 that it was the Father who prepared a human body for Christ. Moreover, the preexistent, eternal Christ is said to have taken upon Himself flesh and blood, as if it were an act of His own individual will (Hebrews 2:14). Clearly, all three Persons of the Trinity were sovereignly involved in bringing about the Incarnation.

How overwhelming the announcement of the Incarnation must have been to young Mary! It is impossible to know the kinds of emotions she felt at the moment of Gabriel's revelation that eternal God would be in her womb. But Mary responded to the announcement in a humble manner: "I am the Lord's servant," she said. "May it be to me as you have said" (Luke 1:38 NIV).

The very important point I want to make, in view of all the above, is that Jesus was and is eternal God. *Mary is not the mother of His deity.* While the child born in her womb was divine, it was not Mary who gave rise to that divinity. Her role was to enable Jesus as eternal God to take on an additional nature: a human nature. And so, Mary is Jesus' mother only in that limited sense. She most certainly is not the mother of God in any sense that she gave rise to the being of God. We need to make sure our Roman Catholic acquaintances understand this distinction.

The Veneration of Mary

We look in vain in the pages of Scripture for any semblance of the kind of veneration Roman Catholics give to Mary. Neither Jesus, nor the apostle Paul, nor any other biblical writer ever exalted Mary the way Catholics do. Now, think about this for a minute. As we read the Gospels, we are given the teachings of Jesus, yet nowhere in the teachings of Jesus do we find that Mary is exalted or venerated. As we read the Epistles, written by the apostles for the spiritual instruction of the church, nowhere do we find anything about the exaltation or veneration of Mary. There is plenty in all these books about worship and salvation and prayer and lots of other very important doctrines, *but nothing about the exaltation or veneration of Mary.*

We would naturally think that if Mary plays the important roles attributed to her by the Roman Catholic Church (co-redemptrix, mediatrix, and the like), there would be at least *something* about all this in the pages of Scripture. *Yet there is nothing.* In the Epistles, Mary's name is virtually absent, and these books are precisely where one would expect Mary's name to be most prominent *if* the Roman Catholic exaltation and veneration of her were correct. But since her name is entirely absent, what are we to make of it? Any Catholic who looks at the biblical evidence is forced to admit that biblical support for the distinctive Roman Catholic doctrines about Mary is lacking.

Ask...

- If we are supposed to venerate Mary, why didn't Jesus say anything about it in the four Gospels?

- If were are supposed to venerate Mary, why is it that Mary's name is *not even mentioned* in any of the Epistles?

Now, as noted above, Roman Catholics are careful to point out that there is a distinction between the adoration given to God (*latria*) and the veneration given to Mary (*hyperdulia*). But in the thinking of Protestants, this is a distinction without a difference. In fact, James White has noted that the words *latria* and *dulia* can be traced back to the Greek words from which they were taken, and an etymological study indicates just how closely related they are. He notes that the words are sometimes used synonymously when speaking of worshiping God. What this means is that the distinction Rome has tried to draw between veneration of Mary and worship of God disappears.[19]

Further, despite the official distinction the Roman Catholic Church draws between *latria* and *hyperdulia*, the reality is that many typical Catholics do in fact end up worshiping Mary by their words and actions. And this is a serious thing in view of God's commandment in Exodus 20:5: "You shall not worship them or serve them; for I, the Lord your God, am a jealous God." It is highly revealing that the Hebrew word for "worship" in this verse (*avad*) is translated in the Septuagint (the Greek translation of the Hebrew Old Testament that predates Christ) using both *dulia* and *latria*.[20]

What About Scott Hahn's Argument for Venerating Mary?

As noted in the previous chapter, Catholic apologist Scott Hahn offered an argument for the veneration of Mary based on the following factors: 1) Christ obeyed the law perfectly; 2) the Ten Commandments sum up that law; 3) one commandment reads, "Honor your father and mother"; 4) because Christ fulfills the law, He fulfills that commandment; 5) hence, Christ bestows honor and glory upon His mother; and 6) we are called to imitate Christ.

This line of thinking is flawed. It is true that Christ obeyed the law perfectly. It is true that the Ten Commandments sum up that law. It is true that one of the commandments reads, "Honor your father and mother." It is true that Christ fulfilled that commandment. It is thus true that Christ bestowed honor upon His mother (in the same sense that all other human beings are called to), *but it is not true that Christ bestowed the kind of glory upon His mother that the Roman Catholic Church has.*

While it is true that the Hebrew word for *honor* (*kabad*) has a secondary meaning of "to glorify,"[21] the primary meaning is "to honor," and that is the meaning in Exodus 20:12. In context the word certainly does not connote giving godlike exaltation to a "co-redemptor" or "mediatrix" or "Queen of heaven," as Roman Catholics have done. Consider the Gospel records. Even though Jesus honored and respected His mother, He *never* exalted her. Indeed, as noted earlier, He is often seen downplaying His relationship with her (see Luke 11:27,28).

According to Hebrew lexicons, the fundamental idea in the word *honor* is rooted in the concept "to be heavy."[22] According to the *Theological Wordbook of the Old Testament*, "From this figurative usage it is an easy step to the concept of a 'weighty' person in society, someone who is honorable, impressive, worthy of respect. This latter usage is prevalent in more than half the occurrences."[23] The underlying idea of the word *honor*, then, is *respect*. Hence, in Exodus 20:12, children are essentially called to *respect* their parents. This Jesus did. But exalt Mary to the level of co-redemptor, mediatrix, and Queen of heaven? *No!*

Jesus Is the Only Mediator and Savior

Catholics often claim that their doctrine of Mary as mediatrix does not in any way detract from, contradict, or do damage to the unique work or position of Jesus Christ. What we must examine is not what Roman Catholicism *claims*, but rather what state of affairs *actually exists*. In other words, despite what Roman Catholicism claims, we must address the issue as to whether Mary as mediatrix *does* detract from the unique mediatory role of Christ.

Scripture is clear that there is only one mediator between man and God, and that is Jesus Christ. No secondary mediatrix is needed: "There is one God, and one mediator also between God and men, the man Christ Jesus" (1 Timothy 2:5). (I will deal with the Roman Catholic interpretation of 1 Timothy 2:5 in chapter 17.) When this one Mediator died on the cross, it was not Mary who offered Him to the Father, but rather Christ "offered Himself without blemish to God" (Hebrews 9:14). This is important, for Roman Catholics often place great weight on their claim that Mary offered Jesus to the Father at the cross.

Jesus is the single Savior of humanity, and this in itself is something that eternally distinguishes Jesus from Mary. For, indeed, the Scriptures are clear that *only God* can be the Savior. God Himself (Yahweh) said in Isaiah 43:11: "I, even I, am the Lord; and there is no Savior besides Me" (Isaiah 43:11). The fact that Jesus is portrayed as this Savior over and over again in the New Testament shows Jesus' unique divinity (for example, Titus 2:13,14). And it is through this one Savior *and Him alone* that "we have redemption, the forgiveness of sins" (Colossians 1:14).

When we consider the biblical doctrine of the Redeemer, one thing that becomes very clear is that it is closely connected to the doctrine of the Incarnation. Humankind's redemption was completely dependent upon the human-divine union in Christ. If Christ the Redeemer had been only God, He could not have died, since God by His very nature cannot die. It was only as a man that Christ could represent humanity and die as a man. As God, however, Christ's death had infinite value—sufficient to provide redemption for the sins of all humankind. Clearly, then, Christ had to be both God and man to secure man's salvation (1 Timothy 2:5).

This is related to the Old Testament concept of the kinsman-redeemer. In Old Testament times, the phrase *kinsman-redeemer* was always used of one who was related by blood to someone he was seeking to redeem from bondage. If someone was sold into slavery, for example, it was the duty of a blood relative—the "next of kin"—to act as that person's "kinsman-redeemer" and buy him out of slavery (Leviticus 25:47-49).

Jesus is the Kinsman-Redeemer for sin-enslaved humanity. For Jesus to become a Kinsman-Redeemer, however, He had to become related by blood to the human race. This indicates the necessity of the Incarnation. Jesus became a man in order to redeem man (Hebrews 2:14-16). And because Jesus was also fully God, His sacrificial death had infinite value (Hebrews 9:11-28).

Further, we must note that the Redeemer as portrayed in Scripture is absolutely sinless. Hebrews 4:15 tells us, "We do not have a high priest who cannot sympathize with our weaknesses, but One who has been tempted in all things as we are, yet without sin" (see also 2 Corinthians 5:21). Just as lambs with no defects were used in Old Testament sacrifices, so the Redeemer was the spotless Lamb of God who was unblemished by sin (1 Peter 1:19).

Jesus' unique qualification as Redeemer is precisely what disqualifies Mary in any role as a co-redemptor, because

1) Mary is a mere human being (she is not divine or even exalted), who 2) is defiled by sin (Romans 3:10-12,23; 5:12), and who 3) herself is in need of the Redeemer (Luke 1:47).

Whereas we look in vain for any Scripture references that portray Mary as a co-redemptor or mediatrix, we find numerous references to the effect that Jesus is *exclusively* man's only means of coming into a relationship with God. Jesus Himself said, "I am the way, and the truth, and the life; no one comes to the Father, but through Me" (John 14:6). A bold Peter proclaimed, "There is salvation in no one else; for there is no other name under heaven that has been given among men, by which we must be saved" (Acts 4:12).

I realize that many Catholics will respond that they agree that Jesus is the primary Mediator, and that Mary's role is secondary. My point is that M*ary has no role whatsoever,* other than being the divinely chosen human instrument through whom the divine Messiah and Redeemer would be born into the world. Once that was accomplished, the biblical record assigns no further role to Mary, and she is hence *not even mentioned* in the Epistles.

There is one other point I must make at this juncture regarding the Roman Catholic portrayal of Christ as a stern Judge, thus making it necessary for us to have a merciful mediator in the person of Mary. Mary is portrayed as the Queen of Mercy, whereas Jesus is portrayed as the King of Justice. It is true, on the one hand, that Jesus is interested in justice. But the alleged need for Mary as a Queen of Mercy evaporates into thin air when it is realized that 1) there is not a shred of biblical evidence that Mary engages in this role, and 2) Jesus Himself is a God of mercy and compassion, and hence there is no need for a "Queen of Mercy."

Examples of Jesus' mercy and compassion abound in the New Testament. Recall that after spending some time alone in a boat, Jesus went ashore and saw a great multitude "and felt compassion for them, and healed their sick" (Matthew 14:14). Later, a crowd of 4000 people who had been listening to Jesus teach became hungry. Jesus called His disciples and said to them: "I feel compassion for the multitude, because they have remained with Me now three days and have nothing to eat; and I do not wish to send them away hungry, lest they faint on the way" (Matthew 15:32). So Jesus multiplied seven loaves of bread and a few small fish so that everyone had plenty to eat (verses 35-39).

Still later, when two blind men pleaded for mercy from Jesus, He did not need to be coerced to help them: "Moved with compassion, Jesus touched their eyes; and immediately they regained their sight and followed Him" (Matthew 20:34).

It is in view of the wonderful mercy and compassion of Jesus Christ that the writer of Hebrews exhorts:

> For we do not have a high priest who cannot sympathize with our weaknesses, but One who has been tempted in all things as we are, yet without sin. Let us therefore draw near with confidence to the throne of grace, that we may receive mercy and may find grace to help in time of need (Hebrews 4:15,16).

The Alleged Bodily Assumption of Mary

There is virtually no scriptural support for the idea that Mary was bodily assumed into heaven at the end of her earthly life. Even Catholic theologian Ludwig Ott admits that "direct and express scriptural proofs are not to be had."[24] But because the Roman Catholic Church teaches the doctrine, we are told that it is true.

Because there is not even a hint of Mary's bodily assumption in Scripture, and because this doctrine did not even become dogma for the Roman Catholic Church until the middle of the twentieth century, we can assume it is not true, but is rather a man-made doctrine. The reality is, the time and circumstances of Mary's death are completely unknown. We can say, though, that the *fact* of her death was something that was generally accepted by the Fathers.[25]

Apparently, her death passed with no unusual notice. Giovanni Miegge, author of *The Virgin Mary: The Roman Catholic Marian Doctrine*, says, "She departed life humbly and modestly as she has lived it, and none remembered the place of her burial, even if a tradition toward the mid-fifth century gave her a sepulchre near Jerusalem in the garden of Gethsemane."[26]

Why did Mary die? She died for the same reason all other human beings die. She, like us, was subject to the penalty of sin, which is death (see Genesis 2:17; Romans 6:23). This is precisely why she, like us, was in need of a Savior (Luke 1:47).

The Alleged Apparitions of Mary

I do not believe that a single genuine appearance of the Virgin Mary has ever taken place. I say this not because I have anything against Mary (I do not—for, as I have said earlier in the book, she is truly blessed among women [Luke 1:28]). I say this because of the scriptural teaching that contact with the dead *in any form* is forbidden by God (Deuteronomy 18:11). We should not expect that God would allow Mary to do something that He has explicitly forbidden. From a scriptural perspective, we will be reunited with the dead only at the second coming of Christ (see 1 Thessalonians 4:13-17), and not before.

Some reputable evangelical scholars who have studied the issue have suggested that people who claim they have seen Mary may have actually encountered a demonic impersonation of Mary.[27] The goal, of course, is to distract people away from the Christ of Scripture.

Kenneth Samples, who himself has visited Medjugorje and has spoken with the visionaries there (who claim to have witnessed appearances of the Virgin Mary), suggests that there might be a number of possible explanations for these apparitions:

> There could be numerous natural explanations. These range from outright human deception, to psychological

projection or hallucination, or even possibly to some physical or natural scientific cause. The cause could even be found in a combination of these factors. However, because of the unbiblical nature of Marian apparitions, if the cause is supernatural in origin then we can only be dealing with the demonic, not with God. I realize that this line of reasoning will be offensive to many Catholics; nonetheless, I believe it is a necessary theological inference.[28]

Scripture indicates that Satan indeed has the power and the motivation to do this kind of thing. Indeed, we are told that Satan "masquerades as an angel of light" (2 Corinthians 11:14 NIV). He has the ability to perform "counterfeit miracles, signs and wonders" (2 Thessalonians 2:9 NIV). In the end times he will inspire false Christs and false prophets who will "perform great signs and miracles to deceive even the elect—if that were possible" (Matthew 24:24 NIV). We are told in the Book of Revelation that the "beast" and the "false prophet"—both inspired by Satan—will perform "great signs," even making "fire come down out of heaven to the earth in the presence of men" (Revelation 13:13).

In view of this, there is no doubt that Satan has the ability to engage in counterfeit appearances of the Virgin Mary. Certainly, he is more than happy to do so if the end result is that many people end up deceived by such doctrines as Mariology, penance, purgatory, the veneration of saints, and the like.

16

The Exaltation of Mary—Part 3
Reasoning from the Scriptures

> "There is salvation in no one else [but Jesus];
> for there is *no other name* under heaven that has been
> given among men, by which we must be saved."[1]
> *The Apostle Peter*

In the previous two chapters we examined a number of issues related to Roman Catholic Mariology and provided a biblical response. In the present chapter, we will focus attention on some of the specific verses that typically come up in debates related to the so-called Immaculate Conception of Mary, the perpetual virginity of Mary, and the veneration of Mary.

The Alleged Immaculate Conception and Sinlessness of Mary

Genesis 3:15—Biblical Support for Mary's Immaculate Conception?

The Roman Catholic Teaching: In Genesis 3:15, right after Adam and Eve fell in sin, we read the words of God in judgment to the serpent: "And I will put enmity between you and the woman, and between your seed and her seed; He shall bruise you on the head, and you shall bruise him on the heel." Roman Catholics such as Ludwig Ott often argue that this verse provides support for the idea of the immaculate conception of Mary:

> Mary stands with Christ in a perfect and victorious enmity towards Satan and his following.... Mary's victory over Satan would not have been perfect, if she had ever been under his dominion. Consequently she must have entered this world without the stain of original sin.[2]

Response: There is virtually no mention of Mary, and not even the slightest hint of the so-called Immaculate Conception in this verse. Taken in its plain sense, the verse indicates that a descendant *of Eve* would defeat the devil. Even Catholic theologian Ludwig Ott concedes that the literal and plain sense of the verse is that "between Satan and his followers on the one hand, and Eve and her posterity on the other hand, there is to be constant moral warfare."[3] It is the literal seed or offspring of Eve that will be victorious over the devil, not that of Mary.

Ask... _____

- Would you please read aloud from Genesis 3:15?

- Doesn't a plain reading of this text indicate only that a descendant of Eve will be victorious over the devil?

- Mary is nowhere in the context of this verse, is she?

_____

Even if by some stretch this verse could be interpreted as referring to Mary and not Eve, that still would not make the doctrine of the Immaculate Conception logically necessary. For, indeed, the text indicates that while there will be *enmity* between the offspring of the woman and that of the devil, nevertheless the *victory itself* lies in the Messiah alone, who is one individual from among the woman's seed. It is never prophesied that "the woman" herself would be victorious, so any need for an Immaculate Conception of the woman vanishes. The woman's only significant role is to give birth to the human-divine Messiah.

Luke 1:28—Biblical Support for Mary's Immaculate Conception?

The Roman Catholic Teaching: In the Catholic New American Bible, we read the words of the angel to Mary at Luke 1:28, "Hail, full of grace!" Roman Catholic theologians argue that the phrase "full of grace" "represents the proper name, and must on this account express a characteristic quality of Mary....However, it is perfect only if it be perfect not only intensively but also extensively, that is, if it extends over her whole life, *beginning with her entry into the world.*"[4] Hence, this verse supports the doctrine of the Immaculate Conception. Mary "was, by sheer grace, conceived without sin as the most humble of creatures, the most capable of welcoming the inexpressible gift of the Almighty."[5]

Response: Roman Catholics are reading something into this text that simply is not there. First, the translation "full of grace" is an inaccurate rendering based on the ancient Vulgate. (The Vulgate is a translation of the Bible by Jerome [A.D. 342–430] from Greek and Hebrew originals into the common Latin of the day.) It is much more accurately translated from the Greek as, "favored one," as in the New American Standard Bible: "Hail, favored one!"

Contextually, the phrase "favored one" is not a proper name* but rather refers to the fact that Mary was highly favored by God in having the wonderful privilege of bearing the Messiah in her womb. The same point is made in verse

---

* Even if we were to take the phrase as a proper name *(which I do not)*, it would not have to be taken extensively back before Mary's birth. The term refers to Mary *at that moment in time*, not to her entire life or to her own conception as a baby.

30 where the angel said to Mary, "You have found favor with God." I. Howard Marshall, an expert on Luke's Gospel, writes that the participle translated "favored one" "indicates that Mary has been especially favored by God in that He has already chosen her to be the mother of the Messiah (1:30). There is no suggestion of any particular worthiness on the part of Mary herself."[6]

Ask... _____

- Were you aware that Greek scholars agree that the translation "full of grace" in Luke 1:28 is an inaccurate rendering based on the ancient Vulgate?

- Since the term really means "favored one," do you think it possible that all the phrase means is that Mary was favored by God in having the wonderful privilege of bearing the Messiah in her womb?

- Isn't that the point of verse 30 too?

- Seen in this light, what justification is there for reading into this verse the idea that Mary was immaculately conceived and was sinless? Where specifically is that stated in the verse?

_____

Scripture is clear that Mary was not sinless. She recognized her sinfulness and her subsequent need for a Savior (Luke 1:47). She also presented an offering to a Jewish priest arising out of her sinful condition (Luke 2:22-24)—something that Old Testament law required (Leviticus 12:2). These verses would not make much sense if Mary was sinless or had been immaculately conceived.

Ask... _____

- How do you reconcile Mary's recognition of her need for a Savior (in Luke 1:47), and her presenting an offering to a Jewish priest arising out of her sinful condition (in Luke 2:22-24), with the Roman Catholic idea of the Immaculate Conception of Mary and her alleged sinlessness?

As I noted in the previous chapter, it is the consistent testimony of Scripture that every single human being—with the one exception of Jesus Christ, whose conception was by the Holy Spirit (Luke 1:35)—has been born into the world with a sin nature. Romans 5:12 tells us that "through one man sin entered into the world, and death through sin, and so death spread to *all* men, because *all* sinned" (emphasis added). We are assured that "*all* have sinned and fall short of the glory of God" (Romans 3:23, emphasis added). "There is *none* righteous, *not even one*; there is *none* who understands, there is *none* who seeks for God; *all* have turned aside…there is *none* who does good, there is *not even one*" (Romans 3:10-12, emphasis added). All these references surely apply to Mary.

Luke 1:42—Biblical Support for Mary's Immaculate Conception and Sinlessness?

The Roman Catholic Teaching: In Luke 1:42 Elizabeth said to Mary, "Blessed among women are you, and blessed is the fruit of your womb!" Roman Catholics often cite this verse in support of Mary's alleged Immaculate Conception and sinlessness. It is claimed that when Elizabeth said, "Blessed are you among women," the "blessing of God which rests upon Mary is made parallel to the blessing of God which rests upon Christ in His humanity. This parallelism suggests that Mary, just like Christ, was from the beginning of her existence, free from all sin."[7] Elizabeth's words "Blessed among women…" are said to communicate the idea, "Mary was the holiest of all women."[8]

Response: There are many objections to the Roman Catholic interpretation of this verse. First, if this is supposed to be Elizabeth's way of saying that Mary was sinless and holy, we are forced to ask how Elizabeth would have come to such knowledge in the first place. She was not a prophet or apostle or any kind of spokesperson for God.

Second, it is a historical fact that a number of the early church fathers such as Origen, Basil, Hillary, John Chrysostom, and Cyril of Alexandria believed that Mary had engaged in sins (such as vanity and ambition) in her life. They certainly did not take Luke 1:42 to indicate that Mary was sinless. Thomas Aquinas, one of Roman Catholicism's greatest scholars in history, declared that the doctrine of the Immaculate Conception is impossible, for Mary, like all other humans (with the exception of Christ), inherited a sin nature from Adam (Romans 5:12).[9]

Ask...

- The Roman Catholic Church pays great respect to the early church fathers, right?

- Did you know that a number of the early church fathers such as Origen, Basil, Hillary, John Chrysostom, and Cyril of Alexandria believed that Mary had engaged in various sins in her life?

- Did you know that Thomas Aquinas, one of Catholicism's greatest scholars in history, declared that the Immaculate Conception is impossible, for Mary, like all other mere humans, inherited a sin nature from Adam?

- Would you please read aloud from Romans 5:12? What do you think this verse means?

Finally, there is not a single lexical source that gives the meaning "sinless" or "holy" for the Greek word for "blessed" (*eulogeo*, in the phrase, "Blessed among women are you"). Catholics are thus reading something into this word that is not there. This verse communicates simply that Mary is "blessed" and "favored" inasmuch as the Messiah would be born through her womb. Nothing more is meant.

The Perpetual Virginity of Mary

Luke 1:34—Support for the Perpetual Virginity of Mary?

The Roman Catholic Teaching: In Luke 1:34 we read Mary's response to the angel who informed her the Messiah would be born in her womb: "How can this be, since I am a virgin?" Some Roman Catholics take this to mean that Mary "had taken the resolve of constant virginity on the ground of special Divine enlightenment."[10] In other words, Mary had taken a vow of lifelong virginity.[11] Hence, her question to the angel carries this idea: *How can the Messiah be born from my womb in view of the fact that I have taken a vow of lifelong virginity?*[12]

Response: The Catholic interpretation of this verse is grasping at straws. Even Catholic theologian Ludwig Ott concedes that the supposition of a vow of virginity on Mary's part seems contrary to the clear statement that *she was engaged to Joseph* (Matthew 1:18).[13]

Scripture makes no mention whatsoever of any vow on Mary's part to a life of virginity. Mary's statement, "How can this be, since I am a virgin?" simply means that at the moment the angel was speaking to her, she was not married (she was betrothed*—Luke 1:27), and was therefore a virgin; any talk of giving birth thus seemed not to make sense. Mary did not say, "How can this be, since I am now and forever will be a virgin?" Rather, she was talking about her present unmarried state.

---

* Because Mary was betrothed, we can rightly assume that she fully intended to engage in sexual relations later. Betrothals in the first century generally lasted a year. Mary's question, "How can this be, since I am a virgin?" was asked in view of her *present state of betrothal,* and it may well be that her marriage to Joseph would not take place for close to a year. Seen in this light, her question makes good sense. We might reflect her thought this way: "I am a virgin, and my upcoming marriage will not take place for close to a year. So how will this pregnancy you speak of come to fruition?"

Ask... _____

- Did you know there is not a single explicit statement in the Bible that Mary took a vow of perpetual virginity?

- How do you reconcile the Roman Catholic claim that Mary took a vow of virginity with the fact that she was clearly betrothed to Joseph when the angel was speaking to her (Luke 1:27)?

- Did you know that the esteemed Catholic theologian Ludwig Ott concedes that this is a problem for the Catholic position?

_____

Some Catholics try to answer this by suggesting that perhaps Mary throughout her life was a married virgin—that is, she ended up getting married to Joseph but engaged in no sexual relations. But such a view goes against Scripture too. After all, we read, "And Joseph arose from his sleep, and did as the angel of the Lord commanded him, and took her as his wife, and kept her a virgin until she gave birth to a Son; and he called His name Jesus" (Matthew 1:24,25). The word *until* clearly shows that Mary was a virgin up to the time Jesus was born, but thereafter Mary and Joseph engaged in a normal marital sexual relationship. To do anything less would violate the nature of marriage in regard to God's instructions that husband and wife are to meet each other's sexual needs (1 Corinthians 7:3).

Ask... _____

- Would you please read aloud from Matthew 1:24,25?

- How do you reconcile the Roman Catholic position on Mary's perpetual virginity with this passage, especially in regard to the word *until*?

_____

Luke 1:38—Biblical Support for the Perpetual Virginity of Mary?

The Roman Catholic Teaching: In Luke 1:38 we read, "And Mary said, 'Behold, the bondslave of the Lord; be it done to me according to your word.' And the angel departed from her." Roman Catholics often cite this verse in support of Mary's alleged perpetual virginity:

> It is significant that Mary, recognizing in the words of the divine messenger the will of the Most High and submitting to his power, says: "Behold, I am the handmaid of the Lord; let it be to me according to your word" (Luke 1:38)....Mary accepted her election as Mother of the Son of God, guided by spousal love, the love which totally "consecrates" a human being to God. By virtue of this love, Mary wished to be always and in all things "given to God," living in virginity.[14]

Response: Roman Catholics are practicing eisegesis, reading something into this verse that simply is not there. All this verse is telling us is that in simple faith and submission, Mary presented herself to the Lord to do with her according to His sovereign will. She submitted to God, despite the possible disgrace, slander, ill repute, or even death she knew she might have to suffer. After all, unfaithfulness in a betrothed person was punishable by death. If she was found to be pregnant during this betrothal period, most people would assume only one thing: unfaithfulness. But Mary's faith in God was such that she unquestioningly submitted to her Lord.

That is why Mary said, "Behold, the bondslave [or handmaid] of the Lord; be it done to me according to your word." She was ready and willing to do anything that her Lord asked of her. But there is not even a hint of perpetual virginity in this verse. Her intention to yet marry Joseph (which would naturally entail sexual relations—Matthew 1:25) in no way compromised her full submission to the Lord. The fact that she was a "bondslave" of the Lord does not in any way prohibit her from marrying, or from engaging in sexual relations within marriage for, throughout the New Testament, Christians (married and unmarried) are called to the same kind of bondslave commitment to the Lord (see Ephesians 6:6).

Ask...

- Did you know that the English word *handmaid* is rooted in the Greek word *doulos*, which means "servant" or "slave"?

- Did you know that all Christians—*married and unmarried*—are called to be Christ's servants (*doulos*), according to Ephesians 6:6 and other verses?

- Since being a servant or slave of Christ does not prohibit someone from being married (or engaging in marital relations), can you see that Mary's life as a handmaid of the Lord does not prohibit her from marrying (and engaging in marital relations) either?

John 19:25-27—Biblical Support
for the Perpetual Virginity of Mary?

The Roman Catholic Teaching: In John 19:25-27 we read:

> But there were standing by the cross of Jesus His mother, and His mother's sister, Mary the wife of Clopas, and Mary Magdalene. When Jesus therefore saw His mother, and the disciple whom He loved standing nearby, He said to His mother, "Woman, behold, your son!" Then He said to the disciple, "Behold, your mother!" And from that hour the disciple took her into his own household.

Roman Catholics argue that "the fact that the dying Redeemer entrusted His Mother to the protection of the disciple John (John 19:26: 'Woman, behold thy Son'), presupposes that Mary had no other children but Jesus."[15] This is said to be in keeping with Mary's vow of perpetual virginity.

Response: The Roman Catholic interpretation is incorrect for a number of reasons. First, we know from other Scriptures that Jesus indeed did have brothers. As noted in the previous chapter, when Jesus spoke in His hometown, some of the people there inquired: "Is not this the carpenter's son? Is not His mother called Mary, and His brothers, James and Joseph and Simon and Judas? And His sisters, are they not all with us?" (Matthew 13:55,56). We also read that Jesus "went down to Capernaum, He and His mother, and His brothers, and His disciples; and there they stayed a few days" (John 2:12). However John 19:25-27 is interpreted, it must be done against the backdrop that Jesus indeed did have brothers. (The Catholic may respond that references to Jesus "brothers" really refer to His "cousins." See chapter 15 for argumentation against this idea.)

Ask... _____

- Would you please read aloud from Matthew 13:55,56?

- Would you please read aloud from John 2:12?

- Do these verses, taken in their plain sense, indicate to you that Jesus had brothers?

_____

Further, it is clear that the reason Jesus did not want to entrust His mother Mary into the hands of His brothers is that His brothers at that time were unbelievers (see John 7:5). Instead, Jesus chose to entrust His mother into the hands of one of His dearest disciples. John is apparently the only one of the disciples with courage enough to take his stand with Mary at the cross. It is understandable that Jesus would want His mother in the care of a strong, committed believer.

Ask... _____

- Does it make sense to you that since Jesus' brothers at the time were not believers, Jesus wouldn't want to entrust His mother into their care (John 7:5)?

• Since John was the disciple closest to Jesus' heart, and since John demonstrated his firm faith by his boldness in being at the foot of the cross, isn't it understandable that Jesus would want to entrust His mother to such a trustworthy man?

Another pertinent factor is that John may have been Jesus' cousin (being Salome's son). So not only was John a relative, but he was also the disciple whom Jesus loved. Understandably, Jesus committed John to Mary and Mary to John, so that in their grief they could care for one another.

The Veneration of Mary

Luke 1:28—Biblical Support for the Veneration of Mary?

The Roman Catholic Teaching: In Luke 1:28 in the Catholic New American Bible we read, "And coming in, he said to her, 'Hail, full of grace, the Lord is with thee.'" Earlier in the chapter, I noted that Catholics often appeal to this verse in support of the Immaculate Conception. But Catholics also appeal to it to show that Mary is entitled to *hyperdulia*—a form of veneration that is higher than that given any other creature, but lower than the worship and adoration given to God. Ludwig Ott tells that "in view of her dignity as the Mother of God and her fullness of grace, a special veneration is due to Mary."[16]

Response: (See the discussion of this verse earlier in the chapter.) This verse refers only to the fact that Mary was highly favored by God in having the wonderful privilege of bearing the Messiah in her womb. As commentator Albert Barnes explains:

> Long had [the Messiah] been predicted; long had the eyes of the nation been turned to him, and long had his coming been an object of intense desire....But now the happy individual was designated who was to be his mother; and on Mary, a poor virgin of Nazareth, was to come this honor.[17]

It is highly revealing that, in the Gospels, it is Jesus who is consistently venerated and worshiped; Mary is *never* venerated. Indeed, when the Magi came to the manger to visit the Christ child, "they fell down and worshiped *Him* [not Mary]" (Matthew 2:11). They gave no veneration to Mary. Nor is veneration ever given to Mary in the Book of Acts or the Epistles. Instead, Mary seems to fade into the background.

Further, Colossians 2:18 and Revelation 22:8,9 make it clear that human beings are not to bow down in veneration before *any* creatures (compare with Exodus 20:4,5; see also Colossians 2:18; Revelation 22:8,9). To venerate Mary—even if it is lesser than the adoration given to God—is a violation of these commandments from God.

Luke 1:42—Biblical Support for the Veneration of Mary?

The Roman Catholic Teaching: In Luke 1:42 we read, "And [Elizabeth] cried out with a loud voice, and said, 'Blessed among women are you, and blessed is the fruit of your womb!'" (insert added). Earlier in the chapter, I noted that Catholics often appeal to this verse in support of the Immaculate Conception. But Catholics also cite this verse in support of the veneration of Mary.[18]

Response: (See the discussion of this verse earlier in the chapter.) Note that no mention whatsoever is made in this verse in regard to venerating Mary. Mary is simply called "blessed." Since Mary is said to be blessed *among* women, it is odd indeed to exalt her *above* all other women, as Roman Catholics have done. Further, from a scriptural perspective, Mary is blessed not because she is incomparably holy or intrinsically worthy but because she is the mother of the Lord (verse 45).

Ask...

- Would you please read aloud from Luke 1:42?

- Why do you think this verse says Mary is blessed "among" women, as opposed to being blessed "above" women?

The Greek word for *bless* in this verse (*eulogeo*) literally means "to speak well of." And indeed, Mary *is* well spoken of as a result of her wonderful role in giving birth to the Messiah. But this does not involve any form of veneration. As noted earlier in the chapter, no such veneration was ever given to Mary by Jesus, the apostles, or anyone else in Scripture. In fact, Scripture seems to downplay Mary and (rightfully) focus all attention on Jesus.

Ask... _____

- Did you know that the Greek word for *bless* (*eulogeo*) means only "to speak well of"?

- Don't you think that veneration goes quite beyond "speaking well" of Mary?

Luke 1:48—Biblical Support for the Veneration of Mary?

The Roman Catholic Teaching: In Luke 1:48 we read the words of Mary: "For He has had regard for the humble state of His bondslave; for behold, from this time on all generations will count me blessed." Many Roman Catholics believe this verse supports the veneration of Mary.[19]

Response: The Greek word for *blessed* in this verse (*makarizo*) literally means "to pronounce happy." And truly, generation after generation of Christians have pronounced Mary blessed and happy as a result of her having the wonderful privilege of giving birth to the Messiah. But there is not a hint of veneration in this verse. It is a great leap in logic to go from "blessedness" and "happiness" to veneration. As commentator Albert Barnes notes:

> It is therefore right to consider [Mary] as highly favored or happy; but this certainly does not warrant us to worship her or to pray to her. Abraham was blessed in being the father of the faithful; Paul in being the apostle to the

Gentiles; Peter in first preaching the gospel to them; but who would think of worshipping or praying to Abraham, Paul, or Peter?[20]

Ask...

- Did you know that Abraham was blessed in being the father of the faithful (Genesis 12)? (*Other biblical men and women were blessed too.*)

- Did you know that every single Christian is blessed "with every spiritual blessing in the heavenly places in Christ" (Ephesians 1:3)?

- Yet in no case do we venerate other humans, do we?

- In the same way, the fact that Mary is called "blessed" is no reason to venerate her, is it?

Luke 11:27—Biblical Support for the Veneration of Mary?

The Roman Catholic Teaching: In Luke 11:27 we read, "It came about while He said these things, one of the women in the crowd raised her voice, and said to Him, 'Blessed is the womb that bore You, and the breasts at which You nursed.'" Ludwig Ott and other Roman Catholic scholars have argued that this verse supports the special veneration due to Mary, the "mother of God."[21]

Response: There is nothing in this verse to support such veneration of Mary. In fact, after an anonymous woman in the crowd called out, "Blessed is the womb that bore You, and the breasts at which You nursed" (verse 27), Jesus immediately replied, "On the contrary, blessed are those who hear the word of God, and observe it" (verse 28). Instead of supporting the veneration of Mary, this verse argues against it.

The Greek word for "on the contrary" (*menounge*), according to *Friberg's Greek Lexicon*, is used especially "in answers to emphasize or correct on the contrary," and carries the idea of "rather."[22] The *Louw-Nida Greek Lexicon* says the word is a marker of contrast, carrying the idea, "but, on the contrary, on the other hand."[23]

Jesus' use of this word should not be taken to mean that He is taking away any honor rightfully due to His mother Mary. We know from Luke 1:28,42,48 that Mary truly is blessed in being the mother of the Messiah. But His quick corrective response is meant to put things into proper perspective by emphasizing that obedience to God's Word is what really matters.

Ask... _____

- Would you please read aloud from Luke 11:27?

- How do you reconcile the Catholic view that this verse supports the veneration of Mary with Jesus' immediate response in verse 28?

_____

Verses 27 and 28 powerfully argue against the veneration of Mary. We might also note that Jesus' exhortation to *obey the Word of God* provides further argumentation. Indeed, as I've previously noted, the Word of God not only provides no support for such veneration of Mary, but also speaks against any veneration paid to any creature.

Ask... _____

- Does the fact that Jesus said obedience to God's Word is the top priority, along with the fact that God's Word warns against venerating any creature, cause you to want to change your view in regard to venerating Mary?

_____

17

The Exaltation of Mary—Part 4
Reasoning from the Scriptures

"To *Him* who loves us, and released us from our sins by His blood, and He has made us to be a kingdom, priests to His God and Father; to *Him* be the glory and the dominion forever and ever. Amen."[1]
The Apostle John

In the previous chapter we examined a number of verses that typically come up in debates related to the Immaculate Conception of Mary, the perpetual virginity of Mary, and the veneration of Mary. In the present chapter, we will focus attention on key verses that relate to Mary's alleged role as co-redemptor and mediatrix, and her alleged bodily assumption into heaven.

Mary as Co-Redemptor and Mediatrix
Genesis 3:15—Biblical Support for Mary as Co-Redemptor?

The Roman Catholic Teaching: In Genesis 3:15 we read God's words of judgment to the serpent: "And I will put enmity between you and the woman, and between your seed and her seed; *He* shall bruise you on the head, and you shall bruise him on the heel" (emphasis added). In the previous chapter I noted that Roman Catholics sometimes appeal to this verse in support of the Immaculate Conception of Mary. But they also appeal to it in support of Mary's alleged role as co-redemptor. More specifically, appeal is made to the Douay Rheims (Catholic) translation of the verse: "I will put enmities between thee and the woman, and thy seed and her seed: *she* shall crush thy head, and thou shalt lie in wait for her heel" (emphasis added).

Response: This Catholic translation is faulty. Instead of basing the translation on the Hebrew text of Genesis 3:15, where the subject is masculine, the Douay Rheims translation is based on the Latin Vulgate,* where the subject is feminine.[2] (Up until the twentieth century no translations of the Bible except those based on the Vulgate were recognized as authoritative by the Roman Catholic Church.) Scholars agree that the Vulgate is faulty at Genesis 3:15. The Hebrew is the original language of the Old Testament, and hence the correct rendering of Genesis 3:15 from the Hebrew points only to the victory of the Messiah (Jesus Christ).

Luke 2:34,35—Biblical Support for Mary as Co-Redemptor?

The Roman Catholic Teaching: In Luke 2:34,35 we read, "And Simeon blessed them, and said to Mary His mother, 'Behold, this Child is appointed for the fall and rise of many in Israel, and for a sign to be opposed—and *a sword will pierce even your own soul*—to the end that thoughts from many hearts may be revealed'" (emphasis added). Here it is argued that because Mary suffered the pain of a sword piercing her soul, she too participated in suffering for human redemption.[3]

Response: Catholics are reading something into the text of Scripture that simply is not there. The suffering that Mary bore was the natural suffering of grief that all humans endure when a loved one dies. Mary's was not any kind of

---

* A Translation of the Bible by Jerome (A.D. 342–430) from Greek and Hebrew originals into the common Latin of the day.

substitutionary suffering for the redemption of man. Nor did Mary die for the sins of man, as Jesus did.

Ask... _____

- Doesn't it make sense to you that Mary's suffering was the natural pain of grief that all humans endure when a loved one dies—especially a son?

- Where in the context of this verse do you see even the smallest clue that Mary's suffering was related in any way to man's redemption?

Jesus *alone* is called the Lamb of God who suffered and took away the sin of the world through His death on the cross (John 1:29,36). First Peter 3:18 tells us that Christ "died for sins once for all, the just for the unjust, in order that He might bring us to God, having been put to death in the flesh, but made alive in the spirit." Romans 6:23 tells us, "For the wages of sin is death, but the free gift of God is eternal life in Christ Jesus our Lord."

Even if it were conceded that Mary suffered in some way for humanity (*which I do not believe*), her suffering would not have had any salvific value. It would have been no more than one human being suffering for another human being. Such willingness to suffer for another might show virtue, but there is no eternal salvation that results from that suffering.

It is entirely different with Jesus Christ, for He is our human-divine Kinsman-Redeemer. As noted earlier in the book, for Jesus to become our Kinsman-Redeemer He had to become related by blood to the human race. This made necessary the Incarnation. Jesus became a man in order to redeem man (Hebrews 2:14-16). And because Jesus was also fully God, His sacrificial death had infinite value (9:11-28).

Christ alone—the Messiah who is fully human and fully divine—is our Redeemer. Mary played no role in man's redemption. Her only role was to serve as the human instrument through whom the human birth of the Messiah would take place. Once that event occurred, Mary's role faded into the background.

Philippians 2:5-11—Did Mary Participate in Christ's Self-Emptying?

The Roman Catholic Teaching: In Philippians 2:5-11 we read the following words about Jesus:

> Have this attitude in yourselves which was also in Christ Jesus, who, although He existed in the form of God, did not regard equality with God a thing to be grasped, but emptied Himself, taking the form of a bondservant, and being made in the likeness of men. And being found in appearance as a man, He humbled Himself by becoming obedient to the point of death, even death on a cross. Therefore also God highly exalted Him, and bestowed on Him the name which is above every name, that at the name of Jesus every knee should bow, of those who are in heaven, and on earth, and under the earth, and that every tongue should confess that Jesus Christ is Lord, to the glory of God the Father.

Some Roman Catholics, while recognizing that these words refer to Jesus Christ, say that Mary too suffered greatly for man, and thus participated by faith in Christ's "self-emptying." For this reason, she is said to have played a role in the redemption of humankind. According to *Redemptoris Mater:*

> On that wood of the Cross her Son hangs in agony as one condemned. "He was despised and rejected by men; a man of sorrows.... He was despised, and we esteemed him not": as one destroyed (cf. Isaiah 53:3-5). How great, how heroic then is the obedience of faith shown by Mary in the face of God's "unsearchable judgments"! How completely she "abandons herself to God" without reserve, "offering the full assent of the intellect and the will" to him whose "ways are inscrutable" (cf. Romans

11:33)! And how powerful too is the action of grace in her soul, how all-pervading is the influence of the Holy Spirit and of his light and power! *Through this faith Mary is perfectly united with Christ in his self-emptying.* For "Christ Jesus, who, though he was in the form of God, did not count equality with God a thing to be grasped, but emptied himself, taking the form of a servant, being born in the likeness of men": precisely on Golgotha "humbled himself and became obedient unto death, even death on a cross" (cf. Phil. 2:5-8). *At the foot of the Cross Mary shares through faith in the shocking mystery of this self-emptying.* This is perhaps the deepest "kenosis" of faith in human history. Through faith the Mother shares in the death of her Son, in his redeeming death; but in contrast with the faith of the disciples who fled, hers was far more enlightened![4]

Response: With all due respect and sympathy for the tremendous suffering Mary bore as she watched her son die on the cross—and with full appreciation for the faith she displayed as it happened—she did not participate in the self-emptying of Christ, nor did her sufferings have any value so far as man's redemption is concerned. Catholics are reading something into this text that has no basis in exegesis.

It is important to understand that the "self-emptying" spoken of in Philippians 2:5-11 had to do with Christ, as God, *taking on human flesh.* Hence, there is no possible parallel in the life of Mary, a mere human being. It is true that once Christ became a man (something that involved "self-emptying"), He did die and suffer on the cross. But strictly speaking, the "self-emptying" had to do not with suffering on the cross but with the Incarnation, which *preceded* the cross.

The context of Philippians 2 indicates that Christ's self-emptying involved a great condescension in taking on the *likeness* (literally "form," or "appearance") of men—that is, unglorified humanity, and taking on the *form* (that is, the "very essence" or "very nature") of a bondservant[5] (see verses

6,7). Christ was thus truly human. This humanity was one that was subject to temptation, distress, weakness, pain, sorrow, and limitation.[6] Yet, at the same time, it must be noted that the word *likeness* suggests *similarity but difference.* As theologian Robert Lightner explains, "Though His humanity was genuine, He was different from all other humans in that He was sinless."[7] Nevertheless, this represented a great *condescension* on the part of the second Person of the Godhead.

According to Philippians 2, the Incarnation was more a gaining of *human* attributes than a giving up of *divine* attributes. Christ did not give up deity; He merely gained humanity. That this is meant by Paul is clear in his affirmation that, in the Incarnation, Christ was "taking the very nature of a servant," "being made in human likeness," and "being found in appearance as a man" (Philippians 2:7,8 NIV). As J. I. Packer puts it, "He was no less God then [in the Incarnation] than before; but He had begun to be man. He was not now God *minus* some elements of His deity, but God *plus* all that He had made His own by taking manhood to Himself. He who made man was now learning what it felt like to be man."[8]

In view of this theological backdrop, can you see how foolish it is to try to argue that Mary by faith participated in the self-emptying of Christ? I say this not with any insensitivity toward Mary in her suffering at the foot of the cross. But whatever suffering she endured bore no relation at all to the self-emptying of Christ as described in Philippians 2:5-11, for this self-emptying related only to Christ *as God* taking on human flesh.

Ask... _____

(First go over the above background material on Philippians 2:5-11.)

• In view of what Scripture indicates about the "self-emptying" of Christ, can you see the folly of trying to argue that Mary by faith participated in this self-emptying?

First Timothy 2:5—Biblical Support for Mary as Mediatrix?

The Roman Catholic Teaching: In 1 Timothy 2:5 we read, "For there is one God, and one mediator also between God and men, the man Christ Jesus." Roman Catholics sometimes try to argue that the word "one" in this verse does not mean "only one." Mark Miraville writes:

> The Greek word used for "one" in the Pauline text of 1 Timothy 2:5 is *"heis,"* which means "one," "first," or "primary." There is another Greek word that St. Paul could have used if he wanted to refer to Christ's mediation as completely exclusive, namely, *"monos,"* which means "sole," "only," or "exclusive one." As O'Carroll, C.S.Sp notes, "The practice of addressing Mary as Mediatrix was not and need not be impeded by the Pauline text. The use of 'one' (*heis* not *monos*) emphasizes Christ's transcendence as a mediator, through the unique value of his redemptive death."[9]

Response: The Catholic view does not make sense. If there is only one (*heis*) God, there is only one (*heis*) mediator: Jesus Christ. The word "one" means the same thing in both cases: "only one." There is exclusively one God. There is exclusively one mediator.

Ask... _____

- Since the same Greek word for "one" is used in referring to *"one* God" and *"one* mediator," is it not clear that in both cases the same meaning for *one* is intended in this verse (that is, "only one")?

_____

Thayer's *Greek Lexicon* tells us that one of the major usages of *heis* is emphatic, carrying the idea, "So that others are excluded."[10] *Friberg's Greek Lexicon* agrees, noting that *heis* can refer to *one* "emphatically, in contrast to more than one."[11] This is the correct usage in 1 Timothy 2:5: There is exclusively one God; there is exclusively one mediator.

Ask... _____

- Since one of the meanings of the Greek word *heis* is "one, so that others are excluded," is it not clear that 1 Timothy 2:5 is teaching that there is exclusively one God and exclusively one mediator between man and God: Jesus Christ?

_____

Another point that bears mentioning is that Jesus is the perfect mediator between God and man precisely because He is both God *and* man (something which is obviously not true of Mary). As God and man, Jesus can perfectly represent God to man and represent man to God.

John 2:1-11—Biblical Support for Mary as a Mediatrix?

The Roman Catholic Teaching: In John 2:1-11 we read the account of Jesus turning water into wine:

> And on the third day there was a wedding in Cana of Galilee, and the mother of Jesus was there; and Jesus also was invited, and His disciples, to the wedding. And when the wine gave out, the mother of Jesus said to Him, "They have no wine." And Jesus said to her, "Woman, what do I have to do with you? My hour has not yet come." His mother said to the servants, "Whatever He says to you, do it." Now there were six stone waterpots set there for the Jewish custom of purification, containing twenty or thirty gallons each. Jesus said to them, "Fill the waterpots with water." And they filled them up to the brim. And He said to them, "Draw some out now, and take it to the headwaiter." And they took it to him. And when the headwaiter tasted the water which had become wine, and did not know where it came from (but the servants who had drawn the water knew), the headwaiter called the bridegroom, and said to him, "Every man serves the good wine first, and when men have drunk freely, then that which is poorer; you have kept the good wine until now." This

beginning of His signs Jesus did in Cana of Galilee, and manifested His glory, and His disciples believed in Him.

Roman Catholics often point to this passage, noting that Mary engaged in an intercessory or mediating role, even early in the Gospel accounts. We read in the *Dogmatic Constitution of the Church:* "In the public life of Jesus, Mary appears prominently; at the very beginning when at the marriage feast of Cana, moved with pity, she brought about *by her intercession* the beginning of miracles of Jesus the Messiah (cf. John 2:1-11)."[12]

Response: Catholics are reading something into this passage that is not there. Note that when Mary informed Jesus in verse 3 that they were out of wine, Jesus responded in verse 4: "Woman, what do I have to do with you? My hour has not yet come." Jesus was making a very important point here. Jesus in His divine power was not subject to her requests, nor do her personal needs have any relationship with His divine mission of redemption. Exegete Edgar J. Goodspeed translates the passage, "Do not try to direct me. It is not yet time for me to act."[13] Jesus came to do *as the Father* instructed Him (John 14–16), not Mary.

Commentators Robert Jamieson, A. R. Fausset, and David Brown note that Jesus' words to Mary were "a gentle rebuke for officious interference."[14] That Jesus ended up turning water into wine was due not to Mary's alleged influence over Him as a mediatrix, but rather to His own graciousness and mercy. There is certainly no warrant for reading into this verse the idea that Mary carries some role up to the present day as mediatrix.

Ask...

* Would you please read aloud from John 2:3,4?

* Does it not seem that Jesus is letting Mary know in a gentle way that it is not her place to request miraculous intervention on His part?

John 19:27—Biblical Support for Mary as Mediatrix?

The Roman Catholic Teaching: In John 19:27 we read Jesus' words to John from the cross: "Then He said to the disciple, 'Behold, your mother!' And from that hour the disciple took her into his own household." In the previous chapter I noted that Catholics often appeal to this verse in support of the perpetual virginity of Mary. But Catholics also argue that by Jesus' words in this verse Mary became the *Mother of the Church*. This being so, it is only good and right to turn to her as mediatrix as a refuge in times of trouble and to seek her in view of her influence over her Son.[15]

Response: In context, Jesus was about to die on the cross. In His presence were His mother Mary and John, the disciple closest to His own heart—and apparently the only disciple with courage enough to take his stand with Mary at the cross. Knowing that His mother and John both would soon be engulfed in deep grief at His death, He entrusted Mary into John's care so that they could mutually comfort and care for one another. To read into this that Mary became the "Mother of the Church" is a wild, wild stretch.

Ask... ───────────────────────────────

- Doesn't the context of this verse indicate that Jesus was entrusting Mary to John so that both could mutually comfort and care for one another in their time of grief?

- Where is there any indication in this verse that Mary became the "Mother of the Church"?

───────────────────────────────

Despite the teachings of Roman Catholicism, the biblical fact of the matter is that *Mary cannot help anyone.* She is a redeemed sinner, and she is in heaven. But she has no power over God Almighty. She has no role as a mediatrix. There is not a single verse of Scripture to support such an idea, but there are many verses that argue against it (for example, 1 Timothy 2:5).

We can go before the presence of God not because of some imagined sway that Mary has in heaven but because of what Jesus has accomplished for us: "We have confidence to enter the holy place by the blood of Jesus" (Hebrews 10:19). "Let us therefore draw near with confidence to the throne of grace, that we may receive mercy and may find grace to help in time of need" (4:16).

Further, it is not Mary who dispenses heavenly graces upon us as "mediatrix," but rather God Himself does this: "Every good thing bestowed and every perfect gift is from above, coming down from the Father of lights, with whom there is no variation, or shifting shadow" (James 1:17).

The Bodily Assumption of Mary

Matthew 27:52,53—Biblical Support for
the Bodily Assumption of Mary?

The Roman Catholic Teaching: In Matthew 27:52,53 we read what took place following Christ's resurrection: "The tombs were opened; and many bodies of the saints who had fallen asleep were raised; and coming out of the tombs after His resurrection they entered the holy city and appeared to many." Some Roman Catholic theologians believe this event shows the "probability" of the bodily assumption of Mary into heaven.[16] "If...the justified of the Old Covenant were called to the perfection of salvation immediately after the conclusion of the redemptive work of Christ, then it is possible and probable that the Mother of the Lord was called to it also."[17]

Response: This passage says virtually nothing about the bodily assumption of Mary. Indeed, Catholic theologian Ludwig Ott concedes that in regard to support for this doctrine, "direct and express scriptural proofs are not to be had."[18]

Ask... _____

• Did you know that Ludwig Ott, one of Catholicism's esteemed theologians, concedes that there are no direct and express scriptural proofs for the doctrine of Mary's bodily assumption?

• Do you know of any verses that explicitly teach this?

It is important to note that the individuals mentioned in this passage were raised out of their graves but they *did not* ascend into heaven. Hence, the primary point of the passage is entirely different from what Roman Catholics would like it to say.

Ask... ———————————————————————————

• Since the individuals mentioned in this verse did not ascend into heaven, and since Mary is not even mentioned, where is the proof of Mary's bodily assumption in this verse?

Further, the context indicates that these individuals did not at this time receive their permanent resurrection bodies, but rather were resuscitated from the dead much like Lazarus was in John 11. All these individuals eventually died again and went back to the grave. The reception of their permanent resurrection bodies is yet future (1 Thessalonians 4:13-17; 1 Corinthians 15:50-52). Hence, the event described in Matthew 27:52 hardly gives support for the bodily assumption of Mary.

Psalm 132:8—A Foreshadowing of the Bodily Assumption of Mary?

The Roman Catholic Teaching: In this verse we read, "Arise, O LORD, to Thy resting place; Thou and the ark of Thy strength." Some Roman Catholics argue that the "ark" in this verse typologically points forward to the bodily assumption of Mary. After all, the ark is made of incorruptible wood, and hence the ark is typological of the incorruptible body of Mary.[19]

Response: It is highly revealing that most Church Fathers and Catholic theologians believe that Mary died.[20] This point alone should give us pause to consider the validity of the doctrine of the bodily assumption of Mary.

Ask... ————————————————————

- Did you know that most Church Fathers and Catholic theologians believe that Mary died?

- What does that say to you?

————————————————————

Further, a typological interpretation of this verse—relating it to Mary's alleged bodily assumption—is unwarranted and unconvincing, especially in view of the fact that there are no *explicit* statements that support the doctrine in the Bible. Trying to find such typological relationships in Scripture shows that Roman Catholics are grasping at straws in search of support.

Moreover, the scriptural testimony is that *all* human beings, by virtue of the sin problem, eventually grow old and die (Romans 3:23; 6:23). Mary was no exception to this. Like other fallen mortals, Mary died and was buried. "Therefore, just as through one man sin entered into the world, and death through sin, and so death spread to all men, because all sinned" (Romans 5:12). There is not a single reference in Scripture that indicates that Mary's body was incorruptible, as Roman Catholics would like to believe.

Ask... ————————————————————

- Would you please read aloud from Romans 5:12?

- Is Mary included in the "all" in this verse? (*If they say no, ask for scriptural proof for her exclusion.*)

- Since Mary considered herself a sinner in need of a Savior (Luke 1:47), and thus presented an offering to the Jewish priest arising out of her state of sin (Luke 2:22-24), is it not clear that Mary too eventually ended up in death as a result of sin, as is true of all other humans (Romans 5:12)?

Revelation 12:1-6—Biblical Support for the Bodily Assumption of Mary?

The Roman Catholic Teaching: In Revelation 12:1-6 we read:

> And a great sign appeared in heaven: a woman clothed with the sun, and the moon under her feet, and on her head a crown of twelve stars; and she was with child; and she cried out, being in labor and in pain to give birth. And another sign appeared in heaven: and behold, a great red dragon having seven heads and ten horns, and on his heads were seven diadems. And his tail swept away a third of the stars of heaven, and threw them to the earth And the dragon stood before the woman who was about to give birth, so that when she gave birth he might devour her child. And she gave birth to a son, a male child, who is to rule all the nations with a rod of iron; and her child was caught up to God and to His throne. And the woman fled into the wilderness where she had a place prepared by God, so that there she might be nourished for one thousand two hundred and sixty days.

Many Roman Catholics believe this passage makes reference to the bodily assumption of Mary: "Scholastic theology sees...the transfigured mother of Christ."[21]

Response: The "woman" mentioned in this verse is not Mary, but is rather the nation of Israel. Theologian John F. Walvoord explains how the backdrop of the Book of Genesis helps us come to this conclusion:

> The statement that [the woman] is clothed with the sun, with the moon under her feet (12:1) is an allusion to Joseph's dream in which he saw the sun, moon, and eleven

stars bowing down to him (Gen. 37:9). The sun and the moon in this context refer to Jacob and Rachel, the fore-bearers of Israel. The woman is also said to have a crown of twelve stars on her head (v. 1). In Joseph's dream also the stars, or the sons of Israel, are intended with the twelfth star, including Joseph himself who was not in the dream as such.[22]

That a woman represents Israel is not unusual in the context of the Book of Revelation. Indeed, another woman named Jezebel is portrayed as representing a false religion in Revelation 2:20. A harlot in Revelation 17 represents the apostate church of the end times. In similar fashion, the woman of Revelation 12 represents the nation of Israel.

Note also that the woman mentioned in Revelation 12 "fled into the wilderness where she had a place prepared by God, so that there she might be nourished for one thousand two hundred and sixty days" (verse 6). There is certainly nothing in Mary's life that remotely resembles what is described in this verse. In context, the verse refers to Israel in the prophetic future.

Moreover, note that only Christ is said to be caught up to God and to His throne (Revelation 12:5), not the woman. There is no bodily assumption of "the woman," let alone Mary.

Further, the fact that this woman was pregnant and cried out in pain goes against the Roman Catholic claim that Mary suffered virtually no pain during the birth of Jesus: "Mary gave birth in miraculous fashion without opening of the womb and injury to the hymen, and consequently also without pains."[23] It makes far more sense to say that Israel as a nation *metaphorically* gave birth to Jesus as the promised Jewish Messiah.

Ask... _____

(Go over the above facts first.)

• Can you see how the backdrop of the Book of Genesis helps us to identify the woman?

- Since the events described in Revelation 12 have no counterpart in the life of Mary, is it not clear that Mary is not being referred to here?

- Who, according to this passage, is caught up to God and His throne? (*Jesus.*)

- Can you find even the slightest clue of Mary's alleged bodily assumption in this verse?

18

The Dos and Don'ts of
Dialoguing with Catholics

"Kindness is a language which the blind
can see and the deaf can hear."[1]
Anonymous

In this book a great deal of effort has been made to answer
Roman Catholic arguments from specific passages in the
Bible. In this closing chapter, which will be short and to the
point, my intention is not to offer further argumentation
against Roman Catholic theology but to offer some final
pointers—some *dos* and *don'ts*—on dialoguing with
Catholics.

Identify with Roman Catholics

The first *do*: *Do identify with Roman Catholics.* We have
a lot in common with Roman Catholics. We share many common Christian beliefs, including (as noted earlier in the book)
the doctrine of the Trinity and the full theistic attributes of
God, God as Creator and Sustainer of the universe, the deity
of Christ, the virgin birth, the Incarnation, the resurrection,
Christ's ascension into heaven, His future return in glory, the

doctrine of the Holy Spirit (including the Holy Spirit's personality, deity, and involvement in the work of redemption), and other key doctrines. Further, Protestants and Catholics agree on basic ethics. This is a lot to build from.

Use this common ground as a launchpad to talk about some of the very important issues related to the gospel (justification, grace, and faith). Your goal is to make sure they end up as members of God's forever family, and that cannot happen unless they believe the true gospel.

Even more basic than our common doctrinal beliefs is our common humanity. Remember that Roman Catholics, like all people, have families and children and all the other things that are important to all of us. They have the need for friendship, the need for love and security, and they are people who laugh and cry like us. Keeping all this in mind will help stir the compassion in your soul and help you relate to them on a real level.

Labor Persistently with Roman Catholics

The second *do: Do labor persistently with Roman Catholics.* Never give up unless he or she decisively refuses further contact. Until the person pulls the plug, hang in there. Don't forget that God blesses His Word. God Himself, in the Book of Isaiah, affirmed of His sovereign Word: "So shall My word be which goes forth from My mouth; it shall not return to Me empty, without accomplishing what I desire, and without succeeding in the matter for which I sent it" (55:11). If you faithfully share God's Word with Roman Catholics, you can be sure that God is at work in their hearts.

I know from personal experience that it is not always easy to "labor persistently." Sometimes when you talk about the Bible, Roman Catholics like to bring tradition into the discussion. When you talk about salvation, they will use the same words we do (*grace, justification, sanctification*) but mean something entirely different. Such factors can make any discussion somewhat of a challenge. But don't get discouraged. Just remember that if you make yourself available to God and share some of the theological points in this book, *you will* see some results.

Answer the Questions of Roman Catholics

The third *do: Do exhaust every effort to answer the questions of Roman Catholics.* We must share not only *what* we believe as Christians, but *why* we believe it as well. We must be able to give convincing reasons for our beliefs. Remember that the apostles were defenders of the faith as well as evangelists. They not only proclaimed Christ, but when they were questioned, they had good, solid reasons for their faith. This is why the apostle Peter said we should always be "ready to make a defense to everyone who asks you to give an account for the hope that is in you, yet with gentleness and reverence" (1 Peter 3:15).

What happens if you do not know the answer to a question that a Roman Catholic brings up? Don't sweat it. Just say, "That's a good question. I am not sure what the answer is, but I am going to do some research this week and find the answer. Can I give you a call when I find the answer?" Your Catholic acquaintance will invariably go along with your request. Hopefully, the book you are holding in your hand will go a long way toward providing the answers you need.

Allow the Roman Catholic to Save Face

The fourth *do: Do allow the Roman Catholic to save face.* When you share the true gospel with a Roman Catholic and defend your position from Scripture, there may come a time in your encounter when you sense you've "won the argument." If and when that moment arrives, you must make every effort to let love shine through and allow him or her to save face. Otherwise, your Catholic friend will resent you and fight you, even though he knows in his heart that you are right.

You might say something like, "I realize that we can get awfully uptight in these areas if we let ourselves. Let us just forget that you are a Roman Catholic and I am a Baptist (or whatever you are). And let's just think of ourselves as two people who want more than anything else to know the whole truth and the whole counsel of God. *Right?*" Disarming the situation in this way will help lower defensive "barriers" and will create an atmosphere in which discussion is much easier and free-flowing.

Try to follow the Golden Rule in your conversations with Catholics. Try to think of how you would want other people to speak to you. Then remember, "however you want people to treat you, so treat them" (Matthew 7:12).

Remain Humble

An important *don't*: *Don't approach a Roman Catholic with a spiritual chip on your shoulder.* A spiritual chip is the communication of the feeling that you are looking down on the Roman Catholic. It communicates the idea, "You're lucky we're having this conversation today, so I can set you straight." Such an attitude will (rightly) turn the person off as fast as anything you could imagine.

Especially for Christians who have thoroughly prepared themselves by learning hard-hitting scriptural answers to Roman Catholic errors, the temptation may be to intellectually *talk down* at the Catholic instead of *conversing with* the Catholic. Don't let this happen. Be on your guard and make every effort, with God's help, to remain humble during your witnessing encounter. Watch out for spiritual pride; *it is deadly!*

Be Patient

Another *don't*: *Don't lose your patience.* This is an extremely important point. Being patient may mean going over the same doctrinal point or reviewing the same verse ten times, if necessary.

If you should lose your patience and raise your voice at your Catholic acquaintance, the likelihood is that he or she will not want to engage in any further religious discussions with you. This is something you do not want to happen. After all, it may take multiple exposures to the truth before the Catholic comes to see that he or she has some wrong beliefs. You need to maintain a witnessing environment such that the Catholic will feel free to engage in religious discussions with you without fearing a verbal assault.

I believe these basic *dos* and *don'ts* will help you as you seek to share the gospel of God's grace with Roman Catholics. But there is one further thing I need to mention. Don't forget the important role of the Holy Spirit in evangelizing others. After all, it is *He* who touches all our souls; it is *He* who convinces us all of sin and of righteousness and of judgment (John 16:8). And we become *in His hands* effective instruments for the Master's use (see 1 Corinthians 6:19; 12:11; Ephesians 5:18).

Be sure to pray fervently for the Holy Spirit's involvement in all your witnessing encounters (Philippians 4:6; 1 Thessalonians 5:17). Pray specifically that God would open your Catholic acquaintance's heart to the glorious gospel of God's grace, and that he or she would see the folly of trying to earn a place in heaven by a life of meritorious works.

If They Convert...

If your Catholic acquaintance ends up trusting in Jesus and His wonderful gospel of God's grace, I believe you should encourage the person to leave the Roman Catholic Church altogether so that he or she can grow spiritually in a good Bible-believing church.

Many will resist this idea and say they want to remain in the Catholic Church in order to win other people to Christ and bring reform in the Church. It is not impossible that God could use such a person for such purposes—assuming he or she grew very strong in Bible doctrine. But reform seems unlikely (John Calvin and Martin Luther would probably want to give you some advice in this regard).

One big problem is that if the person chooses to stay in the Catholic Church, he or she can be guaranteed a steady diet of works theology, which could cause discouragement and doubts, especially in the life of the new believer. This will greatly hinder spiritual growth. It is much better to get out of the works environment and join a church that is spiritually alive—a church that emphasizes a relationship with Jesus over mechanical rituals, a church that emphasizes that the Bible is a Jesus book and not a church book.

Remind your Catholic friend that leaving the Roman Catholic Church does not necessitate breaking off Roman Catholic friendships. Indeed, the person should keep those friendships going strong, not only because the friendships are important in themselves, but because they might also open the door to evangelism down the road.

James McCarthy, a former Catholic who is now an evangelical Christian with a ministry to Catholics, has pointed out that staying in the Roman Catholic Church might send mixed signals. You might tell other people that there are problems in the Church that need remedying, but by your continued presence in the Church, you convey that the problems are not severe enough to cause you to leave.[2] It is better to back up your words with actions, even though it might be painful at first.

One final thing. Don't forget that one of the strongest apologetics (or defenses) of true Christianity is a man or woman who truly walks with God. This is the kind of person that people notice. This is the kind of person whose opinion becomes respected.

A person may have all the right apologetic answers in the world, but if he or she is not walking close with the Lord, his or her answers ultimately mean very little. By contrast, strong answers coming from a person who exudes true commitment to the Lord Jesus is, in my opinion, an apologist in the true biblical sense.

So as you witness to Roman Catholics, first and foremost you must walk with God. Never forget this. It is the true beginning point for effective apologetics. *Walk with Him, and watch Him work through you!*

Appendix A
Infant Salvation

I pointed out in chapter 7 that, in Roman Catholic theology, infants who have been baptized in the Roman Catholic Church before reaching the age of accountability are believed to go straight to heaven at the moment of death, and there they enjoy the "beatific vision" (the happiness of heaven that is involved in seeing the very essence of God). It is believed these infants will not suffer in purgatory because they have accrued no guilt (since they have not reached the age of accountability) and hence deserve no temporal punishment.

Infants that die before the parents bring them in for baptism are viewed as being not bad enough to go to hell, but neither can they go to heaven since baptism is required for entrance into heaven. Some Roman Catholic theologians have suggested that there must be an in-between place—*limbo*—to which unbaptized infants go at the moment of death. There they do not enjoy the glorious benefits and wonders of heaven, but neither do they experience the pain and suffering of hell. This belief in "limbo" is not an official dogma of the Church, but few priests and Roman Catholic theologians deny it either.

It is my personal belief that the Scriptures teach that *every infant bar none* who dies is immediately ushered into God's glorious presence in heaven—*but not because the infant is baptized.* (As I argued in chapter 8, baptism *does not* and *cannot* save anyone.) Rather, I believe that at the moment of death, Jesus applies the benefits of His death on the cross to that child, thereby saving him or her. Following are the critical factors to keep in mind:

The Universal Need of Salvation. At the outset, we must recognize that the whole of Scripture points to the universal need of salvation—even among little children. All of us—including infants who cannot believe—are lost (Luke 19:10), perishing (John 3:16), condemned (John 3:18), and are under God's wrath (John 3:36). In view of this, we cannot say that little children are in a sinless state. That is why it is necessary for Christ to apply the benefits of His death on the cross to each child that dies.

God's Purpose in Salvation. God's primary purpose in saving human beings is to display His wondrous grace. We must ask, Would the "riches of God's grace" be displayed in "wisdom and understanding" (Ephesians 1:7,8 NIV) in excluding little children (before the age of accountability) from His kingdom? I think not. I believe it is the uniform testimony of Scripture that those who are not capable of making a decision to receive Jesus Christ, and who have died, are now with Christ in heaven, resting in His tender arms, enjoying the sweetness of His love. There are several biblical factors supporting this viewpoint.

It is highly revealing that in all the descriptions of hell in the Bible, we *never* read of infants or little children there. Only adults capable of making decisions are seen there. Nor do we read of infants and little children standing at the Great White Throne judgment, which is the judgment of the wicked dead and the precursor to the lake of fire (Revelation 20:11-15). The complete silence of Scripture regarding the presence of infants in eternal torment militates against their being there. And since purgatory and limbo are unbiblical doctrines, (see chapter 13), the only conclusion we can draw is that infants and young children go straight to heaven at the moment of death.

Jesus and the Children. As we examine instances in which Christ encountered children during His earthly ministry, it would seem that children have a special place in His heart and His kingdom. Jesus even said, "Unless you change and become like little children, you will never enter the kingdom of heaven" (Matthew 18:3 NIV). He also said, "Whoever welcomes a little child like this in my name welcomes me" (verse 5 NIV). I do not think there is any way someone could read through Matthew 18 and conclude that it is within the realm of possibility that Jesus could exclude an infant or young child from His kingdom!

King David and His Son. King David in the Old Testament certainly believed he would again be with his young son who died (2 Samuel 12:22,23). David firmly believed in life after death. He had no doubt that he would spend eternity with his beloved little one.

The Basis of the Judgment of the Lost. Another consideration that points to the assurance of infant salvation relates to the basis of the judgment of the lost. We read in Revelation 20:11-13 (NIV) that the lost are judged "according to what they had done." The basis of the judgment of the wicked is clearly *deeds done while on earth.* Hence, infants cannot possibly be the objects of this judgment because they are not responsible for their deeds. Such a judgment against infants would be a travesty.

These and other scriptural factors seem to imply that babies and young children go straight to heaven at the moment of death. But again, this has nothing to do with whether or not they are baptized. The reality is that the infant is in no different state *as far as God is concerned* before or after his or her infant baptism (see chapter 8). In the New Testament, baptism always *follows* the conversion experience (Acts 2:41; 8:13; 18:8); it is not the *cause* of the conversion experience. Baptism does not *cause* initial justification; rather baptism *follows* justification, which comes at the moment of faith in Christ.

Appendix B

Ecumenism in the Roman Catholic Church

In Roman Catholic theology, it has traditionally been taught that there is virtually no salvation outside of the Church. For example, Pope Innocent III said in A.D. 1208: "With our hearts we believe and with our lips we confess but one Church, not that of the heretics, but the Holy Roman Catholic and Apostolic Church, outside which we believe that no one is saved."[1] Pope Pius IX said in A.D. 1854: "It must be held by faith that outside the Apostolic Roman Church, no one can be saved; that this is the only ark of salvation; that he who shall not have entered therein will perish in the flood."[2]

Yet, at Vatican II, a change took place such that Protestants were now labeled "separated brethren."[3] Further, it was suggested that even non-Christians and pagans can become saved. Vatican II's *Declaration on the Relation of the Church to Non-Christian Religions* articulates the Church's new attitude toward non-Christian religions:

> There is found among different peoples a certain awareness of hidden power, which lies behind the course of nature and the events of human life. At times there is present even a recognition of a supreme being, or still more of a Father. This awareness and recognition results in a way of life that is imbued with a deep religious sense. The religions which are found in more advanced civilizations endeavor by way of well-defined concepts and exact language to answer these questions.

The Catholic Church rejects nothing of what is true and holy in these religions. She has a high regard for the manner of life and conduct, the precepts and doctrines which, although differing in many ways from her own teaching, nevertheless often reflect a ray of that truth which enlightens all men. Yet she proclaims and is duty bound to proclaim without fail, Christ who is the way, the truth and the life (John 14:6).[4]

The document specifically focuses upon Muslims and Jews:

The Church has also a high regard for the Muslims. They worship God, who is one, living and subsistent, merciful and almighty, the creator of heaven and earth, who has also spoken to men. They strive to submit themselves without reserve to the hidden decrees of God, just as Abraham submitted himself to God's plan, to whose faith Muslims eagerly link their own. Although not acknowledging him as God, they venerate Jesus as prophet, his virgin mother they also honor, and even at times devoutly invoke. Further, they await the day of judgment and the reward of God following the resurrection of the dead.[5]

The Biblical View: Salvation Is Found Only in Jesus Christ

If people of other religions, including Muslims, are not really lost, then many of the teachings of Christ become absurd. For example, John 3:16 (NIV)—"For God so loved the world that he gave his one and only Son, that whoever believes in him shall not perish but have eternal life"— becomes meaningless.

If people of other religions are not lost, Christ's post-resurrection and pre-ascension commands to His disciples are a mockery. In Luke 24:47 Christ commanded that "repentance for forgiveness of sins should be proclaimed in His name to all the nations." Similarly, in Matthew 28:19 He said, "Therefore go and make disciples of all nations, baptizing them in the name of the Father and of the Son and of the Holy Spirit." These verses might as well be stricken from the Scriptures if human beings without Christ are not lost.

If people of other religions are not really lost, then the Lord's words were meaningless when He said to His disciples, "As the Father has sent me, I am sending you" (John 20:21 NIV). Why did the Father send Him? Jesus Himself explained that "the Son of Man came to seek and to save what was lost" (Luke 19:10 NIV).

If people of other religions do not need Christ and His salvation, then *neither do we.* Conversely, if we need Him, *so do they.* The Scriptures become a bundle of contradictions, the Savior becomes a false teacher, and the Christian message becomes "much ado about nothing" if people of other religions are not lost.

Scripture makes it very plain: "Salvation is found in no one else, for there is no other name under heaven given to men by which we must be saved" (Acts 4:12 NIV). The Bible says, "There is one God and one mediator between God and men, the man Christ Jesus" (1 Timothy 2:5 NIV).

Other religions do not lead to God. The one sin for which God judged the people of Israel more severely than any other was that of participating in heathen religions. Again and again the Bible implies and states that God hates, despises, and utterly rejects anything associated with heathen religions and practices. Those who follow such idolatry are not regarded as groping their way to God, but rather as having turned their backs on Him, following the ways of darkness.

Though Vatican II said many positive things about Islam, it must be pointed out that this religion is not compatible with Christianity.[6] Muslims believe that Allah is the one true God, and that God cannot have a son. They deny the doctrine of the Trinity. In their view, then, Jesus was not the Son of God and He was not God in human flesh. He is to be honored, but no more so than any other prophet of Allah. He is a *lesser* prophet than Muhammad. Further, Jesus did not die on a cross. Salvation is said to come not by faith in Christ but by complete surrender to Allah. So it would seem that Muslims are very much in need of evangelizing.

Having said all this, I must also point out the scriptural teaching that God has given a certain amount of "light" to every single person in the world. Everyone has some sense of God's law in his or her heart. As John Blanchard put it so well, everyone

> has some conception of the difference between right and wrong; he approves of honesty; he responds to love and kindness; he resents it if someone steals his goods or tries to injure him. In other words, he has a conscience which passes judgment on his behavior and the behavior of others, something the Bible calls a law written on his heart.[7]

Paul speaks of this law written on human hearts in Romans 2:15.

God has also given witness of Himself in the universe around us. In beholding the world and the universe, it is evident that there is Someone who made the world and the universe. Since the creation of the world, God's invisible qualities—His eternal power and divine nature—have been clearly seen and understood from that which He created (Romans 1:20).

We know from other Scripture verses that God is an invisible spirit (John 4:24). The physical eye cannot see Him. But His existence is nevertheless reflected in what He has made: the creation. The creation, which is visible, reveals the existence of the Creator, who is invisible.

Because all human beings can see the revelation of God in creation, all people—regardless of whether they've heard about Christ or have read the Bible—are held accountable before God. All are without excuse. Their rightful condemnation, as objects of God's wrath, is justified because their choice to ignore the revelation of God in creation is indefensible (see Psalm 19:1-6; Romans 1:20).

The Scriptures clearly indicate that those who respond to the limited light around them (such as God's witness of Himself in the universe or in the human heart) will receive further, more specific "light." This is illustrated in the life of Cornelius. This Gentile was obedient to the limited amount of "light" he had received—that is, he had been obedient to Old Testament revelation (Acts 10:2). But he didn't have enough "light" to believe in Jesus Christ as the Savior. So God sent Peter to Cornelius's house to explain the gospel, after which time Cornelius believed in Jesus and was saved (Acts 10:44-48).

So what can we conclude? God has given a witness of Himself to all humanity (Romans 1:20; Psalm 19:1-6). Moreover, God desires all to be saved (1 Timothy 2:4) and doesn't want anyone to perish (2 Peter 3:9). He certainly takes no pleasure in the death of the unsaved (Ezekiel 18:23). Further, God is a fair Judge. "It is unthinkable that God would do wrong, that the Almighty would pervert justice" (Job 34:12 NIV). "Will not the Judge of all the earth do right?" (Genesis 18:25 NIV).

At the same time, however, let us not forget that belief in Jesus Christ as Savior is consistently presented as man's only means of coming into a personal relationship with God. Jesus Himself said, "I am the way, and the truth, and the life; no one comes to the Father, but through Me" (John 14:6). And, as noted earlier, Peter proclaimed that "there is salvation in no one else; for there is no other name under heaven that has been given among men, by which we must be saved" (Acts 4:12). The apostle Paul affirmed, "For there is one God, and one mediator also between God and men, the man Christ Jesus" (1 Timothy 2:5).

Appendix C
The Veneration of Relics

In Ludwig Ott's *Fundamentals of Catholic Dogma*, we are told that "it is permissible and profitable to venerate the relics of saints."[1] He suggests that the reason for this is that "the bodies of the saints were living members of Christ and Temples of the Holy Ghost." He points out "that they will again be awakened and glorified and that through them God bestows many benefits on mankind."[2]

The veneration of relics is completely contrary to Scripture. In fact, it is a form of idolatry that is forbidden by God (Exodus 20:4,5). Catholics sometimes respond, however, by arguing that God commanded that certain images be made such as flowered columns in the temple (1 Kings 7:18,19). But Roman Catholics are reading something into the text that is not there. The fact is, the flowered columns were *strictly ornamental*. They were not worshiped.

In what follows, I will briefly summarize four key verses Roman Catholics bring up in support of their view of the veneration of relics. Though my intent will be to keep responses short in this appendix, it will nevertheless become clear that the practice of venerating relics goes against Scripture.

Exodus 13:19—Joseph's Bones—Support for the Veneration of Relics?

The Roman Catholic View: In Exodus 13:19 we read, "Moses took the bones of Joseph with him [out of Egypt], for he had made the sons of Israel solemnly swear, saying, 'God shall surely take care of you; and you shall carry my bones from here with you.'" Roman Catholics say this verse indicates that it is permissible and profitable to venerate the relics of saints.[3]

Response: Such a viewpoint is unwarranted. Indeed, even Ludwig Ott admits that the Bible makes *no explicit mention* of the veneration of relics.[4]

In Exodus 13 there is virtually no mention of venerating Joseph's bones. Joseph's instructions were simple and to the point: "You must carry my bones up with you from this place" (verse 19). Joseph knew that the Israelites would not be permanently settled in Egypt because God had specifically promised Abraham that the Israelites would be led to the promised land (Genesis 12:1-3). We learn from Joshua 24:32 that Joseph's bones were eventually buried at Shechem. And there is no record of *any* Israelite at *any* time *ever* venerating those bones.

We read elsewhere in Scripture that God commanded His people not to make graven images or to bow down to them in an act of religious devotion: "You shall not make for yourself an idol, or any likeness of what is in heaven above or on the earth beneath or in the water under the earth. You shall not worship them or serve them" (Exodus 20:4,5; see also 2 Kings 18:4). To do so is, as the apostle Paul said, to worship and serve the creature rather than the Creator (Romans 1:25). To venerate Joseph's bones clearly goes against the spirit of such passages.

Exodus 25:18—Cherubim—Support for the Veneration of Images?

The Roman Catholic View: In Exodus 25:18 we read that Moses was commanded by God to "make two cherubim of gold, make them of hammered work at the two ends of the mercy seat." Roman Catholic scholars often argue that this verse justifies the veneration of sacred images.[5]

Response: The context of Exodus 25 provides no support for the veneration of the image of the cherubim. In fact, the cherubim were in the most holy place, and only the high priest was allowed to enter the most holy place, and then only once a year (Leviticus 16). It was inaccessible to the average person. That means the cherubim could never be venerated by the average person.[6] Further, note that the cherubim were a part of the ark of the covenant. They were not some separate item that was to be venerated or worshiped. Not even the ark of the covenant was venerated or worshiped. Note further that the whole reason why the high priest would enter into the most holy place once a year to stand before the ark had to do with worship of the one true God, not the veneration of relics.

2 Kings 13:21—God's Miracle through Elijah's Bones— Support for Venerating Relics?

The Roman Catholic View: In 2 Kings 13:21 we read, "As they were burying a man, behold, they saw a marauding band; and they cast the man into the grave of Elisha. And when the man touched the bones of Elisha he revived and stood up on his feet." Some Roman Catholics argue that this verse supports their view regarding the veneration of relics.[7]

Response: There is virtually no mention of venerating Elisha's bones in this verse. This verse simply recounts a mighty and unusual miracle that served to confirm Elisha's earlier promise to Joash of victory over Aram. This miracle took place not because Elisha's bones possessed some mysterious intrinsic power but because God Himself chose to bring about this miracle in a very unusual way. But simply because God did this miracle through Elisha's bones does not mean those bones are to be venerated.

If that were true, this would mean that *any* means God used to bring about a miracle should be venerated, including such things as the mud Jesus used to heal the blind man (John 9:6-15), and the brazen serpent in the wilderness

(Numbers 21). A look at the Old Testament, however, reveals that God Himself condemned the use of the brazen serpent for idolatrous purposes: He "broke in pieces the bronze serpent that Moses had made" (2 Kings 18:4).[8] Idolatry (and veneration) in any form is condemned.

Acts 19:12—Support for Venerating Religious Relics?

The Roman Catholic View: In Acts 19:12 we read that "handkerchiefs or aprons were even carried from [the apostle Paul's] body to the sick, and the diseases left them and the evil spirits went out" (insert added). Some Roman Catholic authorities believe this lends credence to the veneration of relics.[9]

Response: This is reading more into the text than is warranted. First of all, Paul was an apostle, and as such Paul was given the signs of an apostle to confirm God's special revelation through him (2 Corinthians 12:12). Today these signs are no longer with us (see Hebrews 2:3,4).[10]

Further, Acts 19:12 is *descriptive*, not *prescriptive*. The verse simply describes what happened on this one occasion. It does not say that this would happen in future generations, nor does it indicate that relics are to be venerated. The New Testament never affirms that objects used in the performing of miracles are to be venerated. If this weren't the case, we would have to venerate the mud Christ used in healing the blind man's eyes.

Most important, God Himself forbade anything that reeks of idolatry in the Old Testament (see Exodus 20:4,5). When any object that was used by God to do a miracle was venerated, it was considered idolatry (see 2 Kings 18:4).

Appendix D

Understanding Sanctification

The word *sanctification* is rooted in the Greek word *hagiasmos*, which carries the idea "to set apart." Based on its etymology, the word indicates a twofold separation: 1) separation from sin, from the world and its allurements, from the ways of ungodliness, and 2) separation to a life of obedience to God, to fellowship with Him, to devotion to His glory.

Theologians who have carefully examined all the Scripture passages that deal with the issue of sanctification have concluded that there are three different aspects we need to be aware of. The first of these is *positional sanctification,* which (like justification) becomes a reality for the believing sinner from the moment of his conversion (1 Corinthians 6:11; Hebrews 10:10,14,29). The believer is "positionally set apart" from sin and unto God. This position bears no relationship to the believer's daily life. Positional sanctification "is as complete for the weakest saint as it is for the strongest. It depends only on his union and position in Christ."[1] The believer, in God's eyes, is a saint (Romans 1:7; 1 Corinthians 1:2; 2 Corinthians 1:1; Ephesians 1:1).

Second, there is *progressive* or *experiential sanctification,* which has to do with the believer's daily growth in grace, "becoming in practice more and more set apart for God's use."[2] This comes about by yieldedness to God and by separation from sin (1 Peter 1:16). "This experiential sanctification grows as the believer dedicates his life to God (Romans 6:13; 12:1,2) and is nourished by the Word of God

(Psalm 119:9-16)."[3] The believer's "condition" should ideally move closer (in a qualitative sense) to his "position," although sinless perfection will never be reached by mortals. In reality, there may be some fluctuations ("ups" and "downs") in the life of the believer in regard to experiential sanctification.

Third, there is *ultimate sanctification*, which is attained only when we are fully and completely set apart from sin and unto God in heaven (following death). Believers will be "like Him" (1 John 3:2), and conformed to His image (Romans 8:29). The church will be presented "faultless" before the presence of His glory (1 Corinthians 1:8). His bride will be free from every "spot and wrinkle" (Ephesians 5:27). Believers will be totally set apart unto Him.

Our primary concern in this book has to do with the second aspect above—*experiential sanctification*—and how it relates to justification. As noted earlier in the book, Roman Catholicism confuses and merges justification and sanctification. Catholics believe that a person's increasing level of righteousness (sanctification) eventually enables him or her to gain final justification. The goal of the individual Roman Catholic is to continue to cooperate with God's grace and grow in sanctification (righteousness) and good works, and participate in the various Roman Catholic sacraments, with a view to attaining final justification before God. What all this means is that in Roman Catholicism, *good works precede final justification.* Justification is conditioned upon good works.

From a biblical perspective, however, justification is a singular and instantaneous event in which God declares the believing sinner to be righteous. Justification viewed in this way is a judicial term in which God makes a *legal declaration.* It is not based on performance or good works. It involves God's pardoning of sinners and restoring them to a state of righteousness. This declaration of righteousness takes place the moment a person trusts in Christ for salvation

(Romans 3:25,28,30; 8:33,34; Galatians 4:21–5:12; 1 John 1:7–2:2).

Sanctification (or, to be more specific, *experiential sanctification*) follows or comes after justification. That is, once a person trusts in Christ and becomes instantaneously justified (declared righteous), a lifelong process of transformation begins in which the justified sinner becomes more and more holy as a result of the continuous ministry of the Holy Spirit. This work of the Holy Spirit enables the justified sinner to increasingly die unto sin and live unto righteousness.

Experiential sanctification is thus seen to be entirely different from justification. Justification is an instantaneous act that occurs in a moment in time, whereas experiential sanctification is a progressive work. Justification involves a change in the sinner's relationship to the justice of God, whereas experiential sanctification involves a change in the sinner's character. Justification involves one's legal standing, whereas experiential sanctification involves one's internal condition. Justification is an objective reality, whereas experiential sanctification involves subjective growth. Justification is complete and is the same in all believers, whereas experiential sanctification is progressive and is more complete in some people than in others.[4] Justification is entirely God's work, whereas experiential sanctification involves our cooperation. It is critically important that these two not be confused.

Notes

Evangelizing Catholics

1. Edythe Draper, *Bible Illustrations*, electronic media, Parsons Technology.
2. These dates are based on Paul Enns, *The Moody Handbook of Theology* (Chicago: Moody Press, 1989), p. 404.
3. *Catechism of the Catholic Church* (New York: Doubleday, 1994), p. 55.
4. Cited in Karl Rahner, ed., *Teaching of the Catholic Church* (Staten Island, NY: Alba, 1967), p. 203.
5. Enns, *Moody Handbook*, p. 529.
6. Rahner, *Teaching of the Catholic Church*, p. 207.
7. See "On the Mystical Body of Christ and Our Union in It with Christ," encyclical letter by Pope Pius XII, *Mystici Corporis*, First Part: The Church Is the Mystical Body of Christ. See also "That They May Be One," encyclical of Pope John Paul II, *Ut Unum Sint*, The Way of Ecumenism: The Way of the Church. Electronic media, Harmony Media Inc.
8. Austin Flannery, "The People of God," in *Documents of Vatican II: The Conciliar and Post-Conciliar Documents* (Grand Rapids: Eerdmans, 1992), vol. 1, pp. 267-68.
9. Robert Broderick, *The Catholic Concise Encyclopedia* (St. Paul, MN: Simon and Schuster, 1956), p. 170.
10. James McCarthy, *Conversations with Catholics* (Eugene, OR: Harvest House Publishers, 1997), p. 76.
11. Kenneth R. Samples, "What Think Ye of Rome?—An Evangelical Appraisal of Contemporary Catholicism (Part One)," *Christian Research Journal*, Winter 1993, electronic on-line version.
12. Jerry Bridges, *The Discipline of Grace: Study Guide* (Colorado Springs, CO: NavPress, 1994), p. 7.
13. Ibid., p. 8.
14. "Evangelicals and Catholics Together: The Christian Mission in the Third Millennium," published by Truth Ministries, P.O. Box 504M, Bay Shore, NY 11706, vol. 1, no. 10, April 1994, pp. 26-28.
15. Ibid., p. 12.
16. Ibid., p. 4.
17. Samples, "What Think Ye of Rome?"
18. Personal conversation with Ken Samples. See Kenneth R. Samples, "What Think Ye of Rome?—An Evangelical Appraisal of Contemporary Catholicism (Part Two)," *Christian Research Journal*, Spring 1993, on-line electronic version.
19. Harold O. J. Brown, *Heresies* (Garden City, NY: Doubleday & Company, 1984), p. 310.
20. *Catechism of the Catholic Church*, pp. 3-6.

Chapter 1—Dialoguing with Roman Catholics

1. James McCarthy, *Conversations with Catholics* (Eugene, OR: Harvest House Publishers, 1997), p. 63.
2. Ibid., p. 65.

Chapter 2—The Apocrypha

1. Cited in *Bible Illustrations*, (Grand Rapids, MI: Baker Book House), electronic media.
2. See Ron Rhodes, *The Complete Book of Bible Answers* (Eugene, OR: Harvest House Publishers, 1997), pp. 30-32.
3. Wayne Grudem, *Systematic Theology: An Introduction to Biblical Doctrine* (Grand Rapids, MI: Zondervan Publishing House, 1994), p. 59.
4. Norman Geisler and Ralph MacKenzie, *Roman Catholics and Evangelicals: Agreements and Differences* (Grand Rapids, MI: Baker Book House, 1995), pp. 159-60.
5. Documents from the Council of Trent.
6. Geisler and MacKenzie, *Roman Catholics and Evangelicals*, p. 162.
7. W. Graham Scroggie, *A Guide to the Gospels* (Old Tappan, NJ: Revell, n.d.), p. 267.
8. Geisler and MacKenzie, *Roman Catholics and Evangelicals,* p. 162.
9. Eusebius, *Ecclesiastical History*, 4.26.14.
10. Athanasius, *Letter 39*, in *Nicene and Post Nicene Fathers*, Philip Schaff and Henry Wace, eds. (Grand Rapids, MI: Eerdmans, 1978), vol. 4: *Athanasius*, pp. 551-52.
11. Cited in Everett F. Harrison, "The Importance of the Septuagint for Biblical Studies," *Bibliotheca Sacra*, electronic media, Logos Software.
12. John Ankerberg and John Weldon, *Protestants and Catholics: Do They Now Agree?* (Eugene, OR: Harvest House Publishers, 1995), p. 33.
13. Josh McDowell, *Answers to Tough Questions* (Wheaton, IL: Tyndale House Publishers, 1988), p. 48.
14. Nelson Glueck, *Rivers in the Desert* (Philadelphia: Jewish Publications Society of America, 1969), p. 31.
15. Grudem, *Systematic Theology*, p. 59.
16. Geisler and MacKenzie, *Roman Catholics and Evangelicals*, p. 162.
17. This is strongly argued in Samuel J. Schultz, "Augustine and the Old Testament Canon," *Bibliotheca Sacra*, electronic media, Logos Software.

18. Geisler and MacKenzie, *Roman Catholics and Evangelicals*, p. 163.
19. Norman Geisler, class notes for Bibliology, Dallas Theological Seminary.
20. Based on Geisler and MacKenzie, *Roman Catholics and Evangelicals*, p. 168.
21. Ibid., p. 173.
22. Robert Jamieson, A. R. Fausset, and David Brown, *Commentary: Critical and Explanatory, on the Whole Bible*, electronic media, Accordance Software.

Chapter 3—Sola Scriptura Versus Tradition—Part 1

1. John Calvin, cited in Chuck Colson, *Against the Night: Living in the New Dark Ages* (Ann Arbor, MI: Servant Publications, 1989), p. 152.
2. Chrysostom, cited in John Blanchard, *More Gathered Gold* (Hertfordshire, England: Evangelical Press, 1986), p. 31.
3. Issued by the Sacred Congregation for Catholic Education, *Ratio Fundamentalis Institutionis Sacerdotalis XIV*. "The Type of Teaching to be Given," electronic media, Harmony Media Inc.
4. Henry Denzinger, *Sources of Catholic Dogma* (St. Louis: Herder Book Co., 1957), pp. 11-12.
5. *Catechism of the Catholic Church* (New York: Doubleday, 1994), p. 31.
6. *Encyclopedic Dictionary of the Bible*, electronic media, Harmony Media Inc.
7. *The Essential Catholic Handbook: A Summary of Beliefs, Practices, and Prayers* (Liguori, MO: Liguori, 1997), p. 24.
8. *Catechism of the Catholic Church*, p. 31.
9. James R. White, *The Roman Catholic Controversy* (Minneapolis: Bethany House Publishers, 1996), p. 79.
10. Peter Kreeft, *Fundamentals of the Faith* (San Francisco: Ignatius Press, 1988), pp. 274-75.
11. John O'Brien, *Finding Christ's Church*, cited in White, *Roman Catholic Controversy*, p. 92.
12. Loraine Boettner, *Roman Catholicism* (Philadelphia: The Presbyterian and Reformed Publishing Company, 1962), pp. 75-76.
13. B. B. Warfield, *The Inspiration and Authority of the Bible* (Philadelphia: Presbyterian and Reformed, 1948), p. 173.
14. Norman Geisler and William Nix, *A General Introduction to the Bible* (Chicago: Moody Press, 1978), p. 55.
15. Ibid., p. 28.
16. Charles Ryrie, *Bibliotheca Sacra*, January–March 1979, electronic on-line version downloaded from the Dallas Theological Seminary web site.
17. Robert P. Lightner, *Evangelical Theology: A Survey and Review* (Grand Rapids: Baker Book House, 1986), p. 13.
18. *Explaining Inerrancy: A Commentary* (Oakland, CA: International Council on Biblical Inerrancy, 1980), pp. 17-18.
19. I am indebted to Geisler and Nix, *General Introduction*, p. 50, for this chart.
20. James McCarthy, *Conversations with Catholics* (Eugene, OR: Harvest House Publishers, 1997), p. 135.
21. Norman Geisler and Ralph MacKenzie, *Roman Catholics and Evangelicals: Agreements and Differences* (Grand Rapids: Baker Book House, 1995), p. 173.
22. F. F. Bruce, *The Books and the Parchments* (London: Pickering Inglis, 1950), p. 111.
23. Geisler and MacKenzie, *Roman Catholics and Evangelicals*, p. 184.
24. *The Bible Knowledge Commentary*, New Testament, John F. Walvoord and Roy B. Zuck, eds. (Wheaton, IL: Victor Books, 1983), p. 757.
25. Norman L. Geisler and Ralph E. MacKenzie, "What Think Ye of Rome?—Part Three: The Catholic-Protestant Debate on Biblical Authority," *Christian Research Journal*, Spring/Summer 1994, electronic on-line version.
26. Cited in Geisler and MacKenzie, "What Think Ye of Rome?"
27. White, *Roman Catholic Controversy*, p. 71.
28. Geisler and MacKenzie, *Roman Catholics and Evangelicals*, p. 196.
29. Ibid., p. 193.

Chapter 4—Sola Scriptura Versus Tradition—Part 2

1. J. I. Packer, *Knowing Christianity* (Wheaton, IL: Harold Shaw Publishers, 1995), p. 16.
2. David Palm, "Oral Tradition in the New Testament," *This Rock*, May 1995, on-line electronic version.
3. J. Dwight Pentecost, *The Words and Works of Jesus Christ* (Grand Rapids: Zondervan Publishing House, 1982), pp. 43-44.
4. Kenneth L. Barker and John Kohlenberger III, eds., *Zondervan NIV Bible Commentary* (Grand Rapids: Zondervan Publishing House, 1994), p. 16. See also Homer A. Kent, Jr., "A Study in Hermeneutics: Matthew's Use of the Old Testament," *Bibliotheca Sacra*, electronic media, Logos Software.
5. Kent, "A Study in Hermeneutics."
6. Norman Geisler and Thomas Howe, *When Critics Ask* (Wheaton, IL: Victor Books, 1992), p. 328.
7. See James White, "A Response to David Palm's Article on Oral Tradition from *This Rock* magazine, May 1995," downloaded from Alpha and Omega Ministry web site.
8. Kent, "A Study in Hermeneutics."
9. Craig S. Keener, *The IVP Bible Background Commentary* (Downers Grove, IL: InterVarsity Press, 1993), electronic media, Logos Software.

10. William Barclay, *Commentaries on the New Testament*, electronic media, Bible Explorer software.

11. Keener, *IVP Bible Background Commentary.*

12. Palm, *"Oral Tradition in the New Testament."*

13. Ibid.

14. White, *"Response to David Palm's Article."*

15. *The Wycliffe Encyclopedia*, electronic media, Word Processor software.

16. Merrill F. Unger, *Unger's Bible Dictionary*, "Synagogue," in PC Study Bible software.

17. James R. White, *The Roman Catholic Controversy* (Minneapolis: Bethany House Publishers, 1996), p. 100.

18. *The Church of God*, Part I—"The Church in Christian Experience and Reflection," chapter 7; The Ecclesiology of Moehler III: Spiritual Unity; electronic media, Harmony Media Inc. See also White, *The Roman Catholic Controversy*, p. 57.

19. *The Bible Knowledge Commentary: New Testament*, John F. Walvoord and Roy Zuck, eds., electronic media, Parsons Technology.

20. Karl Keating, *Catholicism and Fundamentalism: The Attack on "Romanism" by "Bible Christians"* (San Francisco: Ignatius Press, 1988), p. 136.

21. Palm, "Oral Tradition in the New Testament."

22. Robert Jamieson, A. R. Fausset, and David Brown, *Commentary: Critical and Explanatory, on the Whole Bible*, electronic media, Accordance Software.

23. "Apostolic Tradition," Catholic Answers Home Page, copyright 1996.

24. Archibald Robertson and Alfred Plummer, *A Critical and Exegetical Commentary on the First Epistle of St. Paul to the Corinthians* (Edinburgh: T. & T. Clark, 1978), p. 228.

25. See *Christian Moral Principles*, chapter 33: "Eucharistic Life as Fulfillment in the Lord Jesus," electronic media, Harmony Media Inc.

26. Ibid., chapter 35: "The Truth of Christ Lives in His Church."

27. *Dogmatic Constitution on Divine Revelation*, Dei Verbum Solemnly Promulgated by His Holiness Pope Paul VI on November 18, 1965, electronic media, Harmony Media Inc.

28. James McCarthy, *Conversations with Catholics* (Eugene, OR: Harvest House Publishers, 1997), pp. 132-33.

29. Jamieson, Fausset, and Brown, *Commentary*, inserts added.

30. "Apostolic Tradition," Catholic Answers Home Page, copyright 1996.

31. Ludwig Ott, *Fundamentals of Catholic Dogma* (Rockford, IL: Tan Books and Publishers, 1960), p. 7.

32. *Encyclopedic Dictionary of the Bible*, electronic media, Harmony Media Inc.

33. Palm, "Oral Tradition in the New Testament."

34. See *International Standard Bible Encyclopedia*, electronic media, BibleWorks software.

35. *This Rock*, August 1992, p. 23.

Chapter 5—Papal Infallibility—Part 1

1. John Powell, *Bible Illustrations*, electronic media, Parsons Technology.

2. *The Church of God*, Part I — "The Church in Christian Experience and Reflection," Chapter 7, electronic media, Harmony Media Inc.

3. E. Schuyler English, "Was St. Peter Ever in Rome?" *Bibliotheca Sacra*, CD Version, Logos Software.

4. *Catechism of the Catholic Church* (New York: Doubleday, 1994), p. 254.

5. James McCarthy, *Conversations with Catholics* (Eugene, OR: Harvest House Publishers, 1997), p. 78.

6. *Catechism of the Catholic Church*, p. 249.

7. *The Essential Catholic Handbook: A Summary of Beliefs, Practices, and Prayers* (Liguori, MO: Liguori, 1997), p. 147.

8. McCarthy, *Conversations with Catholics,* p. 117.

9. *The Essential Catholic Handbook*, p. 23.

10. Avery Dulles, "Infallibility: The Terminology," in *Teaching Authority and Infallibility in the Church*, Paul C. Empie, ed. (Minneapolis: Augsburg, 1979), p. 71.

11. John A. Hardon, *Pocket Catholic Dictionary* (New York: Image Books, 1985), p. 194.

12. Henry Denzinger, *The Sources of Catholic Dogma*, electronic media, Harmony Media Inc. See also *Catechism of the Catholic Church*, p. 256.

13. Hardon, *Pocket Catholic Dictionary*, p. 195.

14. Ibid.

15. *The Catholic Catechism*, Part One: "Doctrines of the Faith," electronic media, Harmony Media Inc.

16. *The Essential Catholic Handbook*, pp. 132-33.

17. Ibid.

18. *Catechism of the Catholic Church*, p. 30.

19. Ibid.

20. Ibid., p. 32.
21. Matthias Premm, *Dogmatic Theology for the Laity* (Rockford, IL: Tan Books, 1967), p. 29.
22. James R. White, *The Roman Catholic Controversy* (Minneapolis: Bethany House Publishers, 1996), p. 109.
23. Ibid., p. 110.
24. Ibid.
25. See Norman Geisler and Ralph MacKenzie, *Roman Catholics and Evangelicals: Agreements and Differences* (Grand Rapids: Baker Book House, 1995), p. 218.
26. See *Christian Moral Principles*, chapter 36: "A Critical Examination of Radical Theological Dissent—Some Examples of Alleged Errors in Catholic Teaching," electronic media, Harmony Media Inc.
27. Ibid. See also Geisler and MacKenzie, *Roman Catholics and Evangelicals*, p. 219.
28. *Oxford Dictionary of the Christian Church* (Oxford: Oxford University Press, 1983), p. 66.
29. Geisler and MacKenzie, *Roman Catholics and Evangelicals*, p. 217.
30. Norman L. Geisler and Ralph E. MacKenzie, "What Think Ye of Rome?—Part Four: The Catholic-Protestant Debate on Papal Infallibility," *Christian Research Journal*, Fall 1994, on-line electronic version.
31. Ibid.
32. Norman Geisler and Ron Rhodes, *When Cultists Ask* (Grand Rapids: Baker Book House, 1998), p. 115.
33. Michael Green, *The Second Epistle of Peter and the Epistle of Jude* (Grand Rapids: Eerdmans, 1968), p. 159.
34. Walter Bauer, *A Greek-English Lexicon of the New Testament and Other Early Christian Literature*, William F. Arndt and F. Wilbur Gingrich, trans. (Chicago: University of Chicago Press, 1957), p. 669.
35. Geisler and MacKenzie, *Roman Catholics and Evangelicals*, p. 178.
36. Ibid., p. 215.
37. James McCarthy, *The Gospel According to Rome* (Eugene, OR: Harvest House Publishers, 1995), chapter 11.

Chapter 6—Papal Infallibility—Part 2

1. Martin Luther, *Select Works of Martin Luther*, electronic media, Accordance Bible software.
2. John A. Hardon, *Pocket Catholic Dictionary* (New York: Image Books, 1985), pp. 325-26.
3. William L. Lane, *The Gospel of Mark: The New International Commentary on the New Testament* (Grand Rapids: Eerdmans, 1974), p. 134.
4. Hardon, *Pocket Catholic Dictionary*, pp. 325-26.
5. James White argues this quite convincingly in his book, *The Roman Catholic Controversy* (Minneapolis: Bethany House Publishers, 1996), p. 117.
6. "Pope," *The Catholic Encyclopedia* (New York: Robert Appleton Co., 1912), vol. XII, p. 261.
7. Henry Denzinger, *The Sources of Catholic Dogma*, "Documents of the Roman Pontiffs and of the Councils," electronic media, Harmony Media Inc.
8. Craig S. Keener, *The IVP Bible Background Commentary* (Downers Grove, IL: InterVarsity Press, 1993), electronic media, Logos Software.
9. *Bible Knowledge Commentary*, John F. Walvoord and Roy Zuck, eds., electronic media, Parson's Technology.
10. *Living a Christian Life*, chapter 3: "Charity, the Eucharist and Church Membership," electronic media, Harmony Media Inc.
11. *Encyclopedic Dictionary of the Bible*, electronic media, Harmony Media Inc., insert added.
12. Kenneth Scott Latourette, *A History of Christianity* (New York: Harper, 1953), pp. 223-24.
13. Vatican II, *Dogmatic Constitution on the Church*, no. 22.
14. Ludwig Ott, *Fundamentals of Catholic Dogma* (Rockford, IL: Tan Books and Publishers, 1960), p. 418.
15. Robert Gromacki, "Was the Church Established by Peter?" *The Baptist Bulletin*, April 1964, p. 11, emphasis added.
16. Wayne Grudem, *Systematic Theology: An Introduction to Biblical Doctrine* (Grand Rapids: Zondervan Publishing House, 1994), pp. 889-91.
17. Robert Jamieson, A. R. Fausset, and David Brown, *Commentary: Critical and Explanatory, on the Whole Bible*, electronic media, Accordance Software.
18. John Paul II, *Crossing the Threshold of Hope* (New York: Knopf, 1995), p. 6.
19. Albert Barnes, "Matthew," in *Notes on the New Testament* (Grand Rapids: Baker Book House, 1996), p. 242.
20. Denzinger, *The Sources of Catholic Dogma*, electronic media, Harmony Media Inc.
21. *From Apostles to Orders—Shepherds for the Flock*, electronic media, Harmony Media Inc.
22. Denzinger, *The Sources of Catholic Dogma*, electronic media, Harmony Media Inc.
23. A. Tanquerey, *A Manual of Dogmatic Theology* (New York: Desclee Company, 1959), vol. 1, p. 120.
24. Norman Geisler and Ron Rhodes, *When Cultists Ask* (Grand Rapids, MI: Baker Book House, 1998), p. 192.
25. Ott, *Fundamentals of Catholic Dogma*, p. 417.
26. Ibid., p. 419.
27. Geisler and Rhodes, *When Cultists Ask*, p. 191.
28. E. Schuyler English, "Was St. Peter Ever in Rome?" *Bibliotheca Sacra*, CD version, Logos Software.
29. Ibid.
30. Ibid.

31. See *Catechism of the Catholic Church* (New York: Doubleday, 1994), pp. 248-49.

Chapter 7—Forensic Justification—Part 1

1. Martin Luther; cited in *Draper's Book of Quotations for the Christian World* (Grand Rapids: Baker Book House, 1992), p. 329.
2. Council of Trent, session 6, "Decree on Justification," chapter 6.
3. *Encyclopedic Dictionary of the Bible*, electronic media, Harmony Media Inc.
4. Henry Denzinger, *Sources of Catholic Dogma* (St. Louis: Herder Book Co., 1957), p. 264.
5. *Catechism of the Catholic Church* (New York: Doubleday, 1994), p. 542.
6. See James McCarthy, *Conversations with Catholics* (Eugene, OR: Harvest House Publishers, 1997), p. 46.
7. Council of Trent, session 6, chapter 14.
8. John Paul II, *Crossing the Threshold of Hope* (New York: Knopf, 1994), p. 194.
9. *The Canons and Decrees of the Council of Trent*, H. J. Schroeder, trans. (Rockford, IL: Tan Books, 1978), p. 45, emphasis added.
10. Ibid., p. 43.
11. Ibid., p. 37.
12. Ibid., p. 44.
13. Ludwig Ott, *Fundamentals of Catholic Dogma* (Rockford, IL: Tan Books and Publishers, 1960), p. 262.
14. *Catholic Church History Theological Humanism* (1517–1648), "The Catholic Reformation (1521-85)," electronic media, Harmony Media Inc.
15. The Council of Trent; cited in Wayne Grudem, *Systematic Theology: An Introduction to Biblical Doctrine* (Grand Rapids: Zondervan Publishing House, 1994), p. 728.
16. See James McCarthy, *The Gospel According to Rome* (Eugene, OR: Harvest House Publishers, 1995), p. 22.
17. Ibid., p. 23.
18. Ibid., pp. 26-27.

Chapter 8—Forensic Justification—Part 2

1. Martin Luther, cited in George Sweeting, *Great Quotes and Illustrations* (Waco, TX: Word Books, 1985), p. 158.
2. Wayne Grudem, *Systematic Theology: An Introduction to Biblical Doctrine* (Grand Rapids: Zondervan Publishing House, 1994), p. 723.
3. Martin Luther, cited in J. I. Packer, *Knowing Christianity* (Wheaton, IL: Harold Shaw Publishers, 1995), p. 94.
4. *Bible Illustrations*, electronic media, Hypercard stack, Baker Book House.
5. Norman Geisler and Ralph MacKenzie, *Roman Catholics and Evangelicals: Agreements and Differences* (Grand Rapids: Baker Book House, 1995), p. 477.
6. Cardinal John O'Connor, *New York Times*, February 1, 1990, B4, cited in James McCarthy, *Conversations with Catholics* (Eugene, OR: Harvest House Publishers, 1997), p. 41.

Chapter 9—Forensic Justification—Part 3

1. John Bunyan, cited in *Draper's Book of Quotations for the Christian World* (Grand Rapids: Baker Book House, 1992), p. 540.
2. *Encyclopedic Dictionary of the Bible*, electronic media, Harmony Media Inc.
3. *The Bible Knowledge Commentary*, New Testament, John F. Walvoord and Roy B. Zuck, eds. (Wheaton, IL: Victor Books, 1989), p. 825.
4. Ludwig Ott, *Fundamentals of Catholic Dogma* (Rockford, IL: Tan Books and Publishers, 1960), p. 264.
5. James McCarthy, *The Gospel According to Rome* (Eugene, OR: Harvest House Publishers, 1995), p. 50.
6. Wayne Grudem, *Systematic Theology: An Introduction to Biblical Doctrine* (Grand Rapids: Zondervan Publishing House, 1994), pp. 731-32.
7. Thanks to Norman Geisler for these insights. See Norman Geisler and Ron Rhodes, *When Cultists Ask* (Grand Rapids: Baker Book House, 1998), p. 289.
8. Ott, *Fundamentals of Catholic Dogma*, p. 262. See also Henry Denzinger, *The Sources of Catholic Dogma*, "Documents of the Roman Pontiffs and of the Councils," electronic media, Harmony Media Inc.
9. *Christian Moral Principles*, "Penance, Anointing, and the Life of Self-Denial," electronic media, Harmony Media Inc.
10. *The Ryrie Study Bible* (Chicago: Moody Press, 1986), p. 1622.
11. *The Wycliffe Bible Commentary*, Everett F. Harrison and Charles F. Pfeiffer, eds. (Chicago: Moody Press, 1974), p. 1325.
12. *The NIV Study Bible*, Kenneth Barker, ed. (Grand Rapids: Zondervan Publishing House, 1985), p. 1806.
13. H. C. G. Moule, *Philippians* (Grand Rapids: Kregel Publications, 1977), p. 72.
14. *The Ryrie Study Bible*, p. 1614.
15. *Christian Moral Principles*, "The Truth of Christ Lives in His Church," electronic media, Harmony Media Inc.

16. *Living a Christian Life,* "Life, Health, and Bodily Inviolability," electronic media, Harmony Media Inc.
17. Geisler and Rhodes, *When Cultists Ask,* p. 151.
18. Ibid.
19. *Encyclopedic Dictionary of the Bible,* electronic media, Harmony Media Inc.
20. Ott, *Fundamentals of Catholic* Dogma, p. 265.
21. Matthias Premm, *Dogmatic Theology for the Laity* (Rockford, IL: Tan Books, 1967), p. 262.
22. *Encyclopedic Dictionary of the Bible,* electronic media, Harmony Media Inc. See also Ott, *Fundamentals of Catholic Dogma,* p. 265.
23. Ibid., p. 317.
24. Geisler and Rhodes, *When Cultists Ask,* p. 38.
25. Ott, *Fundamentals of Catholic Dogma,* p. 355.
26. Ibid. See also *Directory on Ecumenism,* issued by the Secretariat for Promoting Christian Unity, *Ad Totam Ecclesiam II,* electronic media, Harmony Media Inc.
27. *Encyclopedic Dictionary of the Bible,* electronic media, Harmony Media Inc.
28. *The Sacraments and Their Celebration,* "Baptism," electronic media, Harmony Media Inc.
29. *Directory on Ecumenism,* electronic media, Harmony Media Inc.
30. *Encyclopedic Dictionary of the Bible,* electronic media, Harmony Media Inc.

Chapter 10—Sacramentalism—Part 1

1. Samuel Shoemaker, cited in *Draper's Book of Quotations for the Christian World* (Grand Rapids: Baker Book House, 1992), p. 526.
2. Cited by Charles C. Ryrie, *A Survey of Bible Doctrine,* electronic media, Parson's Technology.
3. *Catechism of the Catholic Church* (New York: Doubleday, 1994), p. 292.
4. Henry J. Schroeder, *Canons of the Council of Trent* (Rockford, IL: Tan Books and Publishers, 1978), p. 52, canon 4.
5. *The Essential Catholic Handbook: A Summary of Beliefs, Practices, and Prayers* (Liguori, MO: Liguori, 1997), p. 184.
6. Ludwig Ott, *Fundamentals of Catholic Dogma* (Rockford, IL: Tan Books and Publishers, 1960), p. 339.
7. *The Essential Catholic Handbook,* p. 184.
8. John A. Hardon, *Pocket Catholic Dictionary* (New York: Image Books, 1985), pp. 138-39.
9. *The Sacraments and Their Celebration,* "The Sacraments," electronic media, Harmony Media Inc.
10. Council of Trent, session 22, "Teachings and Canons on the Most Holy Sacrifice of the Mass," canon 1.
11. Karl Keating, *Catholicism and Fundamentalism: The Attack on "Romanism" by "Bible Christians"* (San Francisco: Ignatius Press, 1988), p. 248.
12. Robert Broderick, *The Catholic Concise Encyclopedia* (Saint Paul, MN: Simon and Schuster, 1956), pp. 375-76.
13. Hardon, *Pocket Catholic Dictionary,* p. 248.
14. *Catechism of the Catholic Church,* p. 383.
15. Second Vatican Council, "Sacred Liturgy," "On Holy Communion and the Worship of the Eucharist Mystery Outside of Mass," no. 6.
16. Hardon, *Pocket Catholic Dictionary,* pp. 438-39.
17. Liturgy of the Eucharist, First Eucharistic Prayer, the Memorial Prayer.
18. *The Roman Catechism: The Catechism of the Council of Trent,* trans. John A. McHugh and Charles J. Callan, trans. (Rockford, IL: Tan Books and Publishers, 1982), p. 259.
19. *Catechism of the Catholic Church,* pp. 334, 336.
20. Henry Denzinger, *Sources of Catholic Dogma* (St. Louis: Herder Book Co., 1957), p. 268.
21. *Catechism of the Catholic Church,* p. 385.
22. Ibid., p. 332.
23. Broderick, *Catholic Concise Encyclopedia,* p. 402.
24. Karl Rahner, *Teaching of the Catholic Church* (Staten Island, NY: Alba, 1967), pp. 308-09.
25. Ibid., p. 273.
26. Hardon, *Pocket Catholic Dictionary,* p. 87.
27. *The Essential Catholic Handbook,* p. 34.
28. Ott, *Fundamentals of Catholic Dogma,* p. 450.
29. Hardon, *Pocket Catholic Dictionary,* p. 299.
30. *The Essential Catholic Handbook,* p. 187.
31. Ibid.
32. Ott, *Fundamentals of Catholic Dogma,* p. 460.
33. Rahner, *Teaching of the Catholic Church,* p. 354.
34. Ibid., p. 331.
35. Hardon, *Pocket Catholic Dictionary,* p. 22.

36. Harold O. J. Brown, *Heresies: The Image of Christ in the Mirror of Heresy and Orthodoxy from the Apostles to the Present* (Grand Rapids: Baker Book House, 1984), p. 229.

37. Millard Erickson, *Christian Theology* (Grand Rapids: Baker Book House, 1991), p. 1121.

38. Hardon, *Pocket Catholic Dictionary*, p. 468.

39. Wayne Grudem, *Systematic Theology: An Introduction to Biblical Doctrine* (Grand Rapids: Zondervan Publishing House, 1994), pp. 991-94.

Chapter 11—Sacramentalism—Part 2

1. Westminster Confession of Faith, electronic media, Accordance Software.

2. Ludwig Ott, *Fundamentals of Catholic Dogma* (Rockford, IL: Tan Books and Publishers, 1960), p. 374. See also *Living a Christian Life*, Chapter 3: "Charity, the Eucharist and Church Membership," electronic media, Harmony Media Inc.

3. Ibid.

4. Ibid.

5. Robert Jamieson, A. R. Fausset, and David Brown, *Commentary: Critical and Explanatory, on the Whole Bible*, electronic media, Accordance Software, emphasis added, insert added.

6. Norman Geisler and Ralph MacKenzie, *Roman Catholics and Evangelicals: Agreements and Differences* (Grand Rapids: Baker Book House, 1995), p. 262.

7. Ott, *Fundamentals of Catholic Dogma*, p. 375.

8. Ibid.

9. A. Tanquerey, *A Manual of Dogmatic Theology* (New York: Desclee Company, 1959), pp. 267-68.

10. Matthias Premm, *Dogmatic Theology for the Laity* (Rockford, IL: Tan Books and Publishers, 1967), p. 355.

11. Anthony T. Evans, *Biblical Theology and the Black Experience* (Dallas: Black Evangelistic Enterprise, 1977), p. 13.

12. Pope John Paul II, *Crossing the Threshold of Hope*; cited in James McCarthy, *Conversations with Catholics* (Eugene, OR: Harvest House Publishers, 1997), p. 106.

13. McCarthy, *Conversations with Catholics*, p. 109.

14. See Ott, *Fundamentals of Catholic Dogma*, p. 404. See also Denzinger, *The Sources of Catholic Dogma*, "Documents of the Roman Pontiffs and of the Councils," electronic media, Harmony Media Inc.

15. Jamieson, Fausset, and Brown, *Commentary*.

16. *Catechism of the Catholic Church* (New York: Doubleday, 1994), p. 371.

17. Ott, *Fundamentals of Catholic Dogma*, p. 403, insert added.

18. James McCarthy, *The Gospel According to Rome* (Eugene, OR: Harvest House Publishers, 1993), p. 157.

19. Ibid.

Chapter 12—Sin and the Sacrament of Penance

1. Jeremy Taylor, cited in *Draper's Book of Quotations for the Christian World* (Grand Rapids: Baker Book House, 1992), p. 568.

2. *Encyclopedic Dictionary of the Bible,* electronic media, Harmony Media Inc.

3. *The Essential Catholic Handbook: A Summary of Beliefs, Practices, and Prayers* (Liguori, MO: Liguori, 1997), p. 30.

4. Matthias Premm, *Dogmatic Theology for the Laity* (Rockford, IL: Tan Books, 1967), p. 374.

5. *The Essential Catholic Handbook*, p. 30.

6. Premm, *Dogmatic Theology for the Laity*, p. 373.

7. *The Essential Catholic Handbook*, p. 30.

8. Robert Broderick, *The Catholic Concise Encyclopedia* (Saint Paul, MN: Simon and Schuster, 1956), p. 402.

9. *Catechism of the Catholic Church* (New York: Doubleday, 1994), p. 403.

10. Karl Rahner, *Teaching of the Catholic Church* (Staten Island, NY: Alba, 1967), pp. 307-08.

11. Act of Contrition, electronic media, Harmony Media Inc.

12. *The Essential Catholic Handbook*, pp. 52-53.

13. For more on this difficult issue, see my book *The Complete Book of Bible Answers* (Eugene, OR: Harvest House Publishers, 1997) pp. 170-72.

14. *Encyclopedic Dictionary of the Bible*, electronic media, Harmony Media Inc.

15. Ludwig Ott, *Fundamentals of Catholic Dogma* (Rockford, IL: Tan Books and Publishers, 1960), p. 434.

16. William L. Lane, *The Gospel According to Mark* (Grand Rapids: Eerdmans Publishing Company, 1974), p. 307.

17. Ott, *Fundamentals of Catholic Dogma*, p. 423.

18. Colin Kruse, "2 Corinthians," in *New Bible Commentary*, G. J. Wenham, J. A. Motyer, D. A. Carson, R. T. France, eds. (Downers Grove, IL: InterVarsity Press, 1994), p. 1188.

19. Murray H. Harris, *Zondervan NIV Bible Commentary*, Kenneth L. Barker and John Kohlenberger III, eds. (Grand Rapids: Zondervan Publishing House, 1994), p. 667.

20. *The International Bible Commentary*, F. F. Bruce, ed. (Grand Rapids: Zondervan Publishing House, 1979), p. 1393.

21. Ibid.
22. Henry Denzinger, *The Sources of Catholic Dogma*, "Documents of the Roman Pontiffs and of the Councils," electronic media, Harmony Media Inc.
23. *Strong's Greek Lexicon*, electronic media, BibleWorks software.
24. *Friberg's Greek Lexicon*, electronic media, BibleWorks software.
25. *Louw-Nida Greek Lexicon*, electronic media, BibleWorks software.
26. Denzinger, *Sources of Catholic Dogma*.
27. *Strong's Greek Lexicon*.

Chapter 13—Purgatory and Indulgences

1. The apostle Paul, Romans 8:1.
2. *Catholicism,* George Brantl, ed. (New York: Braziller, 1962), p. 232.
3. *Catechism of the Catholic Church* (New York: Doubleday, 1994), p. 291.
4. John A. Hardon, *Pocket Catholic Dictionary* (New York: Image Books, 1985), p. 93.
5. *The Essential Catholic Handbook: A Summary of Beliefs, Practices, and Prayers* (Liguori, MO: Liguori, 1997), pp. 42-43.
6. *Catechism of the Catholic Church*, p. 411.
7. See John Ankerberg and John Weldon, *Protestants and Catholics: Do They Now Agree?* (Eugene, OR: Harvest House Publishers, 1995), p. 104.
8. Anthony Hoekema, *The Four Major Cults* (Grand Rapids: Eerdmans, 1978), p. 354.
9. Ibid., p. 356.
10. Ibid.
11. Ibid.
12. Ankerberg and Weldon, *Protestants and Catholics*, p. 111.
13. Ludwig Ott, *Fundamentals of Catholic Dogma* (Rockford, IL: Tan Books and Publishers, 1960), p. 483.
14. Second Vatican Council, "Sacred Liturgy," "Apostolic Constitution on the Revision of Indulgences," no. 2.
15. *Catechism of the Catholic Church*, p. 291.
16. Wilbur Gingrich and William Arndt, *A Greek-English Lexicon of the New Testament and Other Early Christian Literature* (Chicago: The University of Chicago Press, 1957), p. 525.
17. Douglas Connelly, *What the Bible Really Says: After Life* (Downers Grove, IL: InterVarsity Press, 1995), p. 119.
18. Ibid., p. 118.
19. Merrill F. Unger, *Beyond the Crystal Ball* (Chicago, IL: Moody Press, 1973), p. 63.
20. Ott, *Fundamentals of Catholic Dogma*, p. 483.
21. *Catechism of the Catholic Church*, p. 291.
22. Ott, *Fundamentals of Catholic Dogma*, p. 484.
23. *Encyclopedic Dictionary of the Bible*, electronic media, Harmony Media Inc.
24. *Vine's Expository Dictionary of New Testament Words*, electronic media, the Word Processor software.
25. Ott, *Fundamentals of Catholic Dogma*, p. 484, insert added.
26. Ibid., p. 317.
27. Norman Geisler and Ron Rhodes, *When Cultists Ask* (Grand Rapids: Baker Book House, 1998), p. 246.
28. Ott, *Fundamentals of Catholic Dogma*, p. 317.

Chapter 14—The Exaltation of Mary—Part 1

1. Jesus Christ, John 14:6, emphasis added.
2. See *The Catholic Catechism*, Part Three: "Ritual and Worship," electronic media, Harmony Media Inc.
3. James White, *Mary—Another Redeemer?* (Minneapolis: Bethany House Publishers, 1998), p. 99.
4. Pope Pius IX, *Ineffabilis Deus*.
5. Pope Pius XII, *Mystici Corporis*.
6. White, *Mary—Another Redeemer?* pp. 36-37.
7. Ludwig Ott, *Fundamentals of Catholic Dogma* (Rockford, IL: Tan Books and Publishers, 1960), p. 205.
8. *Catechism of the Catholic Church* (New York: Doubleday, 1994), p. 140.
9. John A. Hardon, *Pocket Catholic Dictionary* (New York: Image Books, 1985), p. 246.
10. See James McCarthy, *The Gospel According to Rome* (Eugene, OR: Harvest House Publishers, 1995), p. 192.
11. Hardon, *Pocket Catholic Dictionary*, p. 272.
12. Ibid.
13. Ott, *Fundamentals of Catholic Dogma*, p. 197.
14. *Catechism of the Catholic Church*, p. 142.
15. Ibid., p. 138.
16. See *The Essential Catholic Handbook: A Summary of Beliefs, Practices, and Prayers* (Liguori, MO: Liguori, 1997), p. 168.
17. This episode is cited in John Ankerberg and John Weldon, *Protestants and Catholics: Do They Now Agree?* (Eugene, OR: Harvest House Publishers, 1995), p. 210.

18. Pope John Paul II, *Redemptoris Mater*, electronic media, Harmony Media Inc.
19. *Mary, Mother of Jesus*, electronic media, Harmony Media Inc.
20. Mark Miraville, *Mary: Co-redemptrix, Mediatrix, Advocate* (Santa Barbara, CA: Queenship Publishing Company, 1993), pp. xv-xvi. See also White, *Mary—Another Redeemer?* p. 118.
21. *The Immaculate Conception*, Apostolic Constitution, Pope Pius IX, *Ineffabilis Deus*, December 8, 1854, electronic media, Harmony Media Inc.
22. Ott, *Fundamentals of Catholic Dogma*, pp. 212-13.
23. Ibid., p. 213.
24. St. Alphonsus Ligouri, *The Glories of Mary* (Brooklyn, NY: The Redemptorist Fathers, 1931), p. 26, emphasis added. See also White, *Mary—Another Redeemer?* p. 61ff.
25. Ibid.
26. Karl Rahner, *The Teaching of the Catholic Church* (Staten Island, NY: Alba, 1967), p. 188.
27. *Catholic Church History*, electronic media, Harmony Media Inc.
28. Hardon, *Pocket Catholic Dictionary*, p. 32.
29. Ibid.

Chapter 15—The Exaltation of Mary—Part 2

1. The apostle Paul, 1 Timothy 2:5, emphasis added.
2. Kenneth R. Samples, "Apparitions of the Virgin Mary—A Protestant Look at a Catholic Phenomenon: Part Two," *Christian Research Journal*, Spring 1991, on-line electronic version.
3. *Bibliotheca Sacra*, (Dallas: Dallas Theological Seminary, 1955), electronic media, Logos Software, insert added.
4. James White, *Mary—Another Redeemer?* (Minneapolis: Bethany House Publishers, 1998), p. 25.
5. Elliot Miller and Ken Samples, *The Cult of the Virgin* (Grand Rapids: Baker Book House, 1992), p. 51.
6. Ibid., p. 23.
7. Paul Enns, *The Moody Handbook of Theology* (Chicago: Moody Press, 1989), p. 531.
8. See Robert Jamieson, A. R. Fausset, and David Brown, *Commentary: Critical and Explanatory, on the Whole Bible*, electronic media, Accordance Software. See also *The Ryrie Study Bible*, Charles Caldwell Ryrie, ed. (Chicago: Moody Press, 1994), p. 861.
9. Ludwig Ott, *Fundamentals of Catholic Dogma* (Rockford, IL: Tan Books and Publishers, 1960), p. 205.
10. J. Dwight Pentecost, *The Words and Works of Jesus Christ* (Grand Rapids: Zondervan Publishing House, 1982), pp. 43-44.
11. John A. Martin, "Luke," in *The Bible Knowledge Commentary*, New Testament, John F. Walvoord and Roy B. Zuck, eds. (Wheaton, IL: Victor Books, 1983), p. 205.
12. Stanley D. Toussaint, *Behold the King: A Study of Matthew* (Portland, OR: Multnomah Press, 1980), p. 42.
13. Robert L. Reymond, *Jesus, Divine Messiah: The New Testament Witness* (Phillipsburg, NJ: Presbyterian and Reformed Publishing Co., 1990), p. 129.
14. Ibid., p. 130.
15. Laurence E. Porter, "Luke," in *The International Bible Commentary*, F. F. Bruce, ed. (Grand Rapids: Zondervan Publishing House, 1986), p. 1188.
16. Martin, *Bible Knowledge Commentary*, p. 205.
17. Pentecost, *Words and Works of Jesus Christ*, p. 45.
18. Robert G. Gromacki, *The Virgin Birth: Doctrine of Deity* (Grand Rapids: Baker Book House, 1984), p. 73.
19. White, *Mary—Another Redeemer?* p. 59.
20. James R. White, *The Roman Catholic Controversy* (Minneapolis: Bethany House Publishers, 1996), p. 210.
21. See *Brown-Driver-Briggs Lexicon*, electronic media, BibleWorks software.
22. Ibid.
23. *Theological Wordbook of the Old Testament*, electronic media, Bible Explorer software.
24. Ott, *Fundamentals of Catholic Dogma*, p. 208.
25. S. Lewis Johnson, "Mary, the Saints, and Sacerdotalism, *Roman Catholicism: Evangelical Protestants Analyze What Divides and Unites Us* (Chicago: Moody Press, 1994), p. 124.
26. Giovanni Miegge, *The Virgin Mary: The Roman Catholic Marian Doctrine*, Waldo Smith, trans. (Philadelphia: Westminster Press, 1955), p. 207.
27. Miller and Samples, *Cult of the Virgin*, p. 130.
28. Samples, "Apparitions of the Virgin Mary—A Protestant Look at a Catholic Phenomenon," on-line electronic version.

Chapter 16—The Exaltation of Mary—Part 3

1. The apostle Peter, Acts 4:12, emphasis added, insert added.
2. Ludwig Ott, *Fundamentals of Catholic Dogma* (Rockford, IL: Tan Books and Publishers, 1960), p. 200.
3. Ibid.
4. Ibid., emphasis added.
5. *Catechism of the Catholic Church* (New York: Doubleday, 1994), p. 208.

6. I. Howard Marshall, *The Gospel of Luke: A Commentary on the Greek Text* (Grand Rapids: Eerdmans, 1978), p. 65.
7. Ott, *Fundamentals of Catholic Dogma*, p. 201.
8. James R. White, *The Roman Catholic Controversy* (Minneapolis, MN: Bethany House Publishers, 1996), p. 200.
9. Thomas Aquinas, *Summa Theologica*, 3, 27, 2.
10. Ott, *Fundamentals of Catholic Dogma*, p. 207.
11. Karl Keating, *Catholicism and Fundamentalism: The Attack on "Romanism" by "Bible Christians"* (San Francisco: Ignatius Press, 1988), p. 283.
12. James White, *Mary—Another Redeemer?* (Minneapolis: Bethany House Publishers, 1998), p. 31.
13. Ott, *Fundamentals of Catholic Dogma*, p. 207.
14. Pope John Paul II, *Mother of the Redeemer (Redemptoris Mater)*, electronic media, Harmony Media Inc.
15. Ott, *Fundamentals of Catholic Dogma*, p. 207.
16. Ibid., p. 215.
17. Albert Barnes, *Barnes Notes on the Old and New Testaments* (Grand Rapids: Baker Book House, 1977), "Luke," p. 7, insert added.
18. Ott, *Fundamentals of Catholic Dogma*, p. 215.
19. Ibid. See also *Catechism of the Catholic Church*, p. 275.
20. Barnes, "Luke," p. 10, insert added.
21. Ott, *Fundamentals of Catholic Dogma*, p. 215.
22. *Friberg's Greek Lexicon*, electronic media, BibleWorks software.
23. *Louw-Nida Greek Lexicon*, electronic media, BibleWorks software.

Chapter 17—The Exaltation of Mary—Part 4

1. The apostle John, Revelation 1:5,6, emphasis added.
2. James McCarthy, *The Gospel According to Rome* (Eugene, OR: Harvest House Publishers, 1993), pp. 208-09.
3. *Catechism of the Catholic Church* (New York: Doubleday, 1994), p. 176.
4. *Redemptoris Mater*, electronic media, Harmony Media Inc., emphasis added.
5. Robert P. Lightner, "Philippians," in *The Bible Knowledge Commentary*, New Testament. John F. Walvoord and Roy B. Zuck, eds. (Wheaton, IL: Victor Books, 1983), p. 654.
6. Ibid., p. 143.
7. Ibid., p. 654.
8. J. I. Packer, *Knowing God* (Downers Grove, IL: InterVarsity Press, 1979), p. 50.
9. Mark Miraville cited in James White, *Mary—Another Redeemer?* (Minneapolis: Bethany House Publishers, 1998), p. 139.
10. *Thayer's Greek Lexicon*, electronic media, BibleWorks software.
11. *Friberg's Greek Lexicon*, electronic media, BibleWorks software.
12. *Dogmatic Constitution of the Church*, electronic media, Harmony Media Inc. emphasis added.
13. Edgar J. Goodspeed, cited in Leon Morris: *The Gospel According to John* (Grand Rapids: Eerdmans, 1971), p. 181.
14. Robert Jamieson, A. R. Fausset, and David Brown, *Commentary: Critical and Explanatory, on the Whole Bible*, electronic media, Accordance Software.
15. Miraville, cited in White, *Mary—Another Redeemer?* p. 129.
16. Ludwig Ott, *Fundamentals of Catholic Dogma* (Rockford, IL: Tan Books and Publishers, 1960), p. 209.
17. Ibid.
18. Ibid., p. 208.
19. Ibid., p. 209.
20. Ibid., p. 71.
21. Ibid., p. 209.
22. John F. Walvoord, *The Prophecy Knowledge Handbook* (Wheaton, IL: Victor Books, 1997), electronic media, Logos Software.
23. Ott, *Fundamentals of Catholic Dogma*, p. 205.

Chapter 18—The Dos and Don'ts of Dialoguing with Catholics

1. George Sweeting, *Great Quotes and Illustrations* (Waco, TX: Word Books, 1985), p. 158.
2. James McCarthy, *Conversations with Catholics* (Eugene, OR: Harvest House Publishers, 1997), p. 81.

Appendix B

1. Henry Denzinger, *Sources of Catholic Dogma* (St. Louis: Herder Book Co., 1957), p. 423.
2. Ibid., p. 1647.
3. Vatican II, *Lumen Gentium*, p. 16.
4. Vatican II, *Declaration on the Relation of the Church to Non-Christian Religions*, no. 2.
5. Ibid., no. 3.

6. See Ron Rhodes, *Islam: What You Need to Know* (Quick-Reference Guide) (Eugene, OR: Harvest House Publishers, 2000).

7. John Blanchard, *Whatever Happened to Hell?* (Durham, England: Evangelical Press, 1993), p. 113.

Appendix C

1. Ludwig Ott, *Fundamentals of Catholic Dogma* (Rockford, IL: Tan Books and Publishers, 1960), p. 319.

2. Ibid.

3. Ibid.

4. Ibid.

5. Ibid., p. 320.

6. Norman Geisler and Ron Rhodes, *When Cultists Ask* (Grand Rapids: Baker Book House, 1997), p. 37.

7. Ott, *Fundamentals of Catholic Dogma*, p. 319.

8. Geisler and Rhodes, *When Cultists Ask*, p. 54.

9. Ott, *Fundamentals of Catholic Dogma*, p. 320.

10. Geisler and Rhodes, *When Cultists Ask*, p. 204.

Appendix D

1. Lewis Sperry Chafer, "Sanctification," in *Major Bible Themes*, John F. Walvoord, ed. (Grand Rapids: Zondervan Publishing House, 1975), p. 207.

2. Charles C. Ryrie, *The Ryrie Study Bible* (Chicago: Moody Press, 1978), p. 1734.

3. Paul Enns, *The Moody Handbook of Theology* (Chicago: Moody Press, 1989), p. 330.

4. Charles Hodge, *Systematic Theology*, 3 vols. (Grand Rapids: Eerdmans, 1986), p. 213.

Bibliography

Ankerberg, John, and John Weldon. *Protestants and Catholics: Do They Now Agree?* Eugene, OR: Harvest House Publishers, 1995.

——— . *The Facts on Roman Catholicism.* Eugene, OR: Harvest House Publishers, 1994.

Armstrong, John, ed. *Roman Catholicism: Evangelical Protestants Analyze What Divides and Unites Us.* Chicago, IL: Moody Press, 1994.

Arndt, William and Wilbur Gingrich. *A Greek-English Lexicon of the New Testament and Other Early Christian Literature.* Chicago, IL: The University of Chicago Press, 1957.

Barnes, Albert. *Notes on the New Testament.* Grand Rapids, MI: Baker Book House, 1996.

The Bible Knowledge Commentary: New Testament. John F. Walvoord and Roy B. Zuck, eds. Wheaton, IL: Victor Books, 1983.

The Bible Knowledge Commentary: Old Testament. John F. Walvoord and Roy B. Zuck, eds. Wheaton, IL: Victor Books, 1985.

Broderick, Robert. *The Catholic Encyclopedia.* Huntington, IN: Our Sunday Visitor, 1976.

Bruce, F. F. *The Hard Sayings of Jesus.* Downers Grove, IL: InterVarsity Press, 1983.

The Canons and Decrees of the Council of Trent, H. J. Schroeder, O.P., trans. Rockford, IL: Tan Books and Publishers, 1978.

Catechism of the Catholic Church. New York, NY: Doubleday, 1994.

The Concise Evangelical Dictionary of Theology. Walter A. Elwell, ed. Grand Rapids, MI: Baker Book House, 1991.

Denzinger, Henry. *The Sources of Catholic Dogma.* St. Louis, MO: B. Herder Book Company, 1957.

Erickson, Millard J. *Christian Theology.* Grand Rapids, MI: Baker Book House, 1987.

The Essential Catholic Handbook: A Summary of Beliefs, Practices, and Prayers. Liguori, MO: Liguori, 1997.

Geisler, Norman, and Ralph MacKenzie. *Roman Catholics and Evangelicals: Agreements and Differences.* Grand Rapids, MI: Baker Book House, 1995.

Geisler, Norman, and Ron Rhodes. *When Cultists Ask.* Grand Rapids, MI: Baker Book House, 1997.

Geisler, Norman, and Thomas Howe. *When Critics Ask: A Popular Handbook on Bible Difficulties.* Wheaton, IL: Victor Books, 1992.

Grudem, Wayne. *Systematic Theology: An Introduction to Biblical Doctrine.* Grand Rapids, MI: Zondervan Publishing House, 1994.

Hahn, Scott and Kimberly. *Rome Sweet Home: Our Journey to Catholicism.* San Francisco, CA: Ignatius Press, 1993.

Hardon, John A. *Pocket Catholic Dictionary.* New York, NY: Doubleday, 1966.

Inerrancy. Norman Geisler, ed. Grand Rapids, MI: Zondervan Publishing House, 1980.

The International Bible Commentary. F. F. Bruce, ed. Grand Rapids, MI: Zondervan Publishing House, 1986.

Kaiser, Walter. *Hard Sayings of the Old Testament.* Downers Grove, IL: InterVarsity Press, 1988.

——— . *More Hard Sayings of the Old Testament.* Downers Grove, IL: InterVarsity Press, 1992.

Keating, Karl. *Catholicism and Fundamentalism: The Attack on "Romanism" by "Bible Christians."* San Francisco, CA: Ignatius Press, 1988.

Kreeft, Peter, and Ronald Tacelli. *Handbook of Christian Apologetics.* Downers Grove, IL: InterVarsity Press, 1994.

Lightner, Robert. *Evangelical Theology: A Survey and Review.* Grand Rapids, MI: Baker Book House, 1986.

——— . *The God of the Bible.* Grand Rapids, MI: Baker Book House, 1978.

——— . *The Last Days Handbook.* Nashville, TN: Thomas Nelson Publishers, 1990.

Marshall, I. Howard. *The Gospel of Luke.* Grand Rapids, MI: Eerdmans Publishing Company, 1978.

McCarthy, James G. *Conversations with Catholics: Catholic Tradition in Light of Biblical Truth.* Eugene, OR: Harvest House Publishers, 1997.

——— . *The Gospel According to Rome: Comparing Catholic Tradition and the Word of God.* Eugene, OR: Harvest House Publishers, 1995.

Miller, Elliot, and Ken Samples. *The Cult of the Virgin.* Grand Rapids, MI: Baker Book House, 1994.

Morris, Leon. *Luke.* Grand Rapids, MI: Eerdmans Publishing Company, 1983.

——— . *The Gospel According to John.* Grand Rapids, MI: Eerdmans Publishing Company, 1987.

New Bible Commentary. R. T. France, D. A. Carson, J. A. Moyer, G. J. Wenham, eds. Downers Grove, IL: InterVarsity Press, 1994.

Ott, Ludwig. *Fundamentals of Catholic Dogma.* Rockford, IL: Tan Books and Publishers, 1974.

Predestination and Free Will: Four Views of Divine Sovereignty and Human Freedom. David Basinger and Randall Basinger, eds. Downers Grove, IL: InterVarsity Press, 1986.

The Quest Study Bible. Edited by *Leadership* and *Christianity Today,* eds. Grand Rapids, MI: Zondervan Publishing House, 1994.

Ramm, Bernard. *Protestant Biblical Interpretation.* Grand Rapids, MI: Baker Book House, 1978.

Reymond, Robert L. *Jesus, Divine Messiah: The New Testament Witness.* Phillipsburg, NJ: Presbyterian and Reformed, 1990.

Rhodes, Ron. *Christ Before the Manger: The Life and Times of the Preincarnate Christ.* Grand Rapids, MI: Baker Book House, 1992.

————— . *Heaven: The Undiscovered Country—Exploring the Wonder of the Afterlife.* Eugene, OR: Harvest House Publishers, 1996.

————— . *The Complete Book of Bible Answers.* Eugene, OR: Harvest House Publishers, 1997.

————— . *The Heart of Christianity: What It Means to Believe in Jesus.* Eugene, OR: Harvest House Publishers, 1996.

————— . *What Did Jesus Mean? Making Sense of the Difficult Sayings of Jesus.* Eugene, OR: Harvest House Publishers, 1999.

Ryrie Study Bible. Charles Caldwell Ryrie, ed. Chicago, IL: Moody Press, 1994.

Ryrie, Charles C. *Basic Theology.* Wheaton, IL: Victor Books, 1986.

————— . *Dispensationalism Today.* Chicago, IL: Moody Press, 1977.

————— . *The Holy Spirit.* Chicago, IL: Moody Press, 1980.

————— . *You Mean the Bible Teaches That...* Chicago, IL: Moody Press, 1974.

————— . *Balancing the Christian Life.* Chicago, IL: Moody Press, 1969.

Saucy, Robert. *The Church in God's Program.* Chicago, IL: Moody Press, 1972.

Sproul, R. C. *Now, That's a Good Question.* Wheaton, IL: Tyndale House Publishers, 1996.

Stein, Robert. *Difficult Passages in the New Testament.* Grand Rapids, MI: Baker Book House, 1990.

Story, Dan. *Defending Your Faith: How to Answer the Tough Questions.* Nashville, TN: Thomas Nelson Publishers, 1992.

Surprised by Truth. Patrick Madrid, ed. San Diego, CA: Basilica Press, 1994.

Toussaint, Stanley D. *Behold the King: A Study of Matthew.* Portland, OR: Multnomah Press, 1980.

Vincent, Marvin R. *Word Studies in the New Testament.* Grand Rapids, MI: Eerdmans Publishing Company, 1975.

Vine's Expository Dictionary of Biblical Words. Merrill F. Unger, W. E. Vine, William White, eds. Nashville, TN: Thomas Nelson Publishers, 1985.

Walvoord, John F. *Jesus Christ Our Lord.* Chicago, IL: Moody Press, 1969.

Walvoord: A Tribute. Donald K. Campbell, ed. Chicago, IL: Moody Press, 1982.

White, James R. *Mary—Another Redeemer?* Minneapolis, MN: Bethany House Publishers, 1998.

————— . *The Roman Catholic Controversy: Catholics and Protestants—Do the Differences Still Matter?* Minneapolis, MN: Bethany House Publishers, 1996.

The Wycliffe Bible Commentary. Everett F. Harrison and Charles F. Pfeiffer, eds. Chicago, IL: Moody Press, 1974.

Zondervan NIV Bible Commentary: New Testament. Kenneth L. Barker and John Kohlenberger III, eds. Vol. 2. Grand Rapids, MI: Zondervan Publishing House, 1994.

Zondervan NIV Bible Commentary: Old Testament. Kenneth L. Barker and John Kohlenberger III, eds. Vol. 1. Grand Rapids, MI: Zondervan Publishing House, 1994.

Subject Index

Scripture Index

Following are the *primary* Scripture passages dealt with in this book:

Other Books by
Ron Rhodes

Angels Among Us

The Complete Book of Bible Answers

Find It Fast in the Bible

Find It Quick Handy Bible Encyclopedia

Reasoning from the Scriptures with Catholics

Reasoning from the Scriptures with the Jehovah's Witnesses

Reasoning from the Scriptures with the Mormons

Reasoning from the Scriptures with Muslims

*The 10 Most Important Things
You Can Say to a Catholic*

*The 10 Most Important Things
You Can Say to a Jehovah's Witness*

*The 10 Most Important Things You
Can Say to a Mormon*

*10 Things You Should Know About
the Creation vs. Evolution Debate*

The Complete Guide to Christian Denominations

Why Do Bad Things Happen If God Is Good?

QUICK REFERENCE GUIDES

Angels: What You Need to Know

Islam: What You Need to Know

Jehovah's Witnesses: What You Need to Know